THE EU, WORLD TRADE LAW AND THE RIGHT TO FOOD

In recent years the European Union has developed a comprehensive strategy to conclude free trade agreements which includes not only prominent trade partners such as Canada, the United States and Japan but also numerous developing countries.

This book looks at the existing WTO law and at the new EU free trade agreements with the Caribbean and sub-Saharan Africa through the lens of the human right to adequate food. It shows how the clauses on the import and export of food included in recent free trade agreements limit the capacity of these countries to implement food security policies and to respect their human rights obligations. This outcome appears to be at odds with international human rights law and dismissive of existing human rights references in EU-founding treaties as well as in treaties between the EU and developing states.

Yet, the book argues against the conception in human rights literature that there is an inflexible agenda encoded in world trade law which is fundamentally conflictual with non-economic interests. The book puts forward the idea that the European Union is perfectly placed to develop a narrative of globalisation considering other areas of public international law when negotiating trade agreements, and argues that the EU does have the competences and influence to uphold a role of international leadership in designing a sustainable global trading system. Will the EU be ambitious enough?

A timely contribution to the growing academic literature on the relation between world trade law and international human rights law, this book imagines a central role for the EU in reconciling these two areas of international law.

Studies in International Trade and Investment Law: Volume 20

Studies in International Trade and Investment Law

Series Editors
Tomer Broude
Krista Nadakavukaren Schefer
Federico Ortino

This series offers a forum for publication of original and scholarly analyses of emerging and significant issues in international trade and investment law—broadly understood to include the whole of the law of the WTO, the public international law of foreign investment, the law of the EU common commercial policy and other regional trade regimes, and any legal or regulatory topic that interacts with global trade and foreign investment. The aim of the series is to produce works which will be readily accessible to trade and investment law scholars and practitioners alike.

Recent titles in this series:

The Right to Development and International Economic Law: Legal and Moral Dimensions
Isabella Bunn

Free Trade and Cultural Diversity in International Law
Jingxia Shi

Tied Aid and Development Aid Policies in the Framework of EU and WTO Law: The Imperative for Change
Annamaria La Chimia

Balancing Human Rights, Environmental Protection and International Trade: Lessons from the EU Experience
Emily Reid

Public Procurement and Labour Rights: Towards Coherence in International Instruments of Procurement Regulation
Maria Anna Corvaglia

The China-Australia Free Trade Agreement: A 21st-Century Model
Edited by Colin Picker, Heng Wang and Weihuan Zhou

Regional Economic Integration and Dispute Settlement in East Asia: The Evolving Legal Framework
Anna G Tevini

The EU, World Trade Law and the Right to Food

Rethinking Free Trade Agreements with Developing Countries

Giovanni Gruni

•HART•
OXFORD • LONDON • NEW YORK • NEW DELHI • SYDNEY

HART PUBLISHING

Bloomsbury Publishing Plc

Kemp House, Chawley Park, Cumnor Hill, Oxford, OX2 9PH, UK

HART PUBLISHING, the Hart/Stag logo, BLOOMSBURY and the Diana logo are trademarks of Bloomsbury Publishing Plc

First published in Great Britain 2018

A catalogue record for this book is available from the British Library.

Library of Congress Cataloging-in-Publication data

Names: Gruni, Giovanni, author.

Title: The EU, world trade law, and the right to food : rethinking free trade agreements with developing countries / Giovanni Gruni.

Other titles: European Union, world trade law, and the right to food

Description: Oxford [UK] ; Portland, Oregon : Hart Publishing, 2018. |

Identifiers: LCCN 2018011668 (print) | LCCN 2018012293 (ebook) | ISBN 9781509916221 (Epub) | ISBN 9781509916207 (hardback)

Subjects: LCSH: Foreign trade regulation—European Union countries. | European Union countries—Commercial policy. | Free trade—European Union countries. | World Trade Organization—European Union countries. | Economic assistance, European—Developing countries. | Right to food—Developing countries. | Food supply—Law and legislation—Developing countries. | European Union countries—Foreign economic relations—Developing countries. | Developing countries—Foreign economic relations—European Union countries.

Classification: LCC KJE6791 (ebook) | LCC KJE6791 .G78 2018 (print) | DDC 382/.456640094—dc23

LC record available at https://lccn.loc.gov/2018011668

ISBN: HB: 978-1-50991-620-7
ePDF: 978-1-50991-621-4
ePub: 978-1-50991-622-1

Typeset by Compuscript Ltd, Shannon

To Antonietta and Stefano

Acknowledgements

For almost 10 years, the pursuit of this book inspired my personal and professional life. Along the way, I received the support of numerous teachers, colleagues and friends who believed in the research making this book possible and shaped me into what I am today. To all of them I am incredibly grateful.

I would like to express my gratitude to Anne Davies who supervised my PhD thesis, which I used as a basis for this book. Our countless meetings in Oxford allowed a first idea to blossom into the defined research agenda that still motivates my work. To her and to the University of Oxford I owe the capacity to think critically and the style of writing I developed during my studies there. At the University of Oxford, I am particularly indebted to Stephen Weatherill, Mark Freedland and Sandra Fredman all of whom were involved in the revision of the manuscript, providing invaluable comments, and to the Faculty of Law, Lincoln College and the Future of Food Programme which hosted my research. I am also thankful to the World Trade Organization (WTO) and the College of Europe that hired me in the final stages of the research, providing unique opportunities to be in touch with high-level trade policy circles in Brussels and Geneva. At the College of Europe I am particularly grateful to Inge Govaere for her guidance on my career and research, and to my former colleagues at the Department of Legal Studies for their support during the completion of the first draft of this book. At the WTO I could not have imagined a more stimulating working environment than I experienced at the Appellate Body and in the negotiations of the Doha Round; two experiences that changed my vision of globalisation.

I am grateful to all the scholars who encouraged me to pursue this research and career. First of all to Silvana Sciarra for her contagious enthusiasm and her invaluable advice and supervision since I was a master's student at the University of Florence. I am also thankful to Marise Cremona and all the professors of the European University Institute who helped me define the line of research during my year there. A special thanks to Michal Bobek for his comments and constructive criticism on the first draft of the manuscript and to Stefaan van den Bogaert, Jorrit Rijpma, Vicky Kosta, Marco Bronckers, Moritz Jesse and all my new colleagues at the University of Leiden for their patience and invaluable support during the completion of this book. I will never forget the inspiring conversations with Francis Snyder at the Centre of Transnational Law in Shenzhen that provided me with many ideas on how to refine the manuscript.

Finally, this book would not have been possible without the help of my family and of all the friends who supported me unconditionally through this endeavour. I will always be indebted to Maurizio Pavesi and Paola Bader, the Pavesi Foundation and the Region of Tuscany for having financed the first steps of this research project.

Giovanni Gruni
February 2018
Twitter: @giovannigruni
Linkedin: https://www.linkedin.com/in/giovannigruni/

Contents

Table of Abbreviations

ACP	African, Caribbean and Pacific
EC	European Economic Community
EPA	Economic Partnership Agreement
EU	European Union
FAO	Food and Agriculture Organization
GATT	General Agreement on Tariffs and Trade
GATS	General Agreement on Trade in Services
GSP	Generalised System of Preferences
ILO	International Labour Organization
OECD	Organisation for Economic Co-operation and Development
SIA	Sustainability Impact Assessment
TDC	Trade and Development Committee
TEU	Treaty on the European Union
TFEU	Treaty on the Functioning of the European Union
UNCTAD	United Nations Conference on Trade and Development
WTO	World Trade Organization
SSG	World Trade Organization Special Safeguard
SSM	World Trade Organization Special Safeguard Mechanism

1

Introduction

ONE OF THE consequences of European integration is that the Member States conferred on the organs of the European Union (EU) the competence to conclude trade agreements with third countries. The centralisation of the trading influence of 28 countries into a single supranational entity created a powerful trading bloc that is emerging as an influential global economic player. In exercising this competence the EU affects the evolution of international trade law through its participation in the WTO and the conclusion of free trade agreements.

In 2005 the EU launched a new trade strategy called 'Global Europe', having the objective to conclude trade agreements with numerous countries, including states vulnerable to food shortages. This policy marked a change of attitude of the EU towards international trade law. In fact, before 2005 the EU aimed to influence international trade law mainly through participation in the World Trade Organization (WTO) and its contribution to multilateral trade negotiations involving the large majority of the countries of the world. After 2005 the EU decided to build its own trade network, outside the WTO, concluding free trade agreements directly with its partner countries. The main objective of these free trade agreements between the EU and developing countries is to eliminate barriers to the trade of goods (including food) and services between the EU and its partners. The traditional understanding of free trade agreements between the EU and the developing world is that they should favour the integration of vulnerable countries into the global market and promote their economic development. Whenever trade negotiations deal with food products the main aim is to open new markets for producers and improve the efficiency of the system, making more food products available at lower prices to more people.

The central project of this book is to challenge this traditional understanding of the free trade agreements between the EU and countries vulnerable to food shortages. This book shows that the EU has produced a new generation of free trade agreements which takes limited account of the human rights, food security and development implications of trade in food, even when the agreement is concluded with countries extremely vulnerable to food shortages. At the same time the book contests the argument that there is an inflexible agenda in world trade law which is fundamentally conflictive with non-economic interests. Consequently, this book advocates that the EU should develop sharper policy instruments to consider the different repercussions of trade in food when negotiating free trade agreements with vulnerable states. This chapter introduces the area of research to which this book aims to contribute, the objective of the book and its general outline.

I. WHY A BOOK ON HUMAN RIGHTS AND INTERNATIONAL TRADE AGREEMENTS?

International trade law has been historically inspired by the theory of comparative advantage, which implies that free trade is beneficial for the countries involved since it boosts specialisation, efficiency and competition.[1] The theory found wide application in the context of the World Trade Organization as well as in regional economic organisations such as the EU, being applied across the board to every product traded internationally. In practice, world trade law evolved through the organisation of successive rounds of international negotiations with the objective to take away tariffs on international trade on goods and to avoid other forms of legal barriers hindering international trade between countries. At global level, the system developed first through the General Agreement on Tariffs and Trade (GATT) system and then, after 1991, through the World Trade Organization and its dispute settlement mechanisms.[2] This area of international law remained across the decades largely separated from other areas of international legislation,[3] and trade negotiations follow dynamics and procedures which differ from other international treaties. For instance, today the WTO is independent from the United Nations and does not incorporate the main international instruments on human rights, environmental protection or development cooperation, so that the extent to which such instruments should be taken into account in trade negotiations remains unclear. This book attempts to address this using the case study of trade in food and the right to adequate food. This case study was chosen because the fragmentation between world trade law and treaties containing economic and social rights is particularly evident, and the two areas of expertise have difficulties with finding common ground.

[1] JH Jackson, 'Global economics and international economic law' (1998) 1 *Journal of International Economic Law* 1; AO Sykes, 'Comparative advantage and the normative economics of international trade policy' (1998) 1 *Journal of International Economic Law* 49; K Bagwell and RW Staiger, 'An Economic Theory of GATT' (1999) 89 *The American Economic Review* 215; K Bagwell and RW Staiger, *The Economics of the World Trading System* (MIT, 2002).

[2] C VanGrasstek, *The History and Future of the World Trade Organization* (WTO, 2013); G Marceau (ed); *A History of Law and Lawyers in the GATT/WTO* (Cambridge University Press, 2015).

[3] J Pauwelyn, 'The Role of Public International Law in the WTO: How Far Can We Go?' (2001) 95 *American Journal of International Law* 535; G Marceau, 'WTO Dispute Settlement and Human Rights' (2002) 13 *European Journal of International Law* 753.

The book takes a constructive position claiming that world trade law and human rights are compatible and that major trade powers like the EU can actively pursue this objective. There are several reasons why at this point in time this area is worthy of attention.

First, the theory of comparative advantage has several limits which are increasingly recognised in mainstream economic theory. In fact, while its capacity to produce wealth is undisputed, it is recognised that the theory has limited ability to distribute such wealth between countries and individuals.[4] In addition some economists claim that unfettered free trade has the capacity to exacerbate social divisions and undermine domestic social bargains[5] and that the economic models utilised oversimplify the reality of the trading system we have today.[6] These limits, which have been well known since the first formulations of the theory, remained unsolved even when free trade agreements started being widely negotiated across the world and in the GATT and WTO systems. At first, economists would simply call for domestic policies to distribute the wealth produced by international trade but today there is increasing recognition that in the absence, or upon the failure, of such domestic policies the system should be corrected already at the level of international law. This opens a space for the design of legal instruments allowing trade negotiators to explicitly consider interests such as equality or food security which have been on the margins of international trade law and policy so far. As the book shows, some early attempts to include such corrective instruments are already present in the WTO system.

Second, trade negotiations have dynamics of their own which are detached from economic theory. Accordingly, even if free trade agreements are inspired by the theory of comparative advantage, the legal details of each treaty depend on the sheer political and economic leverage that countries have during the negotiation process as well as their technical know-how of international trade law and policy.[7] This means that the resulting free trade

[4] See n 1 above; see also D Rodrik, *Straight Talk on Trade: Ideas for Sane World Economy* (Princeton University Press, 2017); JE Stiglitz, *Making Globalization Work* (WW Norton & Company, 2007); P Krugman and AJ Venables, 'Globalization and the Inequality of Nations' (1995) 110 *The Quarterly Journal of Economics* 857.

[5] D Rodrik, *Straight talk on trade* (Princeton University Press, 2018) 1; D Rodrik, *Has Globalization gone too far?* (Columbia University Press, 1997).

[6] See SM Levin, Testimony before the U.S. International Trade Commission, Subject: Trans-Pacific Partnership Agreement: Likely Impact on the U.S. Economy and on Specific Industry Sectors, Investigation No. TPA-105-001; J Bernstein and S Johnson, 'Trade in the real world', *The Washington Post*, 3 May 2015, available at <https://www.washingtonpost.com/posteverything/wp/2015/05/03/trade-in-the-real-world/?utm_term=.133a5356a2fb>; DMG Newbery and JE Stiglitz, 'Pareto Inferior Trade' (1984) 51 *The Review of Economic Studies* 1; W Janeway, 'The Retreat from Hyper Globalization', Institute for New Economic Thinking, 1 December 2016, available at <https://www.ineteconomics.org/perspectives/blog/the-retreat-from-hyper-globalization> accessed 27 December 2017.

[7] E Jones, *Manoeuvring at the Margins: Constraints Faced by Small States in International Trade Negotiations* (Commonwealth Secretariat, 2010).

agreement does not necessarily express the proclaimed economic rationale behind it, and larger countries and economic operators can tilt the balance of the drafting process in their favour even without proper justification in economic theory. At a time when international trade treaties cover increasingly larger areas of legislation, this calls for instruments capable of correcting such political imbalances by protecting countries and groups which do not have the political leverage to influence the negotiating process.

Third, the limits of international trade theory and its implementing legislation have been gaining a more central position in domestic politics with the WTO and free trade agreements being attacked from different sides on the various grounds of social or environmental dumping, wage depression or even as a cause of unemployment.[8] Whereas such political perspectives are at times based on limited technical understanding of the issues at stake, wide political discontent against free trade cannot be disregarded, especially when it contributes to the election of extremist groups which for decades have been kept to the margin of the political landscape. This is a call for international trade specialists to work towards addressing the well-known limits of the global trade system without postponing the debate further.

Finally, international trade treaties have had limited capacity to express the societal values and complexities of some of the goods they regulate. Food, which in the context of trade negotiations is a commodity traded across borders on the basis of offer and demand, incorporates a wealth of interests and needs beyond its economic value. Food is the basis of human life and it defines the quality of life of a person; it affects human health and is a manifestation of culture, societal differences and inequalities. Increasingly food is affected by climate change while its systems of production are one of the main causes. Food is also a strategic commodity which historically has been the cause of international tensions and even wars. Accordingly, the development of additional legal instruments allowing trade negotiators to consider all the societal complexities of food when drafting trade deals would make such agreements easier to promote to the public, and ultimately allow trade law to address some of its fundamental limits.

II. AREA OF RESEARCH

This book is a contribution to the fast-growing area of research that attempts to bridge the gap between international human rights law and international trade law. Even if the attempts to delve into the intricacies

[8] A Lang, *World trade law after neoliberalism. Reimagining the Global Economic Order* (Oxford University Press, 2011); D Rodrik, 'Populism and the Economics of Globalization' NBER Working Paper No. 23559.

of this issue have increased since the explosion of globalisation,[9] each discipline remains largely independent and the different theoretical foundations have been so far difficult to reconcile. On the one hand international trade law is grounded on neoliberal economic principles which encourage the liberalisation of international trade.[10] On the other hand, human rights law is based on individual entitlements derived from the recognition of the dignity of the human person. Accordingly, each human right is considered to require legal protection and fulfilment for every individual.[11]

Looking at the international norms regulating food, the separation of the two disciplines is evident. International human rights law recognises the right of everyone to be free from hunger in the International Covenant on Economic Social and Cultural Rights.[12] International trade law provides the legal infrastructure to the international trade of food through a web of trade agreements, which include the founding treaties of the WTO and around 300 bilateral and plurilateral free trade agreements. International human rights law sees food as an individual entitlement that countries and the international community must protect and actively promote, while in international trade law food is a product traded across the globe on the

[9] See FM Abbott, C Kaufmann and T Cottier (eds), *Trade and Human Rights: foundations and conceptual issues* (Michigan University Press, 2006); T Cottier, J Pauwelyn and E Burgi Bonanomi (eds), *Human rights and international trade* (Oxford University Press, 2005); C McCrudden and A Davies, 'A Perspective on Trade and Labor Rights' (2000) 3 *Journal of International Economic Law* 43. On the right to food and international trade law see O de Schutter, *International Trade in Agriculture and the Right to Food* (Friedrich Ebert Stiftung, 2009); M Jansen and E Lee, *Trade and Employment* (Secretariat of the World Trade Organization and International Labour Office, 2007).

[10] On the economic underpinning of international trade law see JH Jackson, 'Global economics and international economic law' (1998) 1 *Journal of International Economic Law* 1; AO Sykes, 'Comparative advantage and the normative economics of international trade policy' (1998) 1 *Journal of International Economic Law* 49; J Bhagwati, *International trade: selected readings* (MIT Press, 1996); J Bhagwati, *In defense of globalization* (Oxford University Press, 2007); J Bhagwati, 'Free Trade: Old and New Challenges' (1994) 104 *The Economic Journal* 231; C Davidson, S Matusz and D R Nelson, 'Can Compensation Save Free Trade?' (2006) 71 *Journal of International Economics* 167; WJ Samuels, 'Economics as a Science and Its Relation to Policy: The Example of Free Trade' (1980) 14 *Journal of Economic Issues* 163. See WM Corden, *Trade Policy and Economic Welfare* (Oxford University Press, 1997); C Davidson and SJ Matusz, 'Trade liberalization and compensation' (2006) 47 *International Economic Review* 723; AD and V Norman, 'Gains from trade without lump-sum compensation' (1986) 21 *Journal of International Economics* 111; MC Kemp and HY Wan, 'Gains from trade with and without lump-sum compensation' (1986) 21 *Journal of International Economics* 99.

[11] C McCrudden, 'Human Dignity and Judicial Interpretation of Human Rights' (2008) *The European Journal of International Law* 655; C McCrudden, 'In pursuit of human dignity: an introduction to current debates', University of Michigan Public Law Research Paper No. 309; P Capps, *Human Dignity and the Foundations of International Law* (Hart Publishing, 2009); D Kretzmer and E Klein (eds), *The concept of human dignity in the human rights discourse* (Kluwer Law International, 2002).

[12] See K Mechlem, 'Food security and the right to food in the discourse of the United Nations' (2004) 10 *European Law Journal* 631; B van der Meulen, 'The global arena of food law: emerging contours of a meta-framework' (2010) 4 *Erasmus Law Review* 217.

basis of supply and demand. In addition, the two bodies of law do not share the same instruments of enforcement: international human rights law is enforced through the 'soft' supervisory bodies of the United Nations, whereas international trade law is enforced through the dispute settlement regime of the WTO and ad hoc mechanisms in free trade agreements. Finally, international human rights law and international trade law do not have the same research community, since few scholars are trained in both disciplines. In fact, the substantive split between the two bodies of law and the separation of the international organisations dealing with human rights and international trade have provoked a sharp division in the scholarship with few attempts at reconciliation.

The isolation of international trade law from human rights was not perceived as a problem until the intensification of international exchange of goods and services. In fact, the expansion of international trade made the international market a crucial element in the realisation of economic and social rights. In particular, with the intensification of transnational trade the international food market became inextricably linked with the capacity of millions of people to access adequate food. Examples of this interconnection are the recurrent global food crises when oscillations in the price of food on the international market considerably affect the capacity of countries to realise the right to food. For instance, between 2007 and 2008 the international price of several basic food products such as wheat, rice and maize spiked, leaving millions of people without economic access to sufficient food.[13]

Tensions between international trade law and human rights are also present in the external relations of the EU to which this book is dedicated. The EU has longstanding exclusive competences on international commerce and takes part in the evolution and modification of international trade law. Yet, through the new Article 21 of the Treaty on the European Union, economic and social rights could emerge as building blocks of the external action of the EU. Article 21 innovates considerably from previous versions of the EU Treaties, stating that among the guiding principles of EU international relations there are the indivisibility of human rights and the principles of equality and solidarity.[14] How economic and social rights will find a place in the EU external action is not completely clarified by the Treaty or by subsequent policy papers produced by EU institutions. However, in recent years, the intention of giving EU external action a human face emerged unmistakably and it is well demonstrated by the attempt to include socio-economic rights

[13] Food and Agriculture Organization, *The state of food insecurity in the World 2011* (FAO, 2011).

[14] For an analysis of the meaning of solidarity in the EU legal order see S Sciarra, 'Notions of solidarity in times of economic uncertainty' (2010) 39 *Industrial Law Journal* 223.

in EU external trade policies. From the beginning of 2000 the EU Commission produced a wealth of inspiring documents advocating a model of global and regional governance taking stock of the historically weaker part of the international human rights system.[15] These documents make explicit reference to the necessity of reconciling trade and social objectives such as the promotion of food security in vulnerable countries. The inclusion of economic and social rights in EU external action is an ambitious and challenging objective because these rights have had historically limited space in the economic policies of the EU.[16] Internally, recent rulings of the Court of Justice of the European Union have shown how the relation between strong EU competences, especially trade in goods and services, and social rights, can be problematic.[17]

Recent developments in EU external policies present an invaluable opportunity to promote the debate on the relation between international trade law and the right to food by assessing how the EU strikes a balance between the two in its foreign relations. The post-Lisbon EU external agenda is dominated by the Global Europe Strategy, a plan aimed at the conclusion of free trade agreements with numerous countries from the developing world.[18]

[15] On food security see European Commission, 'A EU policy framework to assist developing countries in addressing food security challenges' (Communication) COM(2010) 127 final; European Commission, 'A thematic strategy for food security. Advancing the food security agenda to achieve the MDGs' (Communication) COM(2006) 21 final. On the Right to Health see European Commission, 'The EU role in Global Health' (Communication) COM(2010) 128 final; European Commission, 'EU Strategy for Action on the Crisis in Human Resources for Health in Developing Countries' (Communication) COM(2005) 642 final; European Commission, 'A European Programme for Action to Confront HIV/AIDS, Malaria and Tubercolosis through External Action (2007–2011)' (Communication) COM(2005) 179 final.

[16] See T Novitz, 'Legal Power and Normative Sources in the Field of Social Policy: Normative Power Europe at Work?' in J Orbie (ed), *Europe's Global Role: External Policies of the European Union* (Ashgate, 2008); M Cremona, 'Economic and Social Rights in EU External Policy' in F Bestagno (ed), *I diritti economici sociali e culturali* (Vita e Pensiero, 2009) and C Barnard, 'The External Dimension of Community Social Policy: The Ugly Duckling of External Relation' in Nicholas Emiliou and David O'Keeffe (eds), *The European Union and World Trade Law: After the Gatt Uruguay Round* (John Wiley & Sons, 1996).

[17] In particular, see Case C-438/05 *International Transport Workers' Federation v. Viking Line ABP* [2007] ECR I-10779 and Case C-341/05 *Laval un Partneri Ltd v. Svenska Byggnadsarbetareförbundet* [2007] ECR I-11767. For comments on the tension between economic and social rights see P Syrpis and T Novitz, 'Economic and social rights in conflict: Political and judicial approaches to their reconciliation' (2008) 33 *European Law Review* 411; A Davies, 'One step forward, two steps back? The Viking and Laval cases in the ECJ' (2008) 37 *Industrial Law Journal* 126 and S Sciarra, 'Viking and Laval: Collective Labour Rights and Market Freedoms in the Enlarged EU' (2008) *Cambridge Yearbook of European Law*.

[18] See European Commission, 'Report on progress achieved on the Global Europe strategy, 2006–2010' (Staff working document) SEC(2010) 1268/2 final; European Commission, 'Trade as a driver of prosperity' (Staff Working Document) SEC(2010) 1268 final; European Commission, 'Global Europe: Competing in the World' (Communication) SEC(2006) 567 final. The strategy was recently revised: see Communication from the Commission, 'Trade for All, Towards a more responsible trade and investment policy', available at <http://trade.ec.europa.eu/doclib/cfm/doclib_results.cfm?docid=153846> accessed 27 December 2017.

The fact that free trade agreements are concluded with some of the poorest countries of the world, lacking in social safety nets and in the capacity to absorb trade shocks, makes new free trade agreements an ideal place to study the issue because of the disparity of the relation. In fact, the difference in economic capacity and dimension between the EU and vulnerable developing countries has the consequence that the agreements have minimal impact on EU food security. By contrast, for small or vulnerable developing countries additional imports of food from the EU or the obligation to export certain products to Europe may have consequences for their capacity to ensure food security at domestic level. We will see for instance the case of the Caribbean countries that, under the free trade agreement with the EU, lost the prerogative to regulate their export of food to the EU. This is so even if their contribution to the global food market is minimal and this limits their capacity to intervene during food shortages at domestic level.

This book looks at the details of seven treaties where the imbalance of the relationship is particularly evident, to assess to what extent the EU and its partner countries have protected the right to food from the deficiencies of the international food market. From this book it will emerge that notwithstanding the new external competences acquired with the Lisbon Treaty, food security concerns play a very limited role when the EU concludes agreements regulating the trade of food with vulnerable countries.

III. OBJECTIVE OF THE BOOK

The relation between international trade and the right to food in the external relations of the EU is a vast area of research involving institutional aspects of the EU as well as the study of the obligations that WTO law and international human rights law impose on the EU and its Member States. This book delves into the subject by constructing an analytical model to assess the extent to which the EU considers the right to food when concluding a free trade agreement with a group of countries vulnerable to food shortages. The analytical model is then applied to the case studies of the free trade agreements which the EU concluded in the Caribbean and sub-Saharan Africa. These recent free trade agreements are included in the Global Europe Strategy and involve states that due to their social and economic characteristics are exposed to hunger and malnutrition.

The four chapters preceding the case studies look at the relation between international trade law and the right to food from the perspectives of human rights law, the international food market, EU law and WTO law. The observations made in these chapters are then used to demonstrate that (1) the free trade agreements between the EU and developing countries place legal constraints on the capacity of vulnerable countries to realise the right to food, (2) this outcome is mainly a policy choice of the parties to the free trade agreements independent from the legal obligations of WTO law, and (3) the EU is perfectly placed to launch a reform of world trade law, that, within the free trade model, fully takes into account the right to adequate food.

As recurring global food crises have demonstrated, the international food market is extremely instable and changing market conditions have direct consequences for the realisation of the right to food around the world. Negative effects on the right to food are particularly evident in countries with no safety nets and with scarce domestic production of food. The first statement of this book is based on the premise that since the international food market influences the realisation of the right to food especially in vulnerable countries, it is a human right duty of states to avoid the situation that market failures negatively affect the realisation of the right. This premise is grounded on the normative content of the right to food as defined in the International Covenant on Economic Social and Cultural Rights and its interpretive documents. The Covenant in fact provides that countries have a duty to intervene to protect individuals whenever market conditions affect their fundamental economic and social rights. As clarified by the United Nations Committee on Economic, Social and Cultural Rights, this duty applies to changes in the international food market and especially to global food crises as well as domestic crises requiring modifications of the policies on import or export of food. The book then shows that the free trade agreements increase the legal constraints on the trade instruments that countries can use to defend their citizens from the instability of the international food market or a domestic food crisis. In certain cases the free trade agreement goes as far as forbidding the intervention of Caribbean and sub-Saharan countries at the occurrence of food shortages on their territory.

The second objective of the book is identifying whether the constraints that the free trade agreements pose on the realisation of the right to food are a consequence of WTO law or rather a free choice of the parties to the agreements. In fact, WTO law regulates the conclusion of free trade agreements limiting the policy space of the EU and its partners. In particular, WTO law requires that by definition trade agreements have the main objective to eliminate import and export barriers between the participating countries. These rules apply also to the clauses in free trade agreements regulating the import and export of food. This means that WTO law might have obliged the EU and its partners in developing countries to limit the capacity for intervention of vulnerable states even though this could affect the realisation of the right to food. To identify if this was the case for each clause on the import and export of food of the free trade agreements effectively placing legal constraints on the realisation of the right to food, the book clarifies whether WTO law would have allowed a different outcome. When this is the case the EU and its partners in the developing world could have concluded free trade agreements more in line with the normative content of the right to food. By contrast, when the new constraints are a consequence of

WTO law the free trade agreements manifest the human rights deficiencies of this international organisation. From the book it will emerge that since a different outcome of the trade negotiations was often possible, a reform of the EU external trade policy is required in order to make it more supportive of the realisation of the human right to food. At the same time, with regard to several trade policies relevant for the realisation of the right to food, a different outcome is possible only through an amendment of WTO law.

Finally, this book claims that the EU can, through its Common Commercial Policy, promote a synthesis between human rights and trade policy objectives. This would allow the EU to pull its weight in the development of world trade law to foster a system which balances the macro-economic approach of world trade law with the protection of individual entitlements contained in human rights treaties. This would be in line with an ongoing process of gradual opening of world trade law to substantive and institutional influences from other areas of international law. This would also allow world trade law to correct some of its weaknesses and enable human rights not to stand in the way of economic integration. Ultimately this process would promote a model of globalisation pursuing economic integration in a way which fully protects the individual entitlements recognised by international human rights law. Recent developments in EU law, like the inclusion of sustainable development in the EU external exclusive competences for international commerce, provide the legal infrastructure to pursue such a strategy.

The debate on world trade law and the right to food revolves around all three pillars of the WTO Agreement on Agriculture: import restrictions, export restrictions and domestic support. This book focuses only on legal instruments regulating import and export of food products. This is for reasons of space but also because these two areas were only at the margin of the debate developed around the Doha Round and the Bali and Nairobi packages, which concentrate more on domestic support. As the book will show, the free trade agreements between the EU and the Caribbean and sub-Saharan Africa had a major impact on the parts of world trade law dealing with the import and export of food products.

IV. BOOK OUTLINE

The book is composed of seven chapters plus this Introduction. Chapter two contains the analysis of the normative content of the human right to food on the basis of the International Covenant on Economic, Social and Cultural Rights and its interpretive instruments. The objective of the chapter is identifying whether the normative content of the right to food contains duties that are applicable to the transnational trade of food and its regulation. From that chapter it emerges that the international dimension of the right to food is an essential complement to domestic strategies working toward the fulfilment of the right. In particular, the chapter finds that countries have the duty to ensure that the international food market does not disrupt the realisation of the right to food. This also means that the parties to the Covenant have the obligation to take the human right to food into account when providing the legal infrastructure for international trade of food through the conclusion of trade agreements. Even if world trade law remains largely independent from human rights obligations, the chapter shows that there are already institutional seeds in place allowing a purposive legal dialogue between the fields of international trade law and human rights. This is the opportunity for the EU to promote a less fragmented international legal order where human rights principles are taken into account when negotiating free trade agreements.

Building on this result, Chapter three introduces the main features of the international food market and highlights the most relevant inadequacies of the present system for the realisation of the right to food. We do this by explaining the main failures of the international food market observed during recent decades and identifying the principal categories of countries and individuals that in the present configuration of the international food market remain vulnerable to food shortages. Through this analysis Chapter three defines the policy setting within which the EU external action takes place and identifies some priorities for reconciling the international food market and the realisation of the right to food. The chapter concludes that the EU, to contribute to the realisation of the right to food, should work towards the solution of the market failures of the present system and on the inclusion and protection of the countries and individuals which remain extremely exposed to food insecurity within the international food market.

Chapter four is dedicated to the institutional dimension of EU external trade and human rights policies. The EU is a complex institution and the exercise of its external competences requires the use of the procedures regulated by the Treaty on the European Union and the Treaty on the Functioning of the European Union. This means that the pursuit of the objectives identified in Chapter three is possible only if the EU has the competences and the procedures to pursue them. For this reason Chapter four clarifies how the EU contributes to the evolution and modification of international trade law and what are the policies and the procedures to be followed when concluding international trade agreements. The chapter also identifies the legal basis in the EU Treaties for an external action of the EU in the realm of international trade that also pays attention to the pursuit of the human right to food. The chapter shows that the EU is well aware of the limits of the international food market and of international trade law with regard to the pursuit of food security in vulnerable countries. In particular, the EU has developed a specific policy that is dedicated to the inclusion of development objectives, including food security, in its external trade policy. The policy isolates specific aspects of international trade law that need to be modified in order to make it fully supportive of food security. If this policy is put into practice in the WTO and through the conclusion of free trade agreements the EU could be a driving force in the reconciliation between the regulation of international trade of food and the realisation of the human right to food.

If the EU aims to contribute to the realisation of the right to food through its external trade policy it must do so while duly respecting existing legal obligations that the EU and its trading partners have under the law of the WTO. In fact, the WTO governs the external action of the EU in the realm of trade and places limits on what the EU can do vis-à-vis its trade partners, including countries vulnerable to food shortages. For this reason Chapter five assesses the multilateral rules on the import and export of food from the perspective of the right to food. The chapter defines the policy space that WTO law leaves to countries to include the promotion of food security within the objectives of the negotiations of international trade treaties. The chapter takes into account specific trade instruments (import tariffs and quotas, safeguards, export restrictions) contained in the General Agreement on Tariffs and Trade (GATT) and the WTO Agreement on Agriculture. In addition, Chapter five considers the rules regulating the conclusion of free trade agreements between WTO members, exposing the limits of WTO law with regard to realisation of the human right to food and clarifying the legal space left to states to intervene.

Chapter six and Chapter seven provide the case studies of the EU–Caribbean free trade agreement and of the six free trade agreements that the EU has concluded so far with sub-Saharan Africa. The two chapters contain the demonstration of the two research claims. In order to demonstrate that the free trade agreements between the EU and developing countries limit the capacity of Caribbean countries to realise the right to food, the chapters identify specific trade clauses that reduce the capacity for intervention of vulnerable countries at the occurrence of food shortages due to market instability or natural disasters. In doing so the case studies demonstrate that even though the EU has a policy dedicated to the promotion of food security through modifications of international trade law, the policy does not produce results in practice. In fact, the free trade agreements considered in Chapter six and Chapter seven increase the vulnerability of Caribbean and sub-Saharan countries to food shortages. In addition, the case studies make it clear whether the clauses limiting the capacity of developing countries to realise the right to food are a policy decision by the parties to the trade agreement or rather a consequence of WTO law. In doing so the book separates those cases in which the EU could promote a regulation of the international trade of food more supportive of the realisation of the right to food by modifying its external action, from the cases in which an amendment of WTO law would be necessary. From Chapter six and Chapter seven it emerges that the EU–Caribbean trade agreement and the six free trade agreements between the EU and sub-Saharan countries do not solve any of the human rights inadequacies of WTO law and often create new challenges for the realisation of the right to food.

In the conclusions (Chapter eight) the book provides a tentative analysis of the reasons responsible for such an outcome. These include the lack of institutional mechanisms to include food security objectives across EU external policies and the involvement of private interest groups in all the stages of the conclusion of free trade agreements with vulnerable countries. The book then calls for a reform of the external trade policy of the EU to make it fully supportive of the realisation of global food security. This final chapter identifies two lines of reform of the EU Common Commercial Policy to make it fully supportive of the right to adequate food: defragmenting EU external policies and defragmenting international trade law.

2

The Right to Food in International Law

I. INTRODUCTION

THE RIGHT TO food received express recognition in Article 25 of the Universal Declaration of Human Rights which states that 'everyone has the right to a standard of living adequate for the health and well-being of himself and of his family including food…'.[1] However, the right remained mainly aspirational until the '70s when, in the wake of one of the most disruptive world food crises of the century, it gained the attention of the international community. Legal and economic doctrine followed suit and in the last 20 years of the twentieth century studies on how to solve the problems of hunger and malnutrition flourished across social sciences.[2] Today the right to food is a well-structured human right with a defined normative content, which is already justiciable in domestic courts in several countries around the world.[3]

[1] Universal Declaration of Human Rights, Article 25, available at <www.un.org/en/documents/udhr/> accessed 2 May 2017.

[2] A Sen, *Poverty and Famines: an Essay on Entitlement and Deprivation* (Oxford University Press, 1983); A Sen and Jean Drèze, *Hunger and Public Action* (Clarendon Press, 1989); A Sen, *The Political Economy of Hunger* (Clarendon Press, 1990); A Sen, 'On the Approach to Planning Against Hunger' (1977) 58 *CERES: FAO Review on Agriculture and Development* 14; A Sen, *Hunger and Entitlement* (World Institute of Development Economics Research, 1987); A Sen, 'Food and freedom' (1989) 17 *World Development* 769; A Sen, 'Food Entitlement and Economic Chains' in LF Newman (ed), *Hunger in History* (Blackwell, 1990); A Sen, 'Entitlements and the Chinese Famine' (1990) 15 *Food Policy* 261; A Sen, 'Public Action to Remedy Hunger' (1991) 16 *International Science Reviews* 324. A Eide, 'Human rights requirements to social and economic development: The case of the right to food and nutrition rights' in Uwe Kracht and Manfred Schulz (eds), *Food security and nutrition* (St Martin Press, 1999) at 329; A Eide, 'The Right to Adequate Standard of Living Including the Right to Food' in *Economic, Social and Cultural Rights—A textbook* (Martinus Nijhoff, 2001); A Eide, 'The Importance of Economic and Social Rights in the Age of Globalization' in Wenche Barth Elde and Uwe Kracht (eds), *Food and Human Rights in Development* (Intersentia, 2005); P Alston and K Tomasevski (eds), *The Right to Food* (Martinus Nijhoff, 1984); K Mechlem, 'Food security and the right to food in the discourse of the United Nations' (2004) 10 *European Law Journal* 631, 634; S Joseph, *Blame it on the WTO?* (Oxford University Press, 2017) 181.

[3] C Courtis, 'The Right to Food as a Justiciable Right' (2007) 11 *Max Planck United Nations Yearbook* 317; F Coomans, *Justiciability of Economic and Social Rights* (Intersentia, 2006); S Fredman, *Human Rights Transformed* (Oxford University Press, 2008).

This chapter elucidates the normative content of the right to food and to what extent this can be applied to the negotiations of free trade agreements. The chapter clarifies whether the normative content of the right to food requires governments to take the right into account when concluding trade agreements with third countries. In particular the chapter looks at legal obligations that states have to take into account not just in respect of their own populations but also in respect of the populations of their trading partners and the international community at large. The argument carried on in this chapter is based on the International Covenant of Economic, Social and Cultural Rights—the international convention including the most articulate recognition of the right to food. This chapter is divided into six sections, including this introduction. Section II introduces the right on the basis of the legal obligations contained in the Covenant. Section III identifies the legal obligations stemming from the right that states have to respect in order to comply with the Covenant. The fourth section illustrates the external dimension of such duties, namely the legal obligations stemming from the right to food that states have to respect in their international relations. This section argues that even if the Committee on Economic, Social and Cultural Rights has not identified specific duties to be applied in the context of trade negotiations states cannot disregard the right to food when concluding trade agreements. In addition, the EU explicitly accepted such obligations, adding references to economic and social rights, human rights and food security in its free trade agreements with vulnerable states.

The fifth section shows how world trade and the right to food are an example of extreme fragmentation of international law. The section claims that even though the two fields remain distant there are signs of a purposive institutional dialogue which the EU can exploit to promote a less fragmented international order. This is particularly relevant for free trade agreements which have the explicit objective of supporting economic and social developments of third countries as is the case of recent trade agreements concluded by the EU with developing countries. Section VI concludes.

II. THE CONTENT OF THE RIGHT TO FOOD

A. Introduction

This section presents the content of the right to food emerging from the International Covenant on Economic, Social and Cultural Rights and its interpretive documents. The Covenant is the main international convention including the right, and is the point of reference of the legal doctrine on the subject. This section presents the two main concepts underpinning the right: availability of food and accessibility of food. Even though the two concepts were developed taking into account *domestic* food policies they constitute the theoretical underpinning for all internal and external policies that can have an impact on the realisation of the right to food.

B. Article 11 of the International Covenant on Economic, Social and Cultural Rights

The entry into force of the International Covenant on Economic, Social and Cultural Rights was a watershed in the process of recognition of the right to food at international level. The Covenant in fact included, in its Article 11, a more elaborated version of the right:

> 1. The States Parties to the present Covenant recognize the right of everyone to an adequate standard of living for himself and his family, including adequate food, clothing and housing, and to the continuous improvement of living conditions. The States Parties will take appropriate steps to ensure the realization of this right, recognizing to this effect the essential importance of international co-operation based on free consent.
>
> 2. The States Parties to the present Covenant, recognizing the fundamental right of everyone to be free from hunger, shall take, individually and through international co-operation, the measures, including specific programmes, which are needed:
>
> (a) To improve methods of production, conservation and distribution of food by making full use of technical and scientific knowledge, by disseminating knowledge of the principles of nutrition and by developing or reforming agrarian systems in such a way as to achieve the most efficient development and utilization of natural resources;
> (b) Taking into account the problems of both food-importing and food-exporting countries, to ensure an equitable distribution of world food supplies in relation to need.[4]

The establishment of the Committee on Economic, Social and Cultural Rights allowed, from 1985, the elaboration of the right to food through General Comments and Statements and the analysis of Reports from state parties. It also gave the Committee a central role in international law for the interpretation and clarification of social rights in general and the right to food in particular. This role was strengthened by the 2008 Optional Protocol which granted individual complainants access to the Committee.[5]

[4] Article 11, International Covenant on Economic, Social and Cultural Rights, General Assembly Resolution 2200A 1966, available at <http://www.ohchr.org/EN/ProfessionalInterest/Pages/CESCR.aspx> accessed 5 April 2013.

[5] Optional Protocol on the International Covenant on Economic, Social and Cultural Rights, General Assembly Adopted Resolution A/RES/63/117, 10 December 2008.

Even though Article 11 points out several duties as well as key issues for the realisation of the right it does not clarify its content and has been prone to reductive interpretations that could reach the point of nullifying the essence of the right. As a consequence, in 1999 the Committee on Economic, Social and Cultural Rights felt the need to point out the main normative elements of the right so providing a framework of analysis for the law and policies of state parties. This was done in General Comment 12,[6] a detailed piece of legal analysis completely dedicated to the normative content of the human right to food.

The utility of having the right to food codified in international law is ensuring that the international community works towards a world where every person has a certain amount of food and water, allowing her or him to live healthily, take part in society and have access to the other rights to which they are entitled. The right to food is in fact one of those enabling rights which are necessary for the individual to become an active member of society taking part in economic relationships. To fulfil this objective General Comment 12 clarifies that the individual needs to have both 'physical and economic access … to adequate food or means for its procurement'.[7] In the view of the Committee, the concept of adequacy changes on the basis of prevailing social, economic, cultural, climatic, ecological conditions but cannot be interpreted narrowly as the notion of a 'minimum package of calories, proteins or other specific nutrients'.[8] This means, for instance, that de minimis approaches to food issues, which are satisfied when a threshold of calories per head is reached, do not realise the right to food in its entirety. The individual is able to realise his right to food only if food is available and accessible.

C. Availability of Food

Availability means that the market or the individual produces food in a quantity and quality 'sufficient to satisfy the dietary needs … free of adverse substances, and acceptable within a given culture'. General Comment 12 defines the three concepts:

> [T]he diet as a whole contains a mix of nutrients for physical and mental growth, development and maintenance, and physical activity that are in compliance with human physiological needs at all stages throughout the life cycle and according to gender and occupation …

[6] Committee on Economic, Social and Cultural Rights, Substantive issues arising in the implementation of the International Covenant on Economic, Social and Cultural Rights: General Comment 12 The right to adequate food (art. 11), E/C. 12/1999/5.

[7] Ibid, paragraph 6.

[8] Ibid.

> *Free from adverse substances* sets requirements for food safety and for a range of protective measures by both public and private means to prevent contamination of foodstuffs through adulteration and/or through bad environmental hygiene or inappropriate handling at different stages throughout the food chain; care must also be taken to identify and avoid or destroy naturally occurring toxins.
>
> *Cultural or consumer acceptability* implies the need to take into account, as far as possible, perceived non nutrient-based values attached to food and food consumption and informed consumer concerns regarding the nature of accessible food supplies.[9]

The qualification of availability through the three elements of *dietary needs*, *cultural and consumer acceptability* and *freedom from adverse substances* ensures that the interpretation of the right does not leave room for superficial realisation.[10] Examples are countries, regions or households where the minimum calorie intake per day is respected but there are considerable micronutrients deficiencies. The requirements also highlight the health dimension of the right.[11] A diet which is based on unhealthy food or does not provide the full range of nutrients necessary to the human body to develop does not comply with the right, even if it provides an adequate amount of calories. Through its cultural dimension, the right to food guarantees that food is not used as an instrument of abuse and it is respectful of national and local traditions. Accordingly, human rights approaches to food policies shift the attention from quantity only towards quantity *and quality* of food. If food does not incorporate the characteristics above it does not fulfil human dignity and, as a consequence, the requirement of availability is not respected.

D. Accessibility of Food

Economic evidence shows that violations of the right to food are often a problem of accessibility and not of availability.[12] General Comment 12 addresses this issue, stating that food has to be accessible to the individual both physically and economically. The two elements are both relevant for the definition of the right. Besides, the necessity of granting the individual physical and economic access to foodstuffs opens up a space for interaction of the right with numerous areas of international and domestic law. Whenever a piece of legislation or an international treaty can interfere with

[9] Ibid, paragraphs 9, 10, 11.

[10] K Mechlem, 'Food security and the right to food in the discourse of the United Nations' (2004) 10 *European Law Journal* 631, 638.

[11] Ibid, 636.

[12] See above n. 2.

the access to food of vulnerable groups or its affordability, the right to food is called into question. The Committee on Economic, Social and Cultural Rights defined physical accessibility as requiring that:

> adequate food must be accessible to everyone, including physically vulnerable individuals, such as infants and young children, elderly people, the physically disabled, the terminally ill and persons with persistent medical problems, including the mentally ill. Victims of natural disasters, people living in disaster-prone areas and other specially disadvantaged groups may need special attention and sometimes priority consideration with respect to accessibility of food. A particular vulnerability is that of many indigenous population groups whose access to their ancestral lands may be threatened.[13]

Not every individual has the same risk of exposure to human rights violations. Inequality, poverty and the absence of financial 'safety nets' make some persons more vulnerable than others. Vulnerable categories are different in different societies and depend on culture, customs, economic resources and the structure of the productive system. There are, however, some groups that are statistically more likely to have their basic rights violated, and for them access to food is more difficult. General Comment 12 mentions women, children, elderly and ill people and indigenous populations. To them, international law affords extra protection. Articles 3 and 2(2) of the Covenant contain the obligation not to discriminate on the basis of sex for access to economic, social and cultural rights.

The second dimension of accessibility of food is economic accessibility. Economic accessibility is as relevant as physical accessibility but the protection of economically vulnerable groups has been technically more difficult and politically more controversial. The Committee on Economic, Social and Cultural Rights defines economic accessibility as follows:

> Economic accessibility implies that personal or household financial costs associated with the acquisition of food for an adequate diet should be at a level such that the attainment and satisfaction of other basic needs are not threatened or compromised. Economic accessibility applies to any acquisition pattern or entitlement through which people procure their food and is a measure of the extent to which it is satisfactory for the enjoyment of the right to adequate food. Socially vulnerable groups such as landless persons and other particularly impoverished segments of the population may need attention through special programmes.[14]

The concept of economic accessibility encapsulates the idea that every person shall be able to provide adequate food for themselves and for their dependents. It also refers to the problems of access to land by rural populations

[13] General Comment 12, paragraph 13.
[14] General Comment 12, paragraph 13.

and the marginalisation of segments of society trapped in poverty spirals. Whenever poverty or lack of purchasing power makes food inaccessible to the individual, economic accessibility is not granted and the right to food is violated. This means that price fluctuations and more generally the realm of trade and investment are not alien to the right to food, since they are relevant to the pursuit of economic accessibility.

The concept of economic accessibility clarifies that the market economy is perfectly compatible with the right to food as long as the commodification of food and water does not prevent access to these resources. A fitting example is the ongoing process of privatisation of water resources in numerous countries. Privatisation is not incompatible with the right to food, but when privatisation is followed by the exclusion from a water supply of certain individuals, the right to food is violated.

III. STATE DUTIES

A. Introduction

The normative content of the right to food defines the objective to be achieved by the Members of the Covenant. However, Article 11 is a substantive article, which does not deal with the steps that countries are obliged to take in order to respect the right. In fact, the Covenant makes it explicit that most economic and social rights should be realised progressively through sustained efforts by the Members of the Covenant. This section identifies the duties that countries have to respect in order to be considered as working towards the realisation of the right to food. These duties have been elaborated as duties of governments towards their citizens and the studies on their application concentrate mostly on domestic policies. However, such duties provide the theoretical foundations on the basis of which the Committee on Economic, Social and Cultural Rights has developed external human rights duties applicable to relationships between states. Accordingly, this section sets the scene for the discussion of external human rights duties carried out in the next two sections.

Human rights doctrine, in order to assess the realisation of economic and social rights, identified several duties that states have to observe. This analytical framework distinguishes between the duty to respect, the duty to provide and the duty to fulfil economic and social rights. When Asbjorn Eide wrote his report on the right to food[15] he used these three kinds of obligations on

[15] A Eide, 'The right to adequate food and to be free from hunger', United Nations Economic and Social Council E/CN.4/Sub2/1999/12.

state parties to define the content of the right. The Committee on Economic, Social and Cultural Rights elaborated on this theoretical structure in its General Comment 3,[16] putting Eide's duties in the context of the obligations generally stemming from the Covenant.

B. Duty to Respect

The duty to respect incorporates the vertical dimension of the right to food, sheltering the content of the right in the relationship between the state and its citizens. In social rights theory the duty to respect includes mainly obligations of restraint even if in some cases the duty to respect has been conceptualised as incorporating positive duties as well.[17] The duty to respect is central to the argument human rights lawyers make that the realisation of economic and social rights does not concern only state intervention and expensive budget allocations. This traditional vision of social rights as bundles of positive duties was demolished by recent legal doctrine[18] and, at least in certain countries, has been disavowed by the case law. A recent study of more than 2000 cases from all around the world showed that courts apply the duty to respect by following specific normative patterns.[19] These comprise the duty not to interfere with self-organising efforts or key resources of individuals or associations, and the duty not to deny access by an individual to an existing government programme or employment opportunity. Another dimension, sometimes considered a violation of the duty to fulfil, is the removal of legislative instruments granting or facilitating the realisation of the right. The study refers to removal of legislative protection (for instance the repealing of legislation incorporating the right) or the elimination of government programmes that enable individuals to realise their social rights.[20] In order to distinguish the cases in which state intervention has positive effects on the realisation of the right from the cases where it creates

[16] Committee on Economic, Social and Cultural Rights, General Comment 3, The nature of States parties' obligations (Art. 2, para. 1).

[17] S Fredman, *Human Rights Transformed* (Oxford University Press, 2008) 205.

[18] Ibid; A Pillay, 'Economic and social rights adjudication: developing principles of judicial restraint in South Africa and the United Kingdom' [2013] *Public Law* 599; C Harvey and E Rooney, 'Integrating human rights? Socio-economic rights and budget analysis' (2010) 3 *European Human Rights Law Review* 266; A Nolan and M Dutschke, 'Article 2(1) ICESCR and state parties' obligations: whither the budget?' (2010) 3 *European Human Rights Law Review* 280; S Fredman, 'New horizons: incorporating socio-economic rights in a British Bill of Rights' [2010] *Public Law* 297.

[19] M Langford (ed), *Social rights jurisprudence* (Cambridge University Press, 2009).

[20] Ibid. On the theory of adjudication of economic and social rights see also J King, *Judging Social Rights* (Cambridge University Press, 2012).

new obstacles, the concept of retrogressive measure emerged both in legal practice and doctrine.[21]

The Committee on Economic, Social and Cultural Rights has interpreted the right to food, affirming the complex nature of this right as containing both duties of restraint and positive duties. In order to respect the right to food the state should not act in ways that make access to food more difficult or disrupt existing access to food or instruments for its procurement.[22] In particular, a state should not repeal or suspend legislation necessary for the continued enjoyment of the right, nor should it deny access to food to particular individuals or groups. In the same vein, a state should not adopt legislation or policies which are manifestly incompatible with pre-existing legal obligations relating to the right to food. When a social policy affecting the right to food is abandoned or its budget reduced, the state has the duty to ensure that this does not affect accessibility and availability of food supplies. In internal conflicts or other emergency situations a state cannot prevent access to humanitarian food aid. In extreme scenarios, such as war zones, food cannot be used as a weapon, food embargoes are prohibited and states must not destroy productive resources or impede access for reasons of self-defence.[23]

Among the three core duties, the duty to respect is the least represented in the analysis of the country Reports sent by state parties to the Committee. A reason for this is that the duty to respect is politically sensitive because a violation of the duty generally implies that the Government of the concerned country was directly involved in the starvation or malnutrition of a part of its population or of the population of a foreign country. Besides, the analysis of the Committee is still focused on the state party submission and the party may be more reluctant to show in its Report violations of the duty to respect rather than the duty to fulfil. With regard to the duty to fulfil, it is often possible to give the impression that the state is working towards the objective whereas this is more difficult when the duty to respect has been violated. It is likely that now that individuals can file complaints against state parties, the duty to respect will receive more attention. Even if the practice is rare, there are examples of violations of the duty to respect in the analysis of country Reports.[24]

[21] See A Muller, 'Limitations to and derogations from economic, social and cultural rights' (2009) 9 *Human Rights Law Review* 557.

[22] Committee on Economic, Social and Cultural Rights, General Comment 12: The Right to Adequate Food, E/2004/22 E/C.12/1999/5, paragraph 18.

[23] Ibid, paragraph 19.

[24] See for instance the Report where the Committee, taking into account the respect of social rights in the Russian Federation, noticed that reports indicated that members of military forces received maltreatment including restriction of access to food and water. Committee on Economic, Social and Cultural Rights, Report on the thirtieth and thirty-first sessions,

C. Duty to Protect

The duty to protect expresses the horizontal dimension of the right to food. It obliges states to regulate relationships between private parties so that individuals or enterprises are unable to deprive individuals of their access to adequate food.[25] In international human rights law there is no room for claims by private parties against other private parties. As a consequence, making a state accountable for violations that in practice are committed by private actors can be controversial. The duty to protect provides that the state is responsible for regulating private relationships in a way that does not deprive individuals of their human rights.

Issues linked with the duty to protect are the human rights obligations of states during and after the processes of privatisation of natural resources, and the regulation of businesses providing services necessary for the realisation of social rights. International human rights law is neutral on the economic system that state parties have to adopt, and certainly there is no obligation to keep certain resources or services public. There is, however, the duty to make the private ownership of natural resources or the provision of services compatible with the rights contained in the Covenant. This means, in the context of the right to food, that the operations of private actors in sensitive sectors cannot prevent access to food and water of a part of the population. Sensitive sectors are not only the ones directly involved with the production and distribution of food and water, but also every other economic sector that can impact on the right to food. For instance, mining and drilling should be conducted in ways which are respectful of the local populations and do not disperse adverse substances in water and food staples.

With regard to agriculture and fisheries, the development of intensive means of production and the exploitation of marine resources should serve the objective of improving accessibility and availability of food. On this issue a landmark case in India exemplifies well how more efficient systems of production can have the unintended consequence of making food less accessible for some people. In the case, the Supreme Court of India found that export-oriented coastal shrimp farming resulted in loss of subsistence of local populations.[26] On this point General Comment 12 states that even

E/2004/22 E/C.12/2003/14. An extreme case was the use of food as a weapon by Sudan through the creation of man-made famines in the southern regions of the country. See Committee on Economic, Social and Cultural Rights, Report on the twenty-second, twenty-third and twenty-fourth sessions, E/2001/22 E/C.12/2000/21.

[25] K Mechlem, 'Food security and the right to food in the discourse of the United Nations' (2004) 10 *European Law Journal* 631, 639.

[26] Supreme Court of India, *S. Jagannath v. Union of India and Others* (*Aquaculture* case), 11 December 1996.

if only *states* can be accountable for compliance with the Covenant, all members of society have responsibilities in the realisation of the right to adequate food, and the regulatory environment the state provides should facilitate the implementation of these responsibilities. The duty to protect has received more attention recently because it includes the duty to regulate the activities of multinational corporations so that they do not affect the enjoyment of the right to food. To regulate the issue General Comment 12 proposes a code of conduct agreed between Governments, civil society and private companies. However, under the duty to protect, states parties are obliged to take all appropriate steps to ensure that the activities of private undertakings comply with the right to food. This means that whenever soft regulation is ineffective, states should try other instruments.[27]

In its Statements on globalisation[28] and on the 2008 global food crisis[29] the Committee offers a more comprehensive criticism of the role played by private actors in the contemporary market economy. The Committee recognises that the diminution of the role of the state, the reliance upon the free market and the privatisation and deregulation of activities once considered the exclusive domain of the state, are of some concern for the implementation of economic, social and cultural rights. Even though these processes are not incompatible with the Covenant, there is the need for instituting flanking policies safeguarding the rights it contains. In the statement issued on the occasion of the 2008 world food crisis the Committee urged state parties to introduce regulation of speculation on food staples and avoiding the use of arable land for the production of non-food products such as biofuel.[30]

D. Duty to Fulfil

The duty to fulfil is controversial in domestic jurisdictions because it extends considerably the prerogatives of the judiciary to review acts and policies of

[27] Committee on Economic, Social and Cultural Rights, General Comment 12: The Right to Adequate Food, E/2004/22 E/C.12/1999/5, paragraph 27.

[28] Committee on Economic, Social and Cultural Rights, Globalization and its impact on the enjoyment of economic, social and cultural rights, E/1999/22-E/C.12/1998/26.

[29] Committee on Economic, Social and Cultural Rights, The World Food Crisis, E/C.12/2008/1.

[30] The Special Rapporteur on the Right to Food has given much attention to the issues related to the duty to protect. Jean Ziegler, at first, and Olivier de Schutter, later on, dedicated Reports to the impact of investment and private economic enterprises on the right to food. Even if the documents are not binding they offer a comprehensive account of the tensions between private action and the right to food. They also demonstrate that the actual procedures of the Committee do not allow sufficient penetration into the intricacies of these tensions. For a summary of the work of Jean Ziegler as Special Rapporteur on the Right to Food, see J Ziegler, C Golay, C Mahon and S-A Way, *The Fight for the Right to Food Lessons Learned* (Palgrave MacMillan, 2011). See also O de Schutter (ed), *Transnational Corporations and Human Rights* (Hart, 2006).

the executive and legislative powers.[31] For this reason the duty is often considered unacceptable, and judges refuse to assess the compatibility of formal acts with social rights on the ground that the values involved in the decision can be weighed only by a political body. The duty to fulfil also receives the criticism of being so vague and empty as to be impossible to apply in practice. These arguments have been successfully rebutted on several occasions but thorny problems remain. Key issues are whether the duty imposes a timetable for compliance and how to deal with the fact that the realisation of the right requires budget allocations that might not be available or which the state might be unwilling to make.[32]

In international law the duty to fulfil is a well-established conceptual device that has been in place since the '80s. The Committee, in General Comment 3, clarified that state parties are subject to the duty to fulfil for every right contained in the Covenant. With regard to the right to food, General Comment 12 requires that every state takes whatever steps are necessary to ensure that everyone is free from hunger and as soon as possible can enjoy the right to adequate food. This obligation has two dimensions. First, under the Covenant, there is the positive duty to 'pro-actively engage in activities intended to strengthen people's access to and utilisation of resources and means to ensure their livelihoods, including food security.' Second, whenever an individual or group is unable, for reasons beyond their control, to enjoy the right by the means at their disposal, the states have the obligation to provide the right directly.

The two main interpretative issues concerning the duty to fulfil are the same ones encountered in domestic law: its apparent indeterminacy and the fact that the duty to fulfil allows for progressive realisation of the right.[33]

[31] A Nolan, B Porter and M Langford, 'The justiciability of social and economic rights: an updated appraisal', Center for Human Rights and Global Justice Working Paper 15, 2007, available at <http://www.chrgj.org/publications/docs/wp/NolanPorterLangford.pdf> accessed 23 December 2017; International Commission of Jurists, 'Courts and the legal enforcement of economic, social and cultural rights: comparative experiences of justiciability', Human Rights and Rule of Law Series No. 2, available at <http://www.refworld.org/docid/4a7840562.html>; M Langford, 'Domestic adjudication on economic social and cultural rights: a socio-legal review' (2009) 11 *International Journal on Human Rights* 91.

[32] S Fredman, *Human Rights Transformed* (Oxford University Press, 2008) 66; J King, 'The Justiciability of Resource Allocation' (2007) 2 *Modern Law Review* 197; A Blyberg, 'The case of mislaid allocation: economic and social rights and budget work' (2009) 11 *International Journal on Human Rights* 123; M Langford, 'The justiciability of social rights: from practice to theory' in M Langford (ed), *Social rights jurisprudence: emerging trends in international and comparative law* (Cambridge University Press, 2009); K Roach, 'The challenges of crafting remedies for violations of socio-economic rights' in M Langford (ed), *Social rights jurisprudence: emerging trends in international and comparative law* (Cambridge University Press, 2009).

[33] K Mechlem, 'Food security and the right to food in the discourse of the United Nations' (2004) 10 *European Law Journal* 631, 639.

The duty to fulfil is in fact an obligation as to result, which means that it is necessary to define the standard to be attained to avoid that the obligation becomes void of normative content. General Comment 12 gives an ample description of the content of the right and this is the standard that states should aim to attain.[34] Nutritious, culturally acceptable and healthy food should be available and accessible to everyone without discrimination. Other qualifying elements were given in the General Comment on the right to health, a right with an intricate normative content that can be generalised to the right to food. The efforts to realise the right to food have to be effective, participatory and accountable and respect the principle of equality. This means that the state has the duty to make available sufficient quantities of all the determinants of the right to food. In addition, the state has to involve the population in all decision-making processes involving the right to food and in case of violations of the right it has the duty to justify itself, showing that all possible efforts have been made. Finally, the state has to grant access to the right to every individual without gender or racial bias and including the poor and the disadvantaged. The Committee went beyond these qualifications, suggesting that every state should implement a detailed right to food strategy derived from the normative content of the right. General Comment 12 provides an in-depth explanation of the requirements of the strategy, suggesting the basic elements that a national law implementing the right should have. In case of severe resource constraints, measures should be undertaken to ensure that the right to adequate food is especially fulfilled for vulnerable populations, groups and individuals.[35]

In order to make the duty applicable, it is necessary to qualify the obligations that the state has while it is in the process of realising the right. Article 2 of the Covenant provides that the state has the duty 'to take steps' towards the realisation of the right. This does not mean that the right to food is aspirational.[36] The state has to move towards the objective as expeditiously as possible and retrogressive measures are allowed only if carefully considered and fully justified on the basis of all the rights contained in the Covenant. The state can justify its inaction for reasons of budget allocations only by demonstrating that 'every effort has been made to use all resources that are at its disposition in an effort to satisfy, as a matter of priority, those

[34] Committee on Economic, Social and Cultural Rights, General Comment 15: The Right to Adequate Food, E/2004/22 E/C.12/1999/5, paragraph 27. S Leckie, 'Violations of Economic Social and Cultural Rights' (1998) *SIM Special* 20; R Kunnemann, 'Violations of the Right to Food' in T van Boven, C Flinterman and I Westendorp (eds), *The Maastricht Guidelines on Violations of Economic, Social and Cultural Rights*, Netherlands Institute for Human Rights (1998) *SIM Special* 20.

[35] K Mechlem, 'Food security and the right to food in the discourse of the United Nations' (2004) *European Law Journal* 631, 640.

[36] General Comment 3, paragraph 8.

minimum obligations.' Even when there are budget constraints, the state has to ensure the widest possible enjoyment of the right to food,[37] and has to develop instruments and strategies to monitor the level of fulfilment of the right. When a step towards the realisation of the right is taken it cannot constitute a form of discrimination against certain categories of people.

IV. THE RIGHT TO FOOD AND THE NEGOTIATION OF TRADE AGREEMENTS

A. Introduction

This book concentrates on the relation between international trade law and the right to food in the context of the external action of the EU. The main argument of the book is that in recent trade agreements the EU has concluded with countries vulnerable to food shortages the right to food was not duly taken into account. This section answers the question whether the Covenant on Economic, Social and Cultural Rights imposes human rights duties on states to be respected not only towards their citizens but also in their international action and towards the citizens of third countries. This issue is central to the debate on the inclusion of the right to food in the external relations of the EU, since the EU itself is an expression of the external action of EU Member States, which are all Members of the Covenant. Moreover, it is generally accepted in public international law that states' human rights duties apply also to the action of international organisations to which states are parties.[38]

As will be clarified, the debate on external human rights duties stemming from the Covenant is only a part of the question whether the EU has a duty to take the right to food into account when concluding international agreements with third countries. In fact, human rights obligations on the EU and its Member States stem also from EU law, cooperation agreements concluded between the EU and countries vulnerable to food shortages, as well as the free trade agreements themselves. However, the extraterritorial dimension of the Covenant remains crucial since it is today the only international legal source containing an extensive recognition of the right. When the European Union expressly accepts human rights obligations in the international agreements it concludes, as it did with the Caribbean and sub-Saharan countries, the Covenant is the legal instrument to which reference is made to identify the normative content of the right. This section elucidates

[37] Sandra Fredman, above n. 32.

[38] See A Clapham, *Human Rights Obligations of Non-State Actors* (Oxford University Press, 2010) 162.

the state of the art of the doctrine on extraterritorial obligations to realise the right to food. This section shows that even though extraterritorial duties are less developed than domestic ones, their existence has been recognised in public international law.

B. Extraterritorial Duties in the Covenant

The debate on the existence of extraterritorial obligations under the International Covenant on Economic, Social and Cultural Rights is a longstanding one. Even if extraterritorial human rights duties remained in the shadows for most of the twentieth century, with the increase of the effects of globalisation on people and the thickening of supranational regulation the debate gained momentum. In particular, since the late '90s the Committee has become more explicit in stating the existence of international obligations stemming from the Covenant. However, this has been done through General Comments and Statements rather than via the reporting mechanisms. States in fact do not have to report on their compliance with the Covenant in their relations with other countries. As Coomans suggests,[39] the Committee introduced basic notions but never clarified the normative content of extraterritorial duties arising from the Covenant. The international reach of the Covenant is based on Article 2, which provides that every state party has the obligation: 'to take steps, individually and through international assistance and cooperation, especially economic and technical ... with a view to achieving progressively the full realisation of the rights'.

Articles 22 and 23 imply that the rights contained in the Covenant should be realised also through the action of the United Nations and the provision of technical assistance and in regional meetings by state parties. Moreover, the Committee, in General Comment 3, recalled that under Articles 55 and 56 of the Charter of the United Nations there is the obligation to cooperate for development. The duty received further attention in the UN Declaration on the Right to Development and the Committee maintains that, to be consistent with international law, the concept of development has to contain also the realisation of economic, social and cultural rights. The Committee also noticed that it is evident that the full realisation of the Covenant will remain unfulfilled and aspirational without 'a programme of international assistance and cooperation on the part of all States that are in the position to undertake one'.[40]

[39] F Coomans, 'The extraterritorial scope of the international covenant on economic social and cultural rights in the work of the UN Committee on Economic Social and Cultural Rights' (2011) *Human Rights Law Review* 1.

[40] General Comment 3, paragraph 14.

With regard to the general scope of the Covenant there is a debate on whether the obligation to cooperate internationally goes beyond official cooperation such as development aid and technical support to encompass also the other situations in which states relate with each other.[41] However, the lack of general legal underpinning of extraterritorial duties in certain areas has been supplemented by explicit recognition by the Committee (as in the case of international trade)[42] or in the international practice of certain countries through the inclusion of human rights clauses in international agreements dealing with other issues. This is what happens for instance in the trade agreements the EU concludes with third countries, which always contain a general human rights clause making international human rights law applicable to the treaty in question.[43]

C. Extraterritorial Duties Concerning the Right to Food

In the specific case of the right to food the Committee went beyond the general recognition of the duty to assist and cooperate and suggested that the right to food should be taken into account whenever the external action of the state is relevant for the right. The right to food is in fact one of the few rights in the Covenant that was codified with an intrinsic extraterritorial dimension. Article 11 provides that the right to food should be realised also through 'international cooperation', and identifies in the methods of food production and distribution critical aspects of the realisation of the right. In addition Article 11 paragraph 2(b) explicitly recognises that international cooperation should also pay attention to the different needs of food-importing and food-exporting countries. For these reasons, even though the Committee has never been as exhaustive as when defining internal duties, it clearly recognised that the obligation to realise the right to food through international action goes well beyond the duty to provide aid and technical assistance.[44] For this reason, the Committee included in General

[41] Skogly argued that 'international cooperation and assistance' includes a very wide area of subjects. See SI Skogly, 'Right to adequate food: national implementation and extraterritorial obligations' (2007) 11 *Max Planck United Nations Yearbook* 329.

[42] See section 4.C below.

[43] See section 4.D below on human rights duties the EU creates in free trade agreements.

[44] The explicit recognition of trade as an area of policy making necessary for the realisation of the right to food has a solid economic underpinning. Authoritative economic literature has in fact recognised the limited impact of food aid and development cooperation in general to solve global issues such as hunger and poverty. See P Collier, *The Bottom Billion* (Oxford University Press, 2008); D Moyo, *Dead Aid* (Farar, Straus and Giroux, 2009); W Easterly, *The White Man's Burden: Why the West's Efforts to Aid the Rest Have Done So Much Ill and So Little Good* (Penguin, 2007). In terms of Constitutional Law of the European Union, the Lisbon Treaty provided legal underpinning to the inclusion of economic and social rights in external trade policies through Article 21 paragraph 2 of the Treaty on the European Union.

Comment 12 on the Right to Food a section on the duties of states to realise the right through international cooperation. There the Committee defines the duty to consider the relevant effects on the right to food when the state is involved in treaty-making:

> In implementing this commitment, States parties should take steps to respect the enjoyment of the right to food in other countries, to protect that right, to facilitate access to food and to provide the necessary aid when required. *States parties should, in international agreements whenever relevant, ensure that the right to adequate food is given due attention and consider the development of further international legal instruments to that end.* (emphasis added)[45]

The last sentence of the cited paragraph contains the recognition that the special nature of the right to food requires that the Members of the Covenant take the right into account whenever a treaty they are concluding can have an impact on the realisation of the right. This applies to situations where the conclusion of the agreement can impact on the right to food of the citizens of the trading countries as well as when the consequences fall on third country nationals. This is so because the Committee recognises the international dimension of the realisation of the right to food, which is detached from domestic policies and takes into account the fact that only through a common international effort can the right to food be realised globally. This conclusion is also supported by the wording of Article 11, which explicitly recognises such international dimension of the realisation of the right to food and mentions economic policies such as trade. In the General Comment the Committee also identified specific situations of international action where the right to food should be taken into account. In particular, the Committee established that states should refrain from food embargoes and more generally from using food as an instrument of political and economic pressure. When food aid is provided, this cannot develop into forms of dependency between the donor and the beneficiary. This means also that food aid should not disrupt local producers and local markets and should aim for the return to self-reliance of the beneficiaries. With regard to military occupation, the Committee had occasion to specify that the duties under the Covenant extend to the territories under the effective control of the state party.

Additional obligations have been accepted by the EU in the context of its cooperation agreements with countries vulnerable to food shortages, in particular the Lomé Convention and the Cotonou Agreement. Since the late '90s the European Union has included a human rights clause in every trade agreement it concludes. The clause explicitly recognises that trade is not per se an objective of the treaties but an instrument to improve living conditions and human rights in vulnerable countries.

[45] General Comment 12, paragraph 36.

In conclusion, the Covenant explicitly recognised the existence of international human rights duties which oblige countries to work towards the realisation of economic and social rights through international policies addressed not to their own citizens but to third country nationals or generally to the international community. Undeniably, to what extent this should be done has not always been clarified by the Committee, which mentions only certain international policies as examples of areas of international cooperation within which economic and social rights should be respected. However, the approach has been more pervasive in the specific case of the right to food where the Committee has explicitly recognised that countries should take the right into account when concluding any kind of relevant international agreement. Even though the recognition of external human rights duties with regard to the right to food is extensive the Committee has remained very general with regard to the content of such duties, especially with regard to sector-specific international policies such as trade. This attitude might be explained by the fact that the Committee is attentive not to overstep into areas of international law in which it has not competence or expertise. The absence of detailed human rights duties concerning specific areas of international treaty-making should not be considered, however, as a sign that countries have no duty to realise the right to food when concluding international agreements. In fact, the Covenant and the Committee explicitly recognise the existence of external human rights duties in particular with regard to the right to food. The specific content of these duties will have to be defined case-by-case, taking into account the possible effects of the treaty in question on the realisation of the right to food and the often highly technical details of the area of international law concerned.

D. Extraterritorial Duties to Realise the Right to Food Based on EU Law

The right to food does not have explicit legal bases in EU primary sources. The Treaty of Lisbon does not provide a clear-cut mandate to the EU for the realisation of Economic and Social Rights, and the EU Charter of Fundamental Rights does not contain the right to food. The accession of the EU to the European Convention on Human Rights will not change this legal setting, since the Convention does not contain the right to food either. In addition, the EU has no plans to accede to the International Covenant of Economic, Social and Cultural Rights and the Covenant has a particularly weak status in EU law and policymaking. This situation, however, does not provide the EU with a legal exemption from taking into account the right to food when designing its external policies. This is so for at least four reasons.

First, since the adoption of the Treaty of Lisbon all the external policies of the EU, including the external trade policy, are subject to the general principles of Article 21 of the Treaty on the European Union. The first paragraph of the article explicitly provides that the external action of the EU shall be guided by: 'the universality and indivisibility of human rights and fundamental freedoms, respect for human dignity, the principles of equality and solidarity, and respect for the principles of the United Nations Charter and international law'. This article, referring to the indivisibility of human rights, gives economic and social rights the same legal status as civil and political rights in the external relations of the EU. This clause, which creates the legal foundation for the inclusion of the right to food within the priorities of EU external action beside other EU foreign policy goals,[46] was recently judicially enforced by the Court of Justice of the European Union in its Opinion 2/15.[47] In Opinion 2/15 Article 21 TEU was one of the main reasons for the Court to include sustainable development within the exclusive competence for commerce of the EU.[48]

Second, all the Members of the EU are also parties to the International Covenant of Economic, Social and Cultural Rights and are often parties to the other international instruments codifying the right to food. The Covenant creates not only obligations to realise the right to food on the territory of the state but also the external obligation to progressively realise the right through international cooperation, including through participation in international organisations. Since no external action of the EU can be carried out without the consent of Member States' executive powers through their vote in the European Council, human rights duties of EU Member States directly reflect on the EU.[49] Besides, when the EU carries out its external policies through mixed agreements the resulting agreement also requires the ratification of the national parliaments.

Third, even if the EU is not a Member of the Covenant on Economic, Social and Cultural Rights it can bind itself to respect the Covenant when

[46] Other parts of Article 21 include references to the responsibility of the EU with regard to countries vulnerable to human rights violations and poverty. For instance Article 21.2(d) provides that the European Union shall 'foster the sustainable economic, social and environmental development of developing countries with the primary aim of eradicating poverty'. In the same vein, Article 21.2(g) provides that the EU should assist populations, countries and regions confronting natural or man-man disasters. Also when dealing with EU external trade policy Article 21 contextualises 'progressive liberalisation of international trade' within the wider objective of 'encouraging the integration of all countries into the world economy'.

[47] Opinion 2/15 of the Court, CJEU, 16 May 2017.

[48] G Gruni, 'Towards a Sustainable World Trade Law? The Common Commercial Policy of the European Union after Opinion 2/15' (2018) 13 *Global Trade and Customs Journal* 4.

[49] On indirect human rights obligations of the European Union deriving from the human rights duties of Member States, see T Ahmed and I de Jesus Butler, 'The European Union and Human Rights: An International Law Perspective' (2006) 17 *The European Journal of International Law* 771.

concluding agreements with third countries. An example of this practice is the Cotonou Agreement, the international instrument providing the framework for the cooperation between the EU and 77 developing countries in Africa, the Caribbean and the Pacific.[50] In fact, the Preamble to the Treaty contains an explicit reference to the Covenant. In addition, the parties to the Cotonou Agreement asserted

> their resolve to make ... a significant contribution to the economic, social and cultural development of the ACP States and to the greater well-being of their population, helping them facing the challenges of globalisation ... in the effort to give the process of globalisation a stronger social dimension.

Most of all, Article 9 of the Cotonou Agreement is a human rights clause explicitly binding the parties to respect economic and social rights. The clause produces exactly the same binding legal effects on the EU and on its partners in the African, Caribbean and Pacific regions.[51]

Finally, the EU has a longstanding tradition of including a general human rights clause in any free trade agreements it concludes with third countries. These clauses attracted the attention of legal doctrine for their potential to be a powerful source of human rights duties. Lorand Bartels, for instance, maintains that such clauses produce both negative and positive human rights obligations, including the duty to monitor the realisation of human rights.[52]

[50] For a general introduction to the Cotonou Agreement see A Flint, *Trade, Poverty and the Environment: The EU, Cotonou and African–Caribbean–Pacific Bloc* (Palgrave Macmillan, 2008); O Babarinde and G Faber (eds), *The European Union and the Developing Countries: The Cotonou Agreement* (Martinus Nijhoff, 2008); A Hadfield, 'Janus advances? An analysis of EC development policy and the 2005 Cotonou Partnership Agreement' (2007) 12 *European Foreign Affairs Review* 39; S Kingah, 'The revised Cotonou Agreement between the European Community and African, Caribbean and Pacific States: innovations on security, political dialogue, transparency and social responsibility' (2006) 50 *Journal of African Law* 59.

[51] Article 9 of the Cotonou Agreement provides that: '1. Cooperation shall be directed towards sustainable development centred on the human person, who is the main protagonist and beneficiary of development; this entails respect for and promotion of all human rights. Respect for all human rights and fundamental freedoms, including respect for fundamental social rights, democracy based on the rule of law and transparent and accountable governance are an integral part of sustainable development ... 2. The Parties refer to their international obligations and commitments concerning respect for human rights. They reiterate their deep attachment to human dignity and human rights, which are legitimate aspirations of individuals and peoples. Human rights are universal, indivisible and inter-related. The Parties undertake to promote and protect all fundamental freedoms and human rights, be they civil and political, or economic, social and cultural. In this context, the Parties reaffirm the equality of men and women. ... Respect for human rights, democratic principles and the rule of law, which underpin the ACP–EU Partnership, shall underpin the domestic and international policies of the Parties and constitute the essential elements of this Agreement ... 4. The Partnership shall actively support the promotion of human rights, processes of democratisation, consolidation of the rule of law, and good governance'.

[52] L Bartels, 'Human Rights and Sustainable Development Obligations in EU Free Trade Agreements' University of Cambridge Legal Studies Research Paper Series, Paper No. 24/2012; L Bartels, 'A Legal Analysis of Human Rights Clauses in the EU's Euro-Mediterranean

Accordingly, the Lisbon Treaty provided the EU with a framework, and a mandate, to exercise its external powers in order to contribute to the realisation of human rights, including economic and social rights. In addition, the Member States of the EU have the duty to take the right to food into consideration when taking part in EU external policies. In certain cases, the EU also contracted binding obligations vis-à-vis third countries to respect and realise economic and social rights, as is the case with the Agreement it concluded with the African, Caribbean and Pacific countries.

E. Conclusions

The Covenant on Economic, Social and Cultural Rights imposes on countries the duty to take the right to food into account during the negotiations of trade agreements. In addition the EU has additional duties to consider human rights when concluding free trade agreements with third countries, stemming from its own fundamental treaties and from international treaties, such as the Cotonou agreements concluded with third states. The clarification of the normative prescriptions of such duties is still open to debate. However, countries have the obligation under the Covenant to identify case-by-case the technical legal instruments to take the right to food into account when concluding a trade agreement. In particular countries should avoid the conclusion of trade agreements which limit the capacity of signatory parties to intervene in food shortages on the territory of a state. This duty stems directly from the general duty to progressively realise the right to food of the Covenant and from obligations contained in treaties binding on the EU. In addition to this, several Reports from the UN Human Rights Council have exemplified other ways to protect, respect and fulfil the right to food during the negotiations of trade agreements. Even if these documents are not binding they can provide some ideas to the Members of the Covenant on how to respect their external human rights duties under the Covenant.[53]

Association Agreement' (2004) 9 *Mediterranean Politics* 368. See also H Strydom, 'Will the Cotonou agreement succeed where Lomé I–IV have failed?' (2007) 32 *South African Yearbook of International Law* 125; S Steiner, 'The External Dimension of the European Fundamental Rights Agency' (2006) 11 *Austrian Review of International and European Law* 105; D-C Horng, 'The human rights clause in the European Union's external trade and development agreements' (2003) 9 *European Law Journal* 677; B Brandtner and A Rosas, 'Human Rights and External Relations of the European Community: An Analysis of Doctrine and Practice' (1998) 9 *European Journal of International Law* 468; M Cremona, 'Human Rights and democracy clauses in the EC's trade agreements' (1995) 126 *Law & Justice—Christian Law Review* 105.

[53] United Nations Human Rights Council, Guiding principles on human rights assessment of trade and investment agreements, A/HRC/19/59/Add.5.

Any attempt to introduce human rights in trade negotiations will, however, prove extremely controversial for historical reasons and because the theoretical underpinnings of the two areas of legislation are different and pursue different interests and objectives. In fact, the resistance to the inclusion of human rights in the context of trade negotiations also stems from the concern that having to deal with human rights when negotiating a trade agreement could excessively burden an already complex process to find agreement with the other party. In addition, the reliance on comparative advantage as a justification of world trade law and the risk that human rights might highjack the policy to liberalise trade, leading to protectionism, are all common arguments in trade circles. The following section shows, however, how attempts to create a dialogue between trade law and human rights are already in place and this can lead to the synthesis of different, but complementary visions of international cooperation. Accordingly, this early attempt to imagine human rights duties in trade negotiations could evolve into a permanent laboratory to promote a model of globalisation pursuing economic integration while protecting individual entitlements.

V. DEFRAGMENTING INTERNATIONAL LAW: PATHS OF LEGAL DIALOGUE BETWEEN HUMAN RIGHTS AND TRADE LAW AND THE ROLE OF THE EU

World trade law developed mostly separately from the rest of public international norms, first through the GATT system and then within the WTO institutional mechanisms. Free trade agreements are an additional evolution of that system, based on several exceptions contained in the WTO agreements. The isolation of world trade law has been at times extreme with even the application of the Vienna Convention on the Law of Treaties being an issue of debate.[54] This created a system of rules which developed outside the United Nations framework through successive rounds of international negotiations within a specialised system of knowledge based on free trade, comparative advantage and countries' economic leverage.[55] The liberalisation of world trade remains today a non-Pareto efficient macroeconomic policy, aiming to maximising wealth in the system without protecting individual entitlements.[56] It is often coloured by the aim of

[54] D Plameter and PC Mavroidis, 'The WTO legal system: sources of law' (1998) 92 *American Journal of International Law* 398.

[55] S Meunier, *Trading Voices* (Princeton University Press, 2005); A Hoda and A Gulati, *WTO Negotiations on Agriculture and Developing Countries* (The Johns Hopkins University Press, 2007).

[56] AO Sykes, 'Comparative advantage and the normative economics of international trade policy' (1998) 1 *Journal of International Economic Law* 49; R Schumacher, 'Deconstructing the Theory of Comparative Advantage' (2013) 2 *World Social and Economic Review* 83; D Rodrik,

reducing the intervention of the state in the economy, to avoid distortions of global trade.[57]

Conversely, international human rights law developed separately from world trade law through international treaty-making, often sponsored by the United Nations. Economic and social rights pursue the aim of ensuring human dignity through a minimum level of entitlements which is recognised for every person no matter what is their role in the economic system. Human rights law recognises an active role for signatory parties of international agreements to respect, protect and fulfil human rights also through active intervention in society. However, human rights law does not advocate any specific economic recipe and is considered compatible with the free trade model only as long as it delivers the minimum level of individual entitlements required in human rights treaties.

Even though human rights and world trade law are not mutually exclusive, the history of their relation has been often one of tensions. The legal fragmentation of these two areas of international law caused also an entrenchment of the respective theoretical underpinnings and few occasions of dialogue. The main claim of this section is that even if human rights and world trade law remain largely separate there are seeds of institutional dialogue between the two areas emerging which, if pursued, will allow a synthesis of the objectives pursued and the interests protected. Accordingly, there is an occasion for the EU to take international leadership in the construction of a global economic order which is able to pursue economic integration while ensuring basic human rights protection to every person.

First, the WTO has been slowly softening its traditional stance of complete isolation from the rest of international legal order.[58] Today, the Vienna Convention on the Law of Treaties is recognised by the WTO Dispute Settlement Body[59] and there have been mild signs that other areas of international law might increase in their relevance.[60] This is not to say that we

'Straight talk on Trade', Project Syndicate 15 November 2016, available at <https://www.project-syndicate.org/commentary/trump-win-economists-responsible-by-dani-rodrik-2016-11?barrier=accessreg>.

[57] C Berry, *Globalisation and ideology in Britain Neoliberalism Free Trade and the Global Economy* (Manchester University Press, 2011); D Harvey, *A Brief History of Neoliberalism* (Oxford University Press, 2007); MB Steger, *Globalization: A very short introduction* (Oxford University Press, 2017).

[58] For an evolutional analysis of WTO Law see G Messenger, *The Development of World Trade Organization Law* (Oxford University Press, 2016).

[59] WTO Appellate Body Report, 'United States—Standards for reformulated and conventional gasoline' WT/DS2/9.

[60] J Pauwelyn, 'The role of public international law in the WTO: how far can we go?' (2001) 95 *The American Journal of International Law* 535; J Pauwelyn, 'Interplay between the WTO Treaty and Other International Legal Instruments and Tribunals: Evolution after 20 years of WTO Jurisprudence' in CE Cote, V Guevremont and R Ouellet (eds), *Proceedings of the Quebec City Conference on the WTO at 20* (Presses de l'Université de Laval, 2018);

are anywhere close to an integration of world trade law with the rest of public international law, but a slow pattern of inclusion can be detected in recent years. Besides the Vienna Convention, another example is the WTO use of the Codex Alimentarius.[61] Attempts to link trade policy with food security were also made in the recent Bali and Nairobi WTO Ministerial Conferences, which resulted in some modification of WTO law on domestic support to food production and export subsidies.[62]

Second, even though the WTO remains independent from the United Nations and other organisations concerned with human rights and development cooperation, there have been attempts to involve the WTO machinery in international networks outside traditional trade policy. Notable examples are the International Trade Centre, a multilateral agency where the WTO and the UN work together, and the inclusion of trade and the WTO in the strategy to pursue Sustainable Development Goals.[63] The WTO itself showed some mild openings towards other institutions, allowing some UN representatives to act as observers in certain committees[64] or missions from human rights bodies. This included a mission from the UN Special Rapporteur on the Right to Food at the WTO.[65]

Third, international human rights bodies often have institutions which specialise in trade issues. For instance, within the UN system the United Nations Conference on Trade and Development (UNCTAD) looks at trade policy from the perspective of improving the capacity of developing countries to access its benefits. The UN Human Rights Council also has been covering

J Pauwelyn, 'Sources of International Trade Law: Mantras and Controversies at the World Trade Organization' in S Besson and J d'Aspremont, *Oxford Handbook on the Sources of International Law* (Oxford University Press, 2016); PJ Kuijper, 'Conflicting Rules and Clashing Courts The Case of Multilateral Environmental Agreements, Free Trade Agreements and the WTO', ICTSD Issue Paper No. 10.

[61] M Foltea, *International Organizations in WTO Dispute Settlement How Much Institutional Sensitivity?* (Cambridge University Press, 2014) 245.

[62] A Matthews, 'Food Security and WTO Domestic Support Disciplines post-Bali', ICTSD Issue Paper No. 53; J Hepburn, 'Evaluating agriculture in the Nairobi package', ICTSD Bridges Africa, available at <https://www.ictsd.org/bridges-news/bridges-africa/news/evaluating-agriculture-in-the-nairobi-package> accessed 21 December 2017.

[63] WTO, 'The WTO and the International Trade Centre (ITC)', available at <https://www.wto.org/english/thewto_e/coher_e/wto_itc_e.htm> accessed 21 December 2017.

[64] There is for instance an observer of the United Nations Environment Programme (UNEP) in the WTO Committee on Trade and the Environment see WTO, 'The WTO and United Nations Environment Programme', available at <https://www.wto.org/english/thewto_e/coher_e/wto_unep_e.htm> accessed 27 December 2017; see also 'The WTO and Food and Agriculture Organization', available at <https://www.wto.org/english/thewto_e/coher_e/wto_fao_e.htm> accessed 27 December 2017.

[65] United Nations Human Rights Council, 'Report of the Special Rapporteur on the right to food, Olivier de Schutter Mission to the World Trade Organization', available at <http://carnegieendowment.org/files/Summary_of%20report%20of%20the%20Special%20Rapporteur%20on%20the%20right%20to%20food.pdf> accessed 29 December 2017.

trade issues and its Special Rapporteurs regularly engage the WTO and produce reports on trade law and human rights. The Food and Agriculture Organization (FAO) has trade policy expertise and makes proposals on modifications of world trade law to promote global food security.[66] Even the UN Committee on Economic, Social and Cultural Rights started considering trade law in its statements.[67] These organs are notably marginal to international trade policy and weakened by institutional shortcomings, lack of funding and the absence of legal enforcement. They do, however, represent early examples of interaction between human rights and world trade law.

Fourth, regional organisations such as the EU have, on some limited occasions, already taken a more nuanced position towards the separation between human rights and world trade law. This happened for instance by including references to human rights and labour standards in their free trade agreements with third countries.[68] Even if the marginality of human rights and food security in trade policy, as also this book will show, remains evident, these can be interpreted as early signs of an emerging sensitivity to the limits of international trade theory and the role that trade negotiations can play in the pursuit of interests and objectives which are not central to the theory of international trade law.

Fifth, even though world trade law remains largely separate from the rest of international norms the research on their interplay is flourishing. In the last 20 years there has been an evident effort to create a body of knowledge to identify interactions between trade agreements and other interests, including human rights. This effort, which has often developed under the concept of sustainable development, has created an international network of scholars and think tanks which is increasingly visible and active in high-level trade policy circles. Accordingly, this process of knowledge creation is allowing the world trade community to be less isolated from interests, like

[66] See for instance the FAO trade policy briefs available at: <http://www.fao.org/economic/est/publications/trade-policy-briefs/en/> accessed 29 December 2017.

[67] Statement by the Committee on Economic, Social and Cultural Rights, 'Globalization and its impact on the enjoyment of economic, social and cultural rights' E/C, 12/1998/26; Statement of the Committee to the Third Ministerial Conference of the World Trade Organization E/C 12/1999/11; Statement of the Committee on the world food crisis E/C 12/2008/1.

[68] L Bartels, *Human Rights Conditionality in EU's International Agreements* (Oxford University Press 2005); L Bartels, 'The EU's approach to social standards and the TTIP' in S Khorana (ed), *The Transatlantic Trade and Investment Partnership (TTIP) Negotiations between the EU and the USA* (CIDOB, 2015); G Gruni, 'Law or Aspiration? The EU Proposal for a Labour Rights Clause in the Transatlantic Trade and Investment Partnership' (2016) 43 *Legal Issues of Economic Integration* 399; G Gruni, 'Labor Standards in the EU-South Korea Free Trade Agreement' (2017) 5 *Korean Journal of International and Comparative Law* 100.

human rights, which are absent or left at the margins during the negotiation of trade agreements.[69]

Finally, the traditional theoretical underpinning of the GATT and WTO system is also being questioned and revisited in economic theory. The widespread use of general equilibrium models, for instance, is at the centre of a heated debate between economists, especially after the 2008 financial crisis. Debates on the use of non-Pareto efficient policies and the limited capacity of trade to distribute wealth and avoid inequality are also gaining steam. This shifting theoretical ground could promote the inclusion in trade law of new ideas and concepts to correct the defects of the present system.

In conclusion, the history of the GATT, WTO and free trade agreements has been one of separation from the rest of public international law and in many respects this still holds today. However, the argument that world trade law encodes an inflexible agenda which is in conflict with other areas of international law such as human rights cannot be defended. A plethora of institutional, legal and academic processes are at play which all favour an opening of world trade law to normative and theoretical influences from other fields. Accordingly, the confrontation between world trade law and human rights has no reason to occur in a world where trade specialists and human rights lawyers are increasingly aware of the limits of their respective fields and both engage with the design of the rules of globalisation. This is an occasion for the EU, a major trade power and highly influential member of the WTO, to design policies aimed at defragmenting international law, allowing a synthesis between the macro-economic approach of trade law and the individual entitlements protected by human rights treaties. This is particularly evident with regard to the rules on international trade of food products, which have direct influence on the capacity of individuals to access an adequate amount of food.

[69] E Vranes, *Trade and the Environment Fundamental Issues in International Law, WTO Law, and Legal Theory* (Oxford University Press, 2009); S Droege et al, 'The trade system and climate action: ways forward under the Paris Agreement', Climate Strategies Working Paper, October 2016, 13; O De Schutter, *Trade in the service of sustainable development linking trade to labour rights and environmental standards* (Bloomsbury Hart, 2017); E Reid, *Balancing human rights, environmental protection and international trade* (Bloomsbury Hart, 2017); J Shi, *Free trade and cultural diversity in international law* (Bloomsbury Hart, 2013); International Law Association, 'Mandate of the ILA Committee on Sustainable Development and the Green Economy in International Trade Law', available at <http://www.ila-hq.org/en/committees/index.cfm/cid/1052> accessed 29 December 2017; D Geraets, 'The case of shale gas extraction regulation in light of CETA and TTIP: another example of the frackmentation of international law' (2016) 24 *Environmental Liability* 16; PJ Kuijper, 'Conflicting rules and clashing courts: the case of environmental agreements, free trade agreements and the WTO', International Centre for Trade and Sustainable Development, Issue Paper No. 10.

VI. CONCLUSIONS

The human right to adequate food has a defined normative content providing specific duties to respect, protect and fulfil that states have to observe under international law in order to progress towards the realisation of the right. With regard to international trade, the Committee on Economic, Social and Cultural Rights has clarified that human rights obligations stemming from the right are applicable to international trade institutions and international organisations such as the EU. In particular, the human right to food obliges countries to prevent other areas of international law from creating obstacles to the realisation of the right, and this applies also to international trade law and to the treaties regulating transnational trade of food. However, the Committee has remained general with regard to the specific transnational duties to be considered in the context of the negotiation and conclusion of international trade agreements. Besides international human rights law, duties on the EU are based on its own Treaties and from obligations the EU has accepted in cooperation agreements and in the free trade agreements themselves. All these obligations go in the direction of inclusion of the protection of individual entitlements such as the right to food whenever the EU concludes a free trade agreement with a third country.

This chapter acknowledges that attempts to bridge the gap between world trade law and human rights remain controversial for historical reasons and because the theoretical underpinnings of the two areas of legislation are different and pursue different interests and objectives. In fact, the resistance to the inclusion of human rights in the context of trade negotiations also stems from the concern that having to deal with human rights when negotiating a trade agreement could excessively burden an already complex process of finding agreement with the other party. In addition, the reliance on comparative advantage as a justification of world trade law and the risk that human rights may highjack the policies to liberalise trade, leading to protectionism, are all common arguments in trade circles. This chapter, however, maintains that even if differences remain, the isolation of world trade law from other areas of international law is being challenged by several processes which all favour a more open attitude towards trade law and policy. Accordingly, the argument that human rights law and world trade law are incompatible does not hold in view of such processes and of the increasingly perceived limits of both trade and human rights expertise. In this changing landscape there is an opportunity for the EU to design policies aimed at a synthesis between the macro-economic approach of trade law and the individual entitlements protected by human rights treaties. This would allow trade policy to correct some of its theoretical shortcomings and human rights to engage with the rules regulating globalisation.

3

Realising the Right to Food in the Global Food Market

I. INTRODUCTION

IN THE FACE of the tendency of contemporary international policymaking to favour the integration between national and international food markets, the international dimension of the realisation of the right to food is now an essential complement to domestic strategies working towards the fulfilment of the right.[1] However, even though the International Committee on Economic, Social and Cultural Rights has stressed the importance of international trade for the realisation of the right to food, it did not clarify the mechanisms by which the trade of food between countries links with the fulfilment of the right. It only noted that in capitalist economies, where the realisation of social rights relies on market forces, the Members of the Covenant have the duty to ensure that market behaviour is not disruptive of the realisation of social rights. In other words, whenever pure market conditions do not guarantee the progressive realisation of a right or disrupt its fulfilment, countries have the duty to identify and implement adequate policies. This can be done through domestic social policies when there are budget allocations available and the state is in the position to provide food aid to its citizens directly.[2] When this is not possible because the country does not have public resources available to cope with the crisis the country will have to consider alternative solutions, including trade policies, in order to limit the impact of international food prices on their domestic markets.[3]

[1] See Chapter 2 of this book for the definition of the right to food in international human rights law and the position of the International Committee on Economic, Social and Cultural Rights on globalisation.

[2] Since this book concentrates on the right to food and international trade law there is no space to mention the domestic policies that countries can implement to cope with domestic food shortages even when these are caused by the instability of the international food market. For an example of domestic policies that countries can implement, see Food and Agriculture Organization (FAO), *Voluntary guidelines to support the realisation of the right to adequate food in the context of national food security* (FAO, 2005).

[3] See United Nations Economic and Social Commission for Asia and the Pacific, 'Insulating Domestic Food Markets from International Price Volatility', available at <http://www.uncapsa.org/LIBRARYJournal_detail.asp?VJournalKey=873>.

This is particularly so when the countries affected are vulnerable developing countries with limited financial resources to implement public policies to cope with a domestic food crisis.

Any country taking part in international trade negotiations will have to take these shortcomings into account when including clauses which regulate the international commerce of food products. This is so because at the same time as countries implement international trade law they also have to cope with the instability of international food markets and protect citizens from extreme market behaviour which could affect their capacity to access adequate food. Accordingly, this chapter introduces the main features of the international food market and highlights the most relevant inadequacies of the present system for the realisation of the right to food. The chapter then concentrates on the role that the EU could play in promoting an international legislation of trade, taking stock of these shortcomings. The EU is, in fact, in a decisive position for its influence on international trade law and its leverage during trade negotiations.

The chapter is divided into five further sections. Section II introduces the main failures of the international food market observed recently: price volatility, negative incentives for domestic food production and concentration of market power. Section III highlights why states cannot merely rely on food and development aid to solve the issues, and why international trade law is relevant. Section IV defines the principal categories of countries that in the present configuration of the global agricultural market remain vulnerable to food shortages. The existence of substantial market failures and the presence of extremely exposed categories are stumbling blocks to the realisation of the right to food. Section V argues that the EU is in a privileged position to promote an international legislation of trade which takes these shortcomings into account. This is so because the EU is one of the most prominent trading blocs and its external trade policy is influential of the outcome of international trade negotiations. Accordingly, whenever the EU concludes a trade agreement with a country vulnerable to hunger and malnutrition, it has the leverage and the technical know-how to include clauses attempting to encompass the realisation of the right to food among the objectives of the trade agreement. Section VI concludes.

II. MARKET FAILURES

Since the '70s international trade of food has gained a new dimension, the quantity of food imported and exported has expanded and the variety of food staples included in international exchanges has increased. As a consequence, the international food market has amplified its influence on domestic policy decisions and on the planning of agricultural production. With regard to the realisation of the right to food, the international market has gained a more central position in the capacity of countries and individuals of realising the right. This can be a positive factor as long as the international market contributes to the improvement of living standards of vulnerable categories.

The development of a thriving international market of food does not come, however, without concerns. In fact, a growing international market of food also means that availability and accessibility of commodities crucial for the realisation of the right to food escape the control of national jurisdictions and become increasingly dependent on the market. In fact, market forces changing the quantity of food available to each country and its price can considerably influence the number of people able to realise their basic needs. When this happens, complex economic interactions, often left in the shadows by economic literature, link the supranational dimension of the trade of food with the day-to-day struggle of vulnerable sectors of world society to access basic food staples. In countries with public resources available the failures of global food markets can be coped with through domestic social policies. However, this is more difficult in developing countries, especially when there is limited availability of public resources.

In a perfect world, international markets would always present the ideal conditions for each country and would never be disruptive of national food security. Production of food would be stable and up to the task of satisfying everyone's needs, and the price of basic food staples would be steady and not influential on economic accessibility. Decades of empirical observation of market behaviour, however, have demonstrated a different reality, where the price of food commodities fluctuates continuously for reasons still not well understood, the global food supply is variable, and the global food market proves to be highly unreliable. The emblem of the untrustworthiness of the international food market is the occurrence of global food crises, generally lasting several years, during which the price or quantity of key food commodities gets out of control.[4] In the '70s a major food crisis killed half a million people in Asia and Africa and caused malnutrition and illness for many more.[5] In 2007 the international price of several key staples spiked, causing a step back in the fight against hunger and provoking widespread social unrest. Fluctuations in the price of commodities traded internationally are a common feature of global markets and attempts to artificially set international prices have proved ineffective.[6] When unstable markets affect the capacity of the individual to access an adequate amount of food the realisation of the right food is impaired. During these market-related food crises countries are obliged to do their best to safeguard the right to food

[4] United Nations, *The Global Social Crisis* (United Nations, 2011) 62.

[5] C Gerlach, 'Famine responses in the world food crisis 1972–1975 and the World Food Conference 1974' (2015) 22 *European Review of History* 929.

[6] M Raffaelli, *The rise and demise of commodity agreements* (Woodhead Publishing, 1995).

of their citizens. This can be done through social policies and incentives to domestic agriculture when possible. However, whenever these instruments are not available countries can intervene in their import and export of food products to limit the negative impact of the international market on domestic food security.[7] These policies, however, have to be balanced against the necessity not to damage access to food in third countries or affect the progressive economic integration between countries.

Because international trade of food has grown considerably in the past few decades it is common for producers and consumers to be influenced by its behaviour. Producers plan the variety of their products on the basis of their value on the global market, and consumers' economic access increasingly relies on the prices set at international level. Overall, integration between transnational commerce of food and domestic markets has increased and today the conditions on the global market influence greatly the availability and accessibility of food at domestic level.[8] Even if the trust in global markets to satisfy domestic needs has been augmented, the problem of their reliability has never been properly resolved. Agricultural markets have remained erratic and unpredictable and in recent decades have constantly failed in the task of steadily supporting the realisation of the right to food. Among the shortcomings of the present system three issues are particularly evident and hazardous for the realisation of the right to food: price volatility; negative incentives to domestic food production; and concentration of market power.

A. Price Volatility

The price of food is a crucial factor in the realisation of the right to food because it affects the economic access of individuals to an adequate amount of food. Accordingly, sudden oscillations of food prices disrupt local markets and make economic access to food more difficult for vulnerable individuals. This happens for both downward and upward price oscillations for different reasons.

(i) Upward Oscillations

Agriculture has always been an erratic economic activity, with harvest success depending on weather conditions and exceptional events like floods or earthquakes. Nevertheless, empirical observation in recent decades has

[7] On the necessity to use trade policies to cope with a food crisis see J Stiglitz and A Charlton, *Fair trade for all* (Oxford University Press, 2007) 67.

[8] On the relationship between international trade and domestic food security, see FAO, *Trade reforms and food security: conceptualizing the linkages* (FAO, 2003).

shown that extreme price oscillations on the international market have become more frequent. This market behaviour, called price volatility, has so amplified that it has become an endemic characteristic of global food markets.[9] For instance, during the 2007 food crisis the price of food staples more than doubled in the space of a few months. Economists argue about the causes of this extreme behaviour and reach diverging conclusions. Yet, there is growing agreement that extreme volatility is likely to be the consequence of a multiplicity of factors and transformations that manifested themselves in the second part of the twentieth century. First, more integrated markets made events affecting food supply at national level more easily transmissible to the international level. For instance, a flood, an earthquake or simply a bad harvest in countries crucial to supporting food availability on the international market can cause a critical lack of supply. When this happens, lack of food on the global market provokes food shortages in all the countries relying on it to support their national food security.[10] Second, global warming has made the problem of adverse weather conditions and extreme climatic phenomena more generalised and common. The climatic crisis is also causing a range of issues such as desertification and loss of arable land that make agriculture more vulnerable and unpredictable than in the past.[11] Third, food prices are now linked with other economic parameters that might be highly unstable. A major problem in this area is that food prices now react to fluctuations in the cost of oil. This is so because technological development has made agriculture more

[9] JP Chavas, D Hummels and B Wright, *The economics of food price volatility* (The University of Chicago Press, 2014); P Pinstrup-Andersen, *Food price policy in an era of market instability: a political economy analysis* (Oxford University Press, 2015); R Arezki, *Commodity price volatility and inclusive growth in low-income countries* (International Monetary Fund, 2012); S Joseph, *Blame it on the WTO?* (Oxford University Press, 2017) 181.

[10] G Rapsomanikis, 'Price transimission and volatility spillovers in food markets' in A Prakash (ed), *Safeguarding Food Security in Volatile Global Markets* (FAO, 2011); G Rapsomanikis and H Mugera, 'Price Transmission and Volatility Spillovers in Food Markets of Developing Countries' in I Piot-Lepetit and R M'Barek (eds), *Methods to analyse agricultural commodity price volatility* (Springer, 2011); F Ceballos, MA Hernandez, N Minot and M Robles, 'Transmission of food price volatility from international to domestic markets: evidence from Africa, Latin America, and South Asia' in M Kalkuhl, J von Braun and M Torero (eds), *Food price volatility and its implications for food security and policy* (Springer, 2016); World Bank, 'Transmission of Global Food Prices to Domestic Prices in Developing Countries' Contribution to the G20 Commodity Markets Working Groups; FA Huda, 'Process of global shocks transmission to domestic food price level: case of Bangladesh' (2014) 2(2) *International Journal of Food and Agricultural Economics* 97; HH Lee and CY Park, 'International Transmission of Food Prices and Volatilities: a Panel Analysis', Asian Development Bank Working Paper Series No. 373.

[11] T Hope and M Elizabeth, *Climate Change and Food Security: Africa and the Caribbean* (Routledge, 2016); ME Brown, *Food security, food prices and climate variability* (Routledge, 2014); R Lal, *Climate Change and global food security* (Taylor and Francis, 2005); D Lobell, *Climate change and food security: adapting agriculture to a warmer world* (Springer, 2010); L Li Ching, S Edwards and N Scialabba, *Climate Change and Food Systems Resilience in Sub-Saharan Africa* (FAO, 2011).

productive but also extremely dependent on machines, especially in countries that are major exporters of food.[12] Fourth, several countries implement export control policies limiting the food they make available on international markets. When this is done by major exporters the amount of food available on the market changes significantly and the international price of the food staple fluctuates.[13] Finally, in recent years there has been a growing tendency to market financial derivatives based on food commodities. There is some evidence that this increasing financialisation of international food markets can have arbitrary consequences, especially when food is captured in speculative 'bubbles'.[14]

Having such an unstable international market of food is of great concern for the realisation of the right to food, especially in a time where international policies promote more integration between the domestic market and the international market. Whenever countries or individuals rely too heavily on the international market to feed themselves they are fully exposed to unpredictable fluctuations capable of leaving them without an adequate amount of food from one year to the next. When price spikes happen, they impact the economic accessibility of adequate amounts of food. This is particularly so when the spike includes food staples used in the diet of the most vulnerable sections of the population. In the case of the 2007 crisis, major consequences for the right to food arose from the fact that the price of cereals and rice suffered a substantial increase.

(ii) Downward Oscillations

The evidence of the effects of price spikes on the right to food should not, however, lead to the simplistic conclusion that having cheap food available

[12] PC Westhoff, *The economics of food: how feeding and fueling the planet affects food prices* (FT Press, 2010); World Bank, 'Global Economic Prospects June 2011', 8, available at <http://siteresources.worldbank.org/INTGEP/Resources/335315-1307471336123/7983902-1307479336019/Full-Report.pdf> accessed 19 February 2012. FAO, 'The State of Agricultural Commodity Markets' (2009) 9, available at <ftp://ftp.fao.org/docrep/fao/012/i0854e/i0854e01.pdf> accessed 19 February 2012.

[13] FAO, 'Food Export Restriction: Reviews of the 2007–2010 Experience and Consideration for Disciplining Restrictive Measures', FAO Commodity and Trade Policy Research Working Paper No. 32, available at <http://ictsd.org/downloads/2011/05/sharma-export-restrictions.pdf> accessed 19 February 2012; B Karapinar, 'Export Restrictions and the WTO Law: "Regulatory Deficiency" or "Unintended Policy Space"' in *World Trade Report* (World Trade Organization, 2010).

[14] ILO, 'Investing in food security as a driver to better jobs', available at <http://www.ilo.org/global/publications/books/WCMS_170026/lang--en/index.htm> accessed 14 December 2011; Olivier De Schutter, 'Food Commodities Speculation Food Price Crises', United Nations Special Rapporteur on the Right to Food Briefing Note 02, available at <http://www.srfood.org/images/stories/pdf/otherdocuments/20102309_briefing_note_02_en_ok.pdf> accessed 29 December 2017.

on the international market is always positive. From empirical observations conducted by international organisations, an intricate picture in fact emerges where the effects of price fluctuations at domestic level vary greatly on the basis of national characteristics and level of development. In particular, empirical studies are consistently showing that downwards oscillations of the price of food or periods of price depression can be as detrimental to food security as price spikes. This is so because the majority of malnourished people are farmers in developing countries with their income dependent on agriculture.[15] When extremely cheap food is available on the international market this vulnerable category can be easily displaced. With their principal source of income falling or disappearing, their capacity to afford food for themselves and their dependents is dangerously at risk.[16] This is particularly so at the occurrence of import surges, a trade phenomenon consisting in the sudden increase of imported goods in a certain country.[17]

B. Negative Incentives on Domestic Food Production

For economic operators and countries planning their economic development, global agricultural markets are a business opportunity. The economic opportunities offered by transnational commerce in food can be a positive factor for the realisation of the right to food, for instance, when they contribute to elevating the income of vulnerable categories. However, the global market can also incentivise a utilisation of domestic resources that is damaging for the realisation of the right to food. Negative incentives can lead to unintended consequences such as reduced availability and accessibility of basic food staples or increased price volatility. These negative incentives are obstacles to the realisation of the right to food.

International organisations have documented that international markets can cause negative consequences for the realisation of the right to food in at least four ways. First, global agricultural markets can promote a use of arable land that is not conducive to the realisation of the right to food. This can happen in case of excessive utilisation of arable land to produce cash crops, namely varieties of crops that have high economic value but do

[15] FAO, *State of food insecurity in the world 2013* (FAO, 2013).

[16] FAO, 'The state of food insecurity in the world', available at <http://www.fao.org/docrep/014/i2330e/i2330e.pdf> accessed 19 February 2012; FAO, 'Agricultural Import Surges in Developing Countries', available at <http://www.fao.org/docrep/014/i1952e/i1952e.pdf> accessed 29 December 2017.

[17] FAO, *Agricultural import surges in developing countries* (FAO, 2011); S Joseph, *Blame it on the WTO?* (Oxford University Press, 2017) 181.

not contribute directly to national food security.[18] Empirical cases are the excessive employment of land to develop large-scale cultivations of cocoa, tea, cotton and coffee. Another example is the use of a part of arable land to produce biofuel.[19] The development of large plantations of cash crops and the tendency to use land to produce biofuels has created at times imbalances in the distribution of natural resources and shortages of basic food staples even in countries that would otherwise be rich in arable land.[20]

Second, because international markets are not easily accessible, in order to profit from the opportunities of international commerce, countries need advanced infrastructures and the capacity to meet global standards. In principle, the desire to market products on a global scale is a positive incentive to economic development. The drive towards global markets, however, must be handled with care. In practice, if domestic necessities are ignored, the creation of these capacities can sometimes work against the realisation of the right to food. For instance, there is evidence that several developing countries invested too heavily in infrastructures to link national food production with international markets rather than connecting remote areas of the countries with cities. This conduct has favoured the exclusion of a section of domestic farmers from food production chains, threatening their basic income.[21]

Third, the international food market can incentivise the export of food to third countries even when its national consumption would be fundamental for national food security.[22] This process has been observed in developing countries where basic food staples have been used as export commodities with high value markets in the developed world. This mechanism can go as far as changing traditional diets when local products become over-expensive export commodities. For instance, the International Labour Organization (ILO) observed that in Bolivia quinoa, one the foundations of the local diet, became largely unaffordable when it turned into a major export commodity.[23]

[18] O De Schutter, 'International Trade in Agriculture and the Right to Food, Dialogue on Globalization' Occasional Papers No. 46/ (Geneva, November 2009).

[19] R L Naylor, A Liska, M Burke, W P Falcon, J Gaskell, S Rozelle and K Cassman, 'The Ripple Effect: Biofuels, Food Security and the Environment' (2007) 49 *Environment* 30; T Koizumi, *Biofuels and food security* (Springer, 2014).

[20] J Ziegler, C Golay, C Mahon and S-A Way, *The Fight for the Right to Food* (Palgrave Macmillan, 2011).

[21] S Joseph, *Blame it on the WTO? A human rights critique* (Oxford University Press, 2011) 200; International Assessment of Agricultural Knowledge, Science and Technology for Development, *Agriculture at the Crossroads*, (2009) 459.

[22] See below, section IV.B Agricultural Economies.

[23] See ILO, 'Investing in food security as a driver to better jobs', available at <http://www.ilo.org/global/publications/books/WCMS_170026/lang--en/index.htm> accessed 29 December 2017.

Finally, global food markets can create incentives not to develop national means of production of food. This happens especially in periods when there is cheap food available on the global market. Relying on food imports, countries can underestimate the necessity of producing their own food supply and building up their own food stocks. The United Nations and especially the Food and Agriculture Organization have collected a great deal of evidence on this problem.[24] In fact, because between 1990 and 2005 food prices were relatively stable and low, numerous countries started relying more heavily on food imports. Economic incentives towards the dismantling of national food production had evident consequences for several developing countries that reduced national food production and increased significantly food imports.[25] This produced negative consequences for the realisation of the right to food. To start with, numerous farmers had their income severely affected because the global market de facto substituted their function in the promotion of domestic food security. In addition, these countries remained extremely exposed to volatility of food prices. Even if such exposure could have been counteracted through social policies this was hardly the case for numerous developing countries. When the global market turned its back on them, the strainon the realisation of the right to food was substantial. In fact, this market failure played a significant role in amplifying the effects of the 2007 price spike when numerous countries found themselves suddenly incapable of meeting their food import bill. When the global market puts negative incentives on food production, public policies are needed to support the realisation of the right to food.

C. Concentration of Market Power[26]

In international food markets the distribution of market power is highly uneven. Accordingly, very few countries have the capacity to influence the behaviour of the market through their trade policies. The powerful countries that exert such influence live side by side with a plethora of states with little or no market power. At the same time, the absence of sound competition policies at international level has allowed the rise of private actors that captured substantial shares of the international market of commodities that are key for the realisation of the right to food. These companies have

[24] For an overview of the issue see FAO, *Trade reforms and food security* (FAO, 2003) 67.

[25] See below, section IV.C Net Food-Importing Countries.

[26] This section elaborates the 2011 data of the World Trade Organization on import and export of food products. The raw data used for this section is available at World Trade Organization, 'International Trade Statistics 2015', Food, available at <https://www.wto.org/english/res_e/statis_e/its2015_e/its15_merch_trade_product_e.htm>.

great influence on how food is produced, traded and retailed. Having a global market that should serve every country and individual but that can be influenced by a few public and private actors certainly creates challenges for the realisation of the right to food. The EU is in a privileged position to tackle these challenges, being the foremost trader of food in the world and a powerful actor in the WTO. Because this research concentrates mainly on public international law, the following section leaves aside the problem of multinational corporations and concentrates on states.[27]

(i) Exports

The lion's share of the international food exports comes from the top 10 exporters, with a distinct prominence of the EU, the United States, Brazil, China and Canada in commodities that are crucial for food security. In terms of aggregate share of world exports, these five countries produce more than half of food exchanged internationally.[28] The EU and the US are the world-leading exporters, each providing around 10 per cent of the food available on the international market.[29] Brazil, Canada and Argentina, together with other 16 countries, account for around 30 per cent of world agricultural exports.[30] This group of major exporters is known as the Cairns Group, from the name of the international organisation they created to pursue their common interests. The countries outside the global top 10 provide less than one quarter of the food exchanged internationally.[31] In fact, around 170 countries together generate less external trade of food than the EU or the US alone. The contribution of the remaining countries is in itself highly uneven and numerous developing countries give little contribution to the global food market.[32]

[27] Even from a public law perspective, there is the problem of powerful private actors being able to guide the external action of states. For this timely debate, that certainly touches the European Union, we refer the reader to the relevant literature. See, for instance, RB Hall and TJ Biersteker (eds), *The Emergence of Private Authority in Global Governance* (Cambridge University Press, 2002).

[28] World Trade Organization, 'International Trade Statistics 2015', Food, available at <https://www.wto.org/english/res_e/statis_e/its2015_e/its15_merch_trade_product_e.htm>.

[29] Brazil follows with around the 9%, whereas China and Canada provide around the 6%. The other countries reaching one per cent of global market share are Thailand, Indonesia, Australia, Malaysia, Mexico, India, Russia, New Zealand and Chile.

[30] The Cairns Group is composed of Argentina, Australia, Brazil, Canada, Chile, Colombia, Costa Rica, Guatemala, Indonesia, Malaysia, New Zealand, Pakistan, Paraguay, Peru, the Philippines, South Africa, Thailand, Uruguay and Vietnam.

[31] WTO, 'International Trade Statistics 2015', Leading Importers and Exporters of Food, available at <https://www.wto.org/english/res_e/statis_e/its2015_e/its15_merch_trade_product_e.htm>.

[32] See the section on export restrictions in the Caribbean containing the explanation of the negligible relevance of these countries for global food prices.

Each commodity that is traded internationally has a different sensitivity in terms of realisation of the right to food, depending on its content of nutrients, its affordability and its presence in domestic diets. The Food and Agriculture Organization identified a selected basket of basic staple foods that are particularly important to ensure food security. Taking into account this basket of fundamental foodstuffs, it appears evident that concentration of economic power remains high and generally within the same group of countries that dominate the aggregate ranking. To provide some relevant examples, just nine countries[33] together provide more than 80 per cent of world exports of wheat, with the US, Canada, Russia, Ukraine and the EU being the leading exporters.[34] Six countries provide 84 per cent of rice available on the global market. In fact, Thailand and India alone account for one quarter of world supplies each and Vietnam for around 15 per cent.[35] Exports of dairy products are also extremely concentrated, with the EU, the US, New Zealand and a few other countries having very large shares of the world market.[36] The market in meat has similar levels of concentration, with the EU, the US and the Cairns Group being the main exporters.[37] Because certain crops such as sugar, cocoa and tropical fruit cannot grow in temperate countries, in these markets the balance of power changes, and tropical and equatorial countries have established themselves as major exporters. However, market concentration remains very high across the board with a small number of southern countries maintaining a firm grip on global markets. Still, it is common that the trade of processed food utilising such raw commodities confirms the general rule, and the EU, the US, China and the Cairns Group are often the major exporters of these.

Another significant factor is the variety of food commodities exported. Whereas leading exporters in the developed world trade in a very extended range of products, including both raw and processed food, minor players often concentrate on fewer export commodities. In particular, countries with no processing industries export only raw fruit and vegetables, often to more advanced countries, especially the EU, the US, China and the Cairns Group. The EU is the world leader in terms of variety of food exported,

[33] In this chapter the EU is considered as a country, In this case the calculation includes the 28 Member States of the EU.

[34] United States Department of Agriculture, 'Foreign Agricultural Service, Grain World Markets and Trade', December 2017, available at <https://apps.fas.usda.gov/psdonline/circulars/grain.pdf> accessed 23 December 2017.

[35] Ibid.

[36] European Commission, 'Milk Market Observatory, 12.12.2017', available at <https://ec.europa.eu/agriculture/sites/agriculture/files/market-observatory/milk/pdf/trade-main-competitors_en.pdf> accessed 23 December 2017.

[37] US Department of Agriculture, 'Outlook for U.S. Agricultural Trade', 30 November 2017, available at <https://www.ers.usda.gov/webdocs/publications/85920/aes-102.pdf?v=43069> accessed 23 December 2017.

being able to produce and export virtually every temperate product and processed food. Even among the Cairns Group, the exports of less influential members are much less differentiated and certain countries tend to emerge as world-leading exporters only for certain products.

(ii) Imports

The structure of international imports of food shows a concentration of market power comparable to that of exports. Fifteen countries import 80 per cent of the food traded internationally, with the EU and the US alone importing around 15 per cent each. In fact, the EU, the US, Canada, China, Japan and Russia together capture almost 60 per cent of the food available on the market. The rest of the countries having above a one per centshare of world imports are either developed countries, emerging economies or developing countries with elevated purchasing power such as the United Arab Emirates.[38] Population and need are not necessarily reflected in more food purchased on the global market. For instance, the total value of food India imported in 2009 was the same as that of Hong Kong and lower than that of Saudi Arabia.

With regard to single foodstuffs the setting is more complex and depends on national characteristics, the variety and quantity of food produced at domestic level and the principal diet of the country. As a general tendency, the import of basic food staples is less concentrated than the aggregate trend. In particular, there is a wide group of developing countries that relies heavily on imports of basic foodstuffs to satisfy their domestic necessities.[39] Among developed countries, Japan has been traditionally an exception, having a considerable food deficit for geographical reasons. Accordingly, Japan and the EU, which are the major importers of wheat, count for one per cent of world imports each.[40] The import of cereals is more polarised with the EU, the US and Canada being the largest importers in terms of value. Looking at the quantity, however, numerous low-income countries such as Eritrea, Palestine, Namibia, Kenya and Haiti appear among the top 20 importers. Considering more expensive products such as meat and dairy foods, the import trends are more similar to the aggregate values. For instance, the EU and Japan import respectively around the 10 per cent of poultry meat available on the market, followed by Russia, China and Saudi Arabia.

[38] Mexico 3%, Korea 3%, Saudi Arabia 2%, Hong Kong, India, United Arab Emirates, Malaysia and Switzerland 1.7%, Australia 1.5%. World Trade Organization, 'International Trade Statistics 2011', Food, available at <http://www.wto.org/english/res_e/statis_e/its2011_e/its11_merch_trade_product_e.htm>.

[39] See below section IV.C Net Food-Importing Countries.

[40] Other major importers are Algeria, Egypt, Nigeria, Morocco, Iraq, the US, Mexico, India, Korea, Turkey and the Philippines.

For other meat products and for milk and dairy foods the top 15 importers are generally the same countries as the global trend. Their position in the ranking adjusts depending on national needs and domestic production.

The scenario changes taking into account products that cannot be grown in temperate countries such as sugar, bananas, cocoa and coffee. In these cases the EU is by far the biggest importer and maintains significant distance even on the US. For instance, the International Coffee Organization reports that the EU imports 65 per cent of the raw coffee available on the international market and the US, 20 per cent. In fact, four countries import more than the 90 per cent of the green coffee traded across borders. In the same vein, just four countries import almost 80 per cent of bananas, with the EU alone importing around 40 per cent. This trend applies virtually to every tropical and equatorial crop, including raw sugar, of which the EU is by far the major importer.

(iii) Observations

If the international food market were perfect no country would have the power to influence the price of the commodities exchanged, there would not be information asymmetries and every country would have the same technologies. The structure of the global food market shows, however, that a very few actors dominate the system. This handful of countries can change the price of commodities, own the best technologies and are in a better position to interpret the behaviour of the market.

With regard to export of food, the market is highly fragmented, with very few countries having enough productive capacity to support world consumption and the vast majority of states being scarcely productive and in a position of substantial marginalisation. In particular, the EU and the US dominate the scene and are in fierce competition between each other. These two countries increasingly fear the rising antagonism of emerging economies, in particular Brazil and China. There is then a sort of second division of players that have lower capacity to influence the market of food, or that emerge as leading exporters only for certain commodities. These countries are less influential on their own, but if they coordinate their policies, they become almost as significant as the major global players. This category includes the Cairns Group and a few other countries. The rest of the countries have very little or no trade influence at global level.

This state of things has the consequence that the countries that depend on the international market to feed themselves depend, in fact, on the handful of states that provide food to the global market. Accordingly, modifications of export policies or of the quantity of food produced in major exporting countries can affect heavily their capacity of realising the right to food. For instance, during the 2007 food crisis the decision of several major players to limit their exports exacerbated the scarcity of food in importing countries.

In the same vein, it has been observed that amendments to the EU Common Agricultural Policy have wide consequences for food security all around the world and especially in countries dependent on the global market.[41]

Concentration of *imports* also has consequences for the realisation of the right to food. In fact, major importers have great influence on the revenues of countries *exporting* food staples. This influence increases whenever the exporting country has a minimally differentiated economy based mainly on the export of agricultural goods.[42] This is often the case with regard to equatorial and tropical staples produced in developing countries with scarce manufacturing capacities. In this case the income of the exporting country is highly dependent on their capacity to access the market of major importers. As a consequence, changes of import policies of major players can heavily affect the income of producers in export countries. The coffee and banana markets are examples of this mechanism. If the EU imports 65 per cent of coffee beans and 40 per cent of bananas, every country relying on coffee exports as a source of income is dependent on the EU's import policy. In addition, the ways major importers behave on the market can influence the overall availability of food and its price. For instance, the EU and the US requiring more food from international markets means less availability on a global scale.

III. LIMITS OF DEVELOPMENT AID AND DOMESTIC POLICIES

To the imperfections of the international food market countries can react through domestic policies such as incentives to domestic food production or social safety nets. In addition, vulnerable countries can rely on the development aid from third countries to support the realisation of the right to food on their territory. This section elucidates why even if these instruments remain a viable solution in case of market instability they are not sufficient to ensure the realisation of the right to food in the absence of a comprehensive approach to international policies which also includes international trade law. This is for four reasons that have been clearly identified in economic literature.

First, the impact of development aid on the solutions of the longstanding problems of certain vulnerable states, such as hunger and malnutrition, has been contested. Several prominent economists have in fact investigated the reasons why the efforts of Western countries to aid developing countries have produced so little results, especially in sub-Saharan Africa. Recent

[41] See J Mersing, 'How to Phase Out Rich Country Agricultural Subsidies Without Increasing Hunger in the Developing World' in O De Schutter and KY Cordes (eds), *Accounting for Hunger* (Hart, 2012).

[42] See below, section IV.B Agricultural Economies.

studies argue that development aid to vulnerable countries is of limited use to cope with hunger and malnutrition in the long term. In particular, Paul Collier[43] and William Easterly[44] argue that development aid is very difficult to allocate and that the empirical studies on the effects of development aid on the 50 most vulnerable countries of the world in recent decades show that little success was obtained in the absence of sound policymaking in the areas of trade and economic development. Other authors, such as Dambisa Moyo,[45] go as far as arguing that development aid makes vulnerable countries dependent on wealthier economies and traps them in a spiral of 'corruption, market distortions and further poverty'.[46] Even in the case of international interventions to cope with a major food crisis there is no evidence in economic literature that development aid is in the long term an effective instrument to cope with hunger and malnutrition.[47]

Second, through development aid wealthy countries transfer economic resources to vulnerable states. However, the *amount* of wealth redistributed through development aid is limited if compared to the effects on wealth distribution of international trade.[48] In fact, international trade agreements can affect the share of wealth that each country gathers from trade liberalisation. The United Nations Development Report calculated in 1997 that from the conclusion of the last round of WTO negotiations, the Uruguay Round, sub-Saharan Africa lost around US$1.2 billion per year.[49] In the same vein, Joseph Stiglitz computed that the 70 per cent of the welfare gains produced by the trade agreements concluded in the Uruguay Round went to developed countries, and the large majority of the gains achieved by developing countries were collected by large states such as Brazil.[50] Other analysis estimated that 48 least-developed countries together lost around US$600 million per year as a consequence of the Uruguay Round.[51]

For these reasons if a trade agreement does not take into account the weaknesses of vulnerable countries and does not include specific clauses to support their participation in the international trade system, the consequences are that most of the wealth created goes to more advanced economies which

[43] P Collier, *The Bottom Billion* (Oxford University Press, 2008) 45.

[44] W Easterly, *The White Man's Burden* (Oxford University Press, 2009) 2.

[45] D Moyo, *Dead aid: Why aid is not working and how there is a better way for Africa* (Farrar, Straus and Giroux, 2010) 65.

[46] See CB Barrett and DG Maxwell, *Food Aid After Fifty Years* (Routledge, 2005) 89.

[47] W Easterly and T Pfutze, 'Where does the money go? Best and worst practices in foreign aid' (2008) 22 *Journal of Economic Perspectives* 29; RC Riddel, 'Does Foreign Aid Really Work?' (Oxford University Press, 2007) 145.

[48] WS Grimes, 'International trade law: wealth distribution, free trade, and competition law' (2011) 18 *Southwestern Journal of International Law* 65.

[49] United Nations Development Programme, *Human Development Report 1997: Human Development to Eradicate Poverty* (Oxford University Press, 1997).

[50] J Stiglitz, *Making globalization work* (Penguin Books, 2006) 77.

[51] J Stiglitz and Andrew Charlton, *Fair Trade for All* (Oxford University Press, 2005) 47.

are equipped to compete on the international scene. Whenever trade treaties produce the negative effects mentioned above, the impact of development aid becomes limited.[52] For these reasons, without a holistic approach to global governance which includes trade regulation among the policies to cope with hunger and malnutrition, development aid remains of limited use.

Third, domestic policies to intervene at the occurrence of instability of the international food market require public resources that might not be available, especially in vulnerable countries. In addition, the organisation of domestic policies to cope with food shortages requires complex administrative organisation that might not be available in vulnerable countries where the Government has limited control of the territory. In the absence of public funding to design domestic social policies in vulnerable countries, one of the instruments of state intervention is trade policies.[53] In fact, by intervening in the import or export of food from third countries, vulnerable states can interfere with the quantity and price of food on their territory. This can be done, for instance, by limiting the export of food to third countries so that domestic food production is directed towards the domestic market. When market instability affects domestic producers, countries can raise temporary trade barriers so that vulnerable farmers do not suffer from the competition of more advanced economies.[54]

Finally, international trade treaties have an impact on public revenues. This is so because trade treaties always include limits on the amount of taxes that vulnerable states can impose on the import and export of goods. However, substituting trade revenues with alternative instruments of domestic taxation is not a straightforward process in developing countries, and recent research highlights that alternative instruments of taxation could be too expensive in low-income countries.[55] This is so because in states with a weak administrative apparatus, it is more effective to levy trade taxes than to enforce a domestic tax. A study of the International Monetary Fund, for instance, examining loss of trade revenues between 1975 and 2000, provided evidence that high-income countries recovered them straightforwardly; middle-income countries recouped only 35–55 per cent of revenues; whereas low-income countries recovered 30 per cent for each lost dollar at best.[56]

[52] Ibid. On the benefits and limits of international aid to fight poverty and hunger see P Collier, *The bottom billion* (Oxford University Press, 2008); D Moyo, *Dead Aid* (Farrar Strauss and Giroux, 2009); William Easterly, *The white man's burden* (Oxford University Press, 2007).

[53] Joseph Stiglitz makes the example of the use of temporary import barriers to cope with international market instability. See J Stiglitz, *Making globalization work*, above n 50, 66.

[54] See Chapter 5 of this book.

[55] H-J Chang, *Bad Samaritans* (Bloomsbury Press, 2008) 69.

[56] T Baunsgaard and M Keen, 'Trade Revenue and (or?) Trade Liberalization', International Monetary Fund Working Paper WP/05/112 (International Monetary Fund, 2005).

Accordingly, whenever international trade law does not take into account its impact on public revenues, it affects the capacity of vulnerable states to implement food security policies.

In conclusion, economic literature has identified a connection between international trade and food security in vulnerable countries. This is so because vulnerable states have often limited public resources to organise domestic policies to directly provide emergency food relief. In this situation there are limited alternatives to the intervention in the import and export of food to insulate the domestic market and protect vulnerable producers and citizens. In addition, international treaties limit the capacity of countries to use international trade as a source of public revenues, making it more difficult to gather the resources to intervene domestically to realise the right to food. In addition, international trade has a major impact on the distribution of wealth among countries and the amount of development aid gathered by the international community cannot compete with the economic consequences at domestic level of the redistribution of wealth caused by international trade.

IV. VULNERABLE CATEGORIES

As shown in Chapter two, international human rights law identifies several categories (i.e. indigenous people, women, children) that are more exposed than others to violations of the right to food. Accordingly, human rights law provides a set of international conventions and declarations aiming specifically at their protection. Human rights conventions derive the vulnerability of these categories from their position in society, their exposure to abuses of power or the fact that they are minorities. From the analysis above emerges a different kind of vulnerability to human rights violations, originating from the place certain countries and individuals have in the global market. In fact, the persistence of price volatility, the existence of negative incentives and elevated market concentration make certain categories more exposed to food shortages than others. The following section defines the categories of countries that are more likely to be adversely affected by the limits of the international food market.

A. Developing Countries

Even if food insecurity happens in every country, hunger and malnutrition are extremely polarised in certain areas of the world. The number of hungry people in developed countries is minimal when compared with Africa, South-East Asia and South America. In 2017 of 815 million hungry people, 42 million live in Latin America and the Caribbean, 243 million in

Africa and 520 million in Asia and the Pacific.[57] Endemic poverty, lack of advanced technology and marginalisation from global trade are all factors that contribute to the particular exposure of these areas of the world to food shortages. Low-income countries tend to have less efficient social safety nets and resources to spend in the realisation of the right to food on their territory. Often, their administration is less effective at identifying cases of food insecurity and intervening through adequate policies. In addition, low-income countries have often no influence on the international food market and their citizens have less purchasing power than their counterparts in the developed world. The productivity of their farmers is also lower and many of these countries are characterised by economies based on subsistence agriculture. Lack of resources often means that the state finds it more difficult to intervene to boost production, differentiation and productivity so that subsidisation programmes are more difficult to implement. Finally, with few exceptions, these countries have a shortage of know-how in the economics and law of international trade that makes them less able to interpret global shifts and react accordingly.

These elements mean that the majority of developing countries are less fit to cope with international competition and more exposed to the deficiencies of the international food market. Accordingly, the negative effect of price volatility is more evident across the developing world than in developed countries with price spikes directly affecting the economic accessibility to an adequate amount of food. A lack of solid economic planning means that negative incentives coming from the global market are more effective in shaping national food production. For instance, there is evidence that numerous developing countries in recent decades have specialised excessively in crops needed on the international market without prioritising domestic food security.[58] Moreover, because global food exports are concentrated in the hands of a few exporters, mainly developed countries or transitional economies, the majority of developing countries are exposed to their market power. In addition, because the majority of developing countries are found in tropical and equatorial areas they are often dependent on the import policies of major importers of key crops such as sugar, cocoa, coffee and tropical fruit.

Developing countries are the large majority of states in the world and the group is extremely varied. The World Bank divides countries between *low-income* economies, *middle-income* economies and *high-income* economies. All *low-income* and *middle-income* economies can be defined as developing and are certainly exposed to the problems described above.

[57] See FAO, 'Global hunger declining but still unacceptably high', available at <http://www.fao.org/docrep/012/al390e/al390e00.pdf> accessed 29 December 2017.

[58] FAO, *Trade reforms and food security* (FAO, 2003).

In fact, also numerous countries classified as *high-income economies* can be considered as developing in the sense that they still have substantial economic deficiencies. In terms of realisation of the right to food, even several members of the Organisation for Economic Co-operation and Development have a part of the population endemically exposed to insufficient access to an adequate amount of food. For instance, Mexico contains more malnourished people than all Western Europe. Among developing countries, there are some categories that are certainly more vulnerable than others. These include least-developed countries and small island developing states. Least-developed countries are a group of around 50 countries having extremely low per capita income and particularly fragile economies. Often these countries rely on subsistence agriculture and are very exposed to hunger and malnutrition. Small island developing states are countries that because of their geographical location and small size are more easily marginalised from global markets. These countries are also more prone to economic and natural shocks beyond their control. This category includes the vast majority of Caribbean states and numerous small islands in the Pacific Ocean.

B. Agricultural Economies

A large majority of countries or regions have never developed substantial manufacturing capacity. In these areas, agriculture is the main source of employment and the instrument to gain economic accessibility to an adequate amount of food. Even in numerous transitional economies, a large part of the population still relies on agriculture to survive. This is especially so because in rural societies agriculture not only provides the means of subsistence but also is an embryonic form of welfare. Well-functioning local agricultural markets provide rural populations with the necessary income to realise their right to food and give a crucial contribution to the realisation of other fundamental rights.[59] Frequently, these countries have scarcely differentiated national economies, relying heavily on the cultivation of a small variety of crops or food staples. As a consequence, they are highly vulnerable to changing market conditions affecting their limited means of subsistence. In particular, agricultural economies are vulnerable to changes of import and export policies of influential countries. It is also common that in these countries, rural areas are marginalised from the domestic economy and contain the majority of malnourished and hungry people. The Food and Agriculture Organization reports that of the 900 million undernourished

[59] On the link between food security, employment and social safety nets, see ILO, *Investing in food security as a driver to better jobs*, available at <http://www.ilo.org/global/publications/books/WCMS_170026/lang--en/index.htm> accessed 14 December 2011.

people in the world,[60] 70 per cent are farmers or landless labourers who are too poor to access an adequate amount of food. Accordingly, in agricultural economies the realisation of the right to food requires the improvement of the living conditions of local farmers and support to improve their productivity and integration in the market and society.

C. Net Food-Importing Countries

A net food importer is a country whose value of imported food is higher than its value of exported food in a given period of time. When countries already vulnerable to food shortages become also net food importers they find themselves heavily dependent on international markets to satisfy their food security needs. For this reason, the WTO and the Food and Agriculture Organization recognise that net food-importing developing countries are particularly susceptible to domestic food crises. This is particularly relevant because between the 1990s and 2005 prices of food on the global market favoured the excessive reliance of numerous countries in the developing world and had the consequence that some of them turned into net food importers. For this reason, it is very common today for developing countries to be also net food importers.[61] The WTO Committee on Agriculture produces every year an updated list of net food-importing countries on the basis of statistical evidence provided by its members. The list represents a binding recognition of net food importers applicable in the realm of WTO law.[62] Recently, the Food and Agriculture Organization created a more efficient index of vulnerable countries that takes into account of both income and import necessities. This system allowed the identification of a list of low-income-food-deficit-countries with a very high level of vulnerability to food insecurity.

[60] See O De Schutter, 'Mission to the WTO', Human Rights Council, A/HRC/10/5/Add.2 and Millennium Project, *Halving Hunger: It Can be Done, Summary Version of the Report of the Task Force on Hunger* (The Earth Institute at Columbia University, 2005) 6.

[61] See F Ng and MA Aksoy, 'Who Are Net Food Importing Countries?', World Bank Policy Research Working Paper No. 4457; AA Gurkan, K Balcombe and A Prakash, 'Food import bills: experiences, factors underpinning changes and policy implications for food security of least developed and net food-importing developing countries', FAO, available at <http://www.fao.org/docrep/006/y5117e/y5117e04.htm> accessed 13 December 2015; United Nations Ministerial Conference of the Least Developed Countries, *Globalization, Agriculture and the Least Developed Countries*, available at <http://www.unohrlls.org/UserFiles/File/LDC%20 Documents/Turkey/20June07-Agriculture-Final.pdf> accessed 13 December 2015.

[62] The list is prepared under the framework of the Marrakesh Decision on Measures Concerning the Possible Negative Effects of the Reform Programme on Least-Developed and Net Food-Importing Developing Countries.

V. THE ROLE OF THE EUROPEAN UNION

The previous sections showed that the international food market has some deficiencies which can affect the realisation of the right to food at domestic level. Market failures can be dealt with through domestic social safety nets but this strategy might not be available in numerous vulnerable countries because of budget constraints. Accordingly, international trade policy plays a central role in limiting the negative effects on domestic food security of international market instability and other market deficiencies.

This section elucidates the role that the European Union can have as an international actor to promote an international legislation of trade which takes into account the realisation of the right to food. This section argues that the EU is in a privileged position to influence international trade negotiations so that the right to food is included within the objectives of international trade treaties. In fact, the central position the EU has in international trade has the consequence that it is very difficult to imagine the inclusion of the right to food in trade negotiations without a proactive role of the EU. This is so for at least two reasons. First the EU is the main importer and exporter of goods of the world which means that during trade negotiations the EU has considerable leverage on other countries. Second, the EU has advanced know-how on both food and trade policy which has developed through years of experience in trade law at domestic level. The technical knowledge the EU has developed in more than 50 years of market integration at EU level puts it in a privileged position to propose solutions for including the right to food in international trade law without undermining the objective of more economic integration with other countries.

A. Leverage during Trade Negotiations

In international relations studies it is uncontested that countries do not all have the same bargaining power during trade negotiations. This is true with regard to any kind of trade negotiation, be it a multilateral trade round or the negotiations leading to a free trade agreement.[63] This is so for several reasons, including the fact that during trade negotiations the value of the internal market of a country has a weight that can be used to achieve external objectives. In fact, countries with extremely valuable internal markets can influence the wealth and economic development of third countries,

[63] S Meunier and K Nicolaïdis, 'The European Union as conflicted trade power' (2006) 13 *Journal of European Public Policy* 906, 907.

depending on the degree of access to their market they allow.[64] For this reason the EU, being the biggest market of the world and the foremost exporter, is in a privileged position during trade negotiations, especially with regard to developing countries. In fact, a change in the external trade policy of the EU, for instance the decision to change the tariff on the import of a good from a third country, can have severe consequences on the third country. In addition, since the EU imports and exports virtually every product, it has an evident advantage over those countries which export only certain products and have limited import capacity. In fact, the EU has a much wider variety of benefits to offer to its trade partners in exchange for a beneficial commercial deal than the other way round.[65] Again, this is particularly true when the country involved in the negotiations is a vulnerable economy or an agricultural country which has little to offer to the EU in exchange for trade benefits.[66] This state of things caused Meunier and Nicolaidis to affirm that 'If there is any area in which the European Union has become an uncontested power in the international system, it is clearly in the field of trade policy'.[67]

In multilateral trade negotiations the influence of the EU had already been acknowledged at the end of the Uruguay Round[68] and today the European Commission maintains that the EU 'is the biggest player on the global trading scene'[69] and that 'the EU has achieved a strong position by acting together with one voice on the global stage, rather than with 28 separate trade strategies'.[70] More generally since the Member States of the EU created the Common Commercial Policy and gave the EU exclusive competence to negotiate international trade agreements, studies flourished in law and political science pointing at the fact that the EU is one of the most influential

[64] S Meunier, *Trading Voices: The European Union in International Commercial Negotiations* (Princeton University Press, 2007) 166.

[65] Meunier and Nicolaidis maintain that 'The EU is a formidable power in trade … there is little doubt that it has become, after the last enlargement, the biggest trading block in the world. As a result its potential hegemonic power, based on the capacity to grant or withhold access to its internal market, has become as strong as the US.' S Meunier and K Nicolaidis, 'The European Union as a Trade Power' in Christopher Hill and Michael Smith (eds), *The International Relations of the European Union* (Oxford University Press, 2005).

[66] E Jones, *Negotiating Against the Odds: A Guide for Trade Negotiators from Developing Countries* (Palgrave Macmillan 2013); A Narlikar, *International Trade and Developing Countries* (Routledge, 2003); P Drahos, 'Four lessons for developing countries from the trade negotiations over access to medicines' (2007) 28 *Liverpool Law Review* 1; JS Odell (ed), Negotiating Trade Developing Countries in the WTO and Nafta (Cambridge University Press 2006); J Stiglitz and A Charlton, *Fair trade for all* (Oxford University Press, 2007) 67.

[67] S Meunier, *Trading Voices: The European Union in International Commercial Negotiations* (Princeton University Press, 2005) 248.

[68] C Bretherton and J Vogler, *The European Union as a Global Actor* (Routledge, 1999) 46.

[69] European Commission, DG Trade, Official Website, <http://ec.europa.eu/trade/policy/eu-position-in-world-trade>.

[70] Ibid.

actors with regard to international trade policies and one of the few trading block able to have a clear impact on the development of international trade law.[71] The European Commission is aware of the leverage the EU has during international trade negotiations and developed a comprehensive strategy to use trade negotiations to achieve EU economic interests.[72]

B. Technical Know-How in International Trade Law

The economic and political leverage the EU has on the evolution of international trade law is strengthened by its almost unmatched know-how in the field. Having intellectual resources in the area of trade that can be rivalled only by the ones of few other countries provides the EU with an additional advantage whenever it is negotiating a trade agreement with a third country. This is so for two reasons. First, as Meunier and Nicolaidis maintained, 'more than forty years of experience negotiating international trade agreements on behalf of its members have made the EU an essential player and a powerful bargainer in the multilateral trading system'.[73] In particular, the EU Commission is one of the few administrative bodies in the world which has been taking part in the evolution of international trade law since its early stages of the negotiations linked with the General Agreements on Tariffs and Trade. Trough subsequent participation to such negotiations the EU Commission developed a profound understanding of international trade practices that few other governments can equal. The advanced know-how the EU Commission achieved is demonstrated by the fact that it is able to litigate international trade disputes without the support of any private law firms. Even powerful global players such as China are unable to appear before international trade courts through their own administrative bodies and are represented by a private law firm.[74] The practice of dispute

[71] PA Messerlin, 'The influence of the EU on the World Trade System' in M Daunton, A Narlikar and RM Stern (eds), *The Oxford Handbook on the World Trade Organization* (Oxford University Press, 2012); H Zimmermann, 'Realist Power Europe? The EU in the Negotiations about China's and Russias's WTO Accession' (2007) 45 *Journal of Common Market Studies* 813; M Elsig, 'The EU's Choice of Regulatory Venues for Trade Negotiations: A Tale of Agency Power?' (2007) 45 *Journal of Common Market Studies* 927.

[72] See for instance the Communication From the Commission, 'Trade, Growth and World Affairs' COM(2010) 612 final, 15 where the Commission states that 'Trade and trade policy reinforce the EU's international influence and concerted action at EU level should pursue and support EU economic interests in third countries.'

[73] S Meunier and K Nicolaidis, 'The European Union as a Conflicted Trade Power' (co-authored with Kalypso Nicolaidis) (2006) 13 *Journal of European Public Policy* 906.

[74] See, 'Where are China's WTO lawyers?', Forbes, 27/4/2009, available at <http://www.forbes.com/2009/04/27/china-wto-law-business-economy-trade.html> accessed 12 February 2014; EU Commission, The legal service of the European Commission, available at <http://ec.europa.eu/dgs/legal_service/pdf/sj_en.pdf> accessed 12 February 2014.

resolution in the WTO Appellate Body provided the Commission with further insights in the application of international trade treaties which most countries do not have since they are represented in trade disputes by a third party. The difference in legal know-how is particularly evident with regard to developing countries which joined the WTO only recently and were not part of the GATT system. In addition, most of developing countries have never brought a case in front of an international trade court which means they completely lack of practice in litigation.[75]

Second, most of the legal instruments negotiated at international level are already present in the legal structure of the European Union. In fact most of the issues of economic integration discussed during trade negotiations were already dealt with by European countries during their own process of regional integration. Being the most advanced example of regional integration of the world gives the EU an edge on all the countries which lack of experience in transnational trade regulation. This means that when the EU Commission negotiates a trade agreement it can also rely on the expertise developed in its internal process of economic integration. This applies to basic trade instruments such as tariffs and other restrictions as well as more specialised domains such as investment law, competition law and intellectual property.

This discrepancy in domestic experience with highly complex economic legislation is again particularly obvious with regard to vulnerable developing countries. These countries in fact are often members of regional organisations which are less developed than the EU.[76] In addition, regional organisations in Africa, the Caribbean and the Pacific lack of the highly specialised administrative bodies of the EU and the level of regional integration achieved often does not allow them to speak as a single voice during trade negotiations.[77] Finally, the difference in legal development between the EU and vulnerable countries is so wide that sometimes the legislation discussed in the trade agreement does not even exist at domestic level in the developing countries. This means that the developing country cannot rely

[75] R Abbott, 'Are developing countries deterred from using the WTO dispute settlement system?' ECIPE Working Paper 01/2007.

[76] United Nations Conference on Trade and Development, *Strengthening Regional Economic Integration for Africa's Development* (United Nations, 2009); JF Hornbeck, 'CARICOM: Challenges and Opportunities for Caribbean Economic Integration', CRS Report for Congress, available at <http://doczine.com/bigdata/2/1367212967_0be99a5735/crscaricom_challenges_e.pdf> accessed 12 February 2014.

[77] A Jessem and E Rodriguez, 'The Caribbean Community: Facing the Challenges of Regional and Global Integration', ITD Occasional Paper 2, available at <http://books.google.be/books?id=W8XcZ_51wbAC&pg=PA42&lpg=PA42&dq=caricom+external+relations&source=bl&ots=ynKEjqVFd3&sig=YmQ_h10ZAW3QIxX8VelyvcyGNaY&hl=en&sa=X&ei=Pn_7UtXoOc2qhQeN3YH4Cg&ved=0CD4Q6AEwBA#v=onepage&q=caricom%20external%20relations&f=false> accessed 12 February 2012.

on domestic know-how of the legal field when negotiating the agreement and has very little understanding of the consequences of the trade agreement on its domestic legislation. When new legal fields such as competition law or intellectual property are introduced in the developing country through the trade agreement domestic EU law is often used as a blueprint for the clauses of the treaty.[78] In these cases the difference in legal development means that the developing country relies on domestic EU law to shape its own domestic legislation in the field.

C. The Position of Vulnerable Countries in Trade Negotiations

European economic and political leverage and technical know-how put vulnerable countries in a particular weak position when negotiating a trade agreement with the EU. This applies to multilateral negotiations where countries are weighed in the negotiation process on the basis of their economic influence, and the more influential countries take part in the drafting process of the treaties from the very beginning while the other countries join at a later stage.[79] In multilateral negotiations, however, developing countries have the advantage of being the large majority of the countries taking part in the negotiations, which means that they can develop strategies to influence the negotiations or at least to provoke a stalemate in case of strong disagreement with more influential international actors such as the EU. In fact, evidence is emerging in literature that the influence of developing countries in WTO negotiations has increased since 2001 and that a comprehensive revision of WTO agreements is unlikely without substantial trade benefits being guaranteed to the developing world.[80]

The negotiating strategies that vulnerable countries can utilise in the WTO are not available when the EU negotiates a trade agreement directly with a country or a group of countries having little economic influence. In this situation the EU is in a position of evident advantage because it is by far the country with the strongest bargaining power. Through this position the EU can have great influence on the results of the agreement and the content of the trade treaty.[81] In fact, even though vulnerable countries still

[78] See for instance the impact of EU competition law on the clauses of trade agreements between the EU and developing countries S Papadopoulos, *The International Dimension of EU Competition Law and Policy* (Oxford University Press, 2010) 93.

[79] Sarah Joseph, *Blame it on the WTO? A human rights critique* (Oxford University Press, 2011) 200.

[80] SE Rolland, 'Developing countries coalitions at the WTO: in search of legal support (2007) 48 *Harvard International Law Journal* 483.

[81] As will be shown in Chapter 7 on the EU–African trade agreements, the influence of the EU can be easily demonstrated by looking at the text of the trade agreements. The similarities in the wording of the agreements in fact suggest that the European Commission pursues the same objectives in negotiations with all ACP countries.

have to sign and ratify the trade deal they might do so only to maintain a commercial relationship with the EU or to prevent other developing countries from gaining access to the EU internal market under better conditions. Inequality of bargaining power means that the external trade policies of the EU are a driving force in the evolution of international trade law and that the decisions taken in Brussels by the EU Commission and the other organs of the EU are likely to affect how food is traded anywhere in the world. Accordingly, it is unlikely that the right to food is taken into account during trade negotiations without the EU developing a specific external policy on the issue. As it will be shown in Chapter four, there are some mild signs that the EU is developing specific policies to include non-trade objectives in trade negotiations.

D. Conclusions

Economic and intellectual dominance in the field of international trade has put the EU in a privileged position to influence the evolution of international trade law. Since the EU has the leverage to affect the global trade agenda, its external trade policy is a key factor in defining if and how the right to food is taken into account during trade negotiations. In addition, the EU Commission, being at the forefront of legal know-how and research in the field of international trade, is one of the few institutions in the world which is in the position to develop new ideas and legal devices to embed the realisation of the right to food in the rules regulating international trade. Even though the EU is not the only influential actor and other countries have economic and political leverage, it is unlikely that the right to food will be taken into account during trade negotiations without a proactive stance by the EU. In addition, the EU, as will be explained in Chapter four, has an explicit mandate in its founding Treaties to take into account human rights in all areas of its external action, including its Common Commercial Policy.

VI. CONCLUSIONS

This chapter has shown that the international market of food is persistently failing to reinforce the realisation of the right to food and substantial empirical studies exposed market imperfections that work against the realisation of the right to adequate food. Price volatility, negative incentives for domestic food production and concentration of market power have been identified as central issues that need to be addressed in order to make the international food market more responsive to the necessities of providing food security to everyone.

The analysis proposed also rejected the interpretation of the international food market as a global marketplace having the function of delivering an adequate food supply to every country. International exchanges of food are unstable, supply is far from steady and affordable to everyone and the excessive reliance on international trade can reduce the capacity of countries to progress in the realisation of the right to food. In addition, the international food market is not really 'global' in that it is mainly a form of economic interaction between a small number of players. The failures of the international food market also make certain groups of countries and people prone to food insecurity because of the vulnerable position that they occupy in the market. In this respect, the chapter has identified developing countries, net food-importing countries and agricultural economies as sectors of world society that require particular attention in international policies addressing the failures of the international food markets. These categories are in fact the ones that suffer more directly from market failures and are more dependent on the external trade policies of the major economic players.

This situation bears profound consequences for the definition of the role that import and export policies play in the realisation of the right to food. In fact, from the essential features of international agricultural markets defined above, it emerges that public intervention in the import and export of food can play a crucial role in the realisation of the right to food at domestic level and in third countries. As far as the EU is concerned, the chapter has shown that the Union is in the ideal position to address the deficiencies of the system and to promote a conformation of international trade that is more supportive of the realisation of the right to food. In fact, the EU is the most prominent trader of food in the world, and has extended technical knowledge in both the production and trade of food. Furthermore, the EU has great market and political leverage on third countries and its export and import policies can influence the availability of food everywhere in the world. In addition, the EU is a powerful actor in the WTO and it is at the centre of an intricate web of trade and development agreements with numerous vulnerable countries. In fact, the influence of the EU on global food markets is so strong that it is difficult to imagine a full realisation of the right without the support of EU external trade policy.

In particular, from the elements above three general policy priorities emerge. Firstly, the EU should attempt, when possible, to fix the major failures of international food markets such as price volatility and the presence of negative incentives for domestic food production. Secondly, the EU should facilitate the realisation of the right to food in third countries, avoiding that its external action limits the policy space these countries have for the realisation of the right. For instance, it should avoid creating international obligations that forbid policies necessary for the realisation of the right to food at domestic level. Finally, the EU should avoid implementing import and export policies that affect categories of countries and individuals that are particularly vulnerable to food shortages. This means, for example, avoiding those alterations of its import or export policies that would affect vulnerable farmers in developing countries.

Because import and export policies of food are crucial for the realisation of the right to food, the EU[82] should use extreme care when it designs its external trade policies or takes part in international law-making affecting the ways in which food is traded, especially when this action has an impact on vulnerable countries. In the development of its external trade action, however, the EU is bound to respect existing legal obligations applicable to the trade of food commodities. In particular, the EU is subjected to the law of the WTO, which includes norms on the import and export of food. Accordingly, any assessment of the EU external action cannot disregard the fact that the policy space of the EU is limited both in terms of implementation of import and export policies and capacity to negotiate new rules for international trade of food. In consideration of this, Chapter five evaluates existing multilateral obligations applicable to the import and export of food from the perspective of the realisation of the right to food. The chapter will clarify the legal space that the EU and its trade partners have in which to regulate international trade of food.

Before entering into the details of WTO law, the next chapter looks at the relation between trade and the right to food within the institutional dynamics of the external action of the EU.

[82] For an overview of the human rights obligations of the EU, see below Chapter 4 of this book.

4

The EU External Trade Policy and the EU External Food Security Policy

I. INTRODUCTION

THIS CHAPTER LOOKS at the relation between the right to food and international trade law from the perspective of the policies with which the EU intervenes in international trade law. The main purpose of this chapter is to clarify how the EU contributes to the evolution and modification of international trade law and what are the policies that inspire its external action. This is done in three steps. First the chapter presents the institutional dimension of the EU external trade policy, explaining the EU organs involved in the policies and the procedures to be followed in concluding international trade agreements. Second, the chapter provides a picture of the policy objectives the EU pursues internationally with regard to the international trade of food. Third, the chapter offers a perspective on the policies the EU has put in place to promote food security in vulnerable countries. The chapter concludes with some observations on cross-fertilisation between the policies of the EU aiming at the modification of international trade law and the policies directed to the promotion of food security in third countries through international co-operation.

II. THE INFLUENCE OF THE EU ON INTERNATIONAL TRADE LAW: INSTITUTIONAL DIMENSION

WTO law provides the multilateral framework of international trade relations between states. The Organization has 164 Members out of 198 countries in the world and aspires to universal coverage. Since all major global players and the large majority of developing countries are WTO Members, the organisation is the accepted point of reference for international trade law. In addition, since the creation of the WTO over 400 bilateral and plurilateral arrangements on goods and services have been notified to the WTO, making the legislation more complex and the bigger picture more difficult to obtain. These additional trade agreements remain outside the WTO institutional framework and can provide rules on import and export of food that may go considerably beyond existing multilateral trade law in terms of the elimination of trade barriers. Bilateral and plurilateral trade agreements such as the Economic Partnership Agreements considered in the case studies in Chapters six and seven supplement multilateral trade law in the relationship between the parties but create no obligations for other countries.

The EU has a plethora of ways to intervene in this complex body of norms and uses them extensively. The Directorate General for External Trade of the European Commission, one of the largest, put in place a broad policy to participate in the evolution of international trade law and promotes the modification of that law alongside precise policy objectives defined by EU institutions. These policies are designed completely at EU level because the Treaty of Lisbon gives EU institutions exclusive competence on external trade. Accordingly, the EU Commission represents Member States during WTO negotiations and negotiates free trade agreements with partner countries. This section introduces four aspects of the EU external trade policy. First, we present the legal basis for the EU external action with regard to international trade law. Second, we explain the procedures and the institutions involved in the design and conclusion of international trade agreements. Third, we provide a brief reflection on the role of Member States during trade negotiations. Finally, the section summarises the ways with which the EU intervenes in international trade law within the WTO framework and outside of it (through free trade agreements).

A. Competence

Since the Treaty of Rome the international commerce of goods between Members of the European Economic Community (EC) and third states has been a core competence of its institutions. To this crucial but limited prerogative the EC and the EU added additional external powers through treaty amendments and the case law of the European Court of Justice. The Treaty of Lisbon represents today the point of arrival of more than 50 years of evolution of EU competences in the realm of external trade, and provides the EU with an extensive and exclusive ground to act with regard to international trade regulation.[1] Notably, the Treaty of Lisbon extended the

[1] For a complete history of the development of EC and EU eternal powers in the realm of trade, see P Eeckout, *External Relations of the European Union* (Oxford University Press, 2009) 9–57; M Cremona, 'The Completion of the Internal Market and the Incomplete Commercial Policy of the European Community' (1990) 15 *European Law Review* 283–97; M Cremona, 'A Policy of Bits and Pieces? The Common Commercial Policy After Nice' [2002]

EU's exclusive competence well beyond the international trade of goods, fully including international trade in services and trade-related issues such as intellectual property and direct investment.[2] In particular, the Treaty on the Functioning of the European Union includes a general part on EU external relations that provides a list of objectives that the EU should pursue in its relationships with third countries and through its action in international organisations. Article 21 provides several objectives closely linked with the EU's international commercial policy. Paragraph (e) of Article 21 provides that the EU shall 'encourage the integration of all countries into the world economy including progressive abolition of restrictions on international trade' and paragraph (d) requires that the EU 'foster[s] the sustainable economic, social and environmental development of developing countries with the primary aim of eradicating poverty'.[3] In addition, paragraph (h) provides that the EU should promote an international system based on multilateral co-operation and good global governance. Within this general framework, Article 3 of the Treaty on the Functioning of the European Union recognises the exclusive competence of the EU for the Common Commercial Policy. The policy is then defined in Articles 206 and 207 of the same Treaty, which also outline the procedure for the conclusion of trade agreements with third countries. Article 206 identifies the areas involved in the policy as

> changes in tariff rates, the conclusion of tariff and trade agreements relating to trade in goods and services, and the commercial aspects of intellectual property, foreign direct investment, the achievement of uniformity in measures of liberalisation, export policy and measures to protect trade such as those to be taken in the event of dumping and subsidies.

Cambridge Yearbook of European Legal Studies 61–91; M Cremona, 'EC External Commercial Policy after Amsterdam: Authority and Interpretation within Interconnected Legal Orders' in JHH Weiler (ed), *Towards a Common Law of International Trade?: The EU, the WTO and the NAFTA* (Oxford University Press, 2000); M Cremona, 'Balancing Union and Member State interests: Opinion 1/2008, choice of legal base and the common commercial policy under the Treaty of Lisbon' (2010) 35 *European Law Review* 678–94.

[2] GV Puig and B Al-Haddab, 'The common commercial policy after Lisbon: an analysis of the reforms' (2011) 36 *European Law Review* 289–301. The legal meaning of EC and EU external exclusive competences has changed over time. For an analysis of the significance of exclusivity in the common commercial policy, see P Koutrakos, *EU International Relations* Law (Hart Publishing, 2006) 7–134.

[3] On the relation between the concept of sustainable development and external trade, see MW Gehring and M-C Cordonnier-Segger, *Sustainable development in world trade law* (Kluwer Law International, 2005); V Barral, 'Sustainable development in international law: nature and operation of an evolutive legal norm' (2012) 23 *European Journal of International Law* 377–400; HG Ruse-Khan, 'A real partnership for development? Sustainable development as treaty objective in European economic partnership agreements and beyond' (2010) 13 *Journal of International Economic Law* 139; C George and C Kirkpatrick, 'Trade and development: assessing the impact of trade liberalisation on sustainable development' (2004) 38 *Journal of World Trade* 441.

Recently, in Opinion 2/15 on the EU–Singapore Free Trade Agreement, the Court of Justice of the European Union provided a rather extensive interpretation of this clause which includes most of these areas within the exclusive competence of the EU.[4]

As we shall see below, the EU external commercial policy is much more than that, and is one of the most complex areas of EU policymaking, with strands reaching out to other policy areas such as development co-operation and human rights promotion. The conclusion of trade agreements with third countries and the participation in the WTO fully reside within the common commercial policy. Accordingly, the planning and execution of the policies directed at the modification of international trade law happen entirely at European level through the mechanisms identified in the two EU Treaties. The following section defines the procedure to be followed for the conclusion of international trade agreements and the EU organs involved.

B. Procedure and Institutions

The European Commission performs a central role in defining European commercial strategies. In particular, the Commission plans ahead future free trade agreements and takes stock of the evolution of international trade law within the WTO framework.[5] Until the Lisbon Treaty, the policymaking on international trade and the conclusion of trade agreements mainly took the form of a dual institutional dialogue between the Commission and the Council, with limited involvement of the European Parliament.[6] The Lisbon Treaty changed the situation, providing the European Parliament with more intrusive powers in the procedure to define and carry out the EU's external trade policy. Most notably, the Lisbon Treaty created a procedure whereby after the signature of new trade agreements of which the EU is a party the consent of the EU Parliament is required for the conclusion of the agreement. In addition, all internal EU legislation necessary to implement the agreement has to be adopted through the ordinary co-decision procedure. However, the role of the Parliament during negotiations of trade agreements is weakened by the fact that during the negotiations it has no procedural rights except that of being informed.

[4] G Gruni, 'Towards a Sustainable World Trade Law? The Common Commercial Policy of the European Union after Opinion 2/15 CJEU' (2018) 13 *Global Trade and Customs Journal* 4–12.

[5] The bulk of policymaking with regard to international trade happens in the Directorate General for Trade of the European Commission.

[6] D Kleimann, 'Taking stock: EU Common Commercial Policy in the Lisbon Era', Centre for European Policy Studies Working Document No. 345, April 2011.

The Treaty on the Functioning of the European Union regulates the procedure to be followed in concluding a trade agreement. The procedure can be divided into three main steps: planning, negotiation and ratification.

The European Commission plans the Common Commercial Policy identifying the policy objectives to be pursued and the most suitable legal instruments. Accordingly, the Common Commercial policy is included in the general European strategies as was the case with the Lisbon Strategy, the renewed Lisbon Strategy and the EU 2020 Strategy.[7] This is so because the Common Commercial Policy is considered a key pillar of the EU's action to improve European competitiveness and create new jobs. As it happens in other policy areas, the Commission initiative is conducted in close political consultation with other EU organs.

When the European Commission wants to initiate the negotiation of a trade agreement, it needs to receive the authorisation of the Council, generally through qualified majority voting. The Council also provides the Commission with negotiating directives, sketching the priorities to be followed during the negotiations. The European Commission informs the Council of the state of the negotiations and the Council can address directives to the negotiators and designate a special committee in consultation with which negotiations must be conducted.

When the final draft of the treaty is ready the Council authorises its signature and conclusion. Before the Council provides the authorisation to conclude the trade agreement it has to consult the European Parliament. In certain cases provided by Article 218 of the TFEU but covering all economic and trade agreements, the Council has to obtain the consent of the Parliament before concluding the treaty. This procedure provides the EU Parliament with a final veto power on the treaty similar to national parliaments' power to ratify. Notwithstanding its limited role during the negotiations the EU Parliament has to be immediately informed of all the stages of the procedure.[8]

[7] See Communication from President Barroso to the Spring European Council, 'Working together for growth and jobs. A new start for the Lisbon Strategy', COM(2005) 24 final; Communication from the Commission, 'Trade Growth and World Affairs. Trade Policy as a core component of the EU's 2020 strategy' COM(2010) 612 final.

[8] The fact that the Parliament has acquired the power to reject trade agreements could develop into a more pervasive supervision of the negotiations. Signals of this new attitude of the European Parliament came from the rejection of the Anti-Counterfeiting Agreement and the Resolution requesting a delay of the negotiations for a free trade agreement with Japan. However, Members of the European Parliament are not allowed to take part in the negotiations. See 'European Parliament rejects ACTA', available at <http://www.europarl.europa.eu/news/en/pressroom/content/20120703IPR48247/html/European-Parliament-rejects-ACTA> accessed 11 October 2012, and Reuters, 'EU Parliament flexes new muscle on Japan free trade deal', available at <http://uk.reuters.com/article/2012/06/13/uk-eu-trade-parliament-idUKBRE85C18420120613> accessed 11 October 2012.

C. Role of Member States

Since the Common Commercial Policy is an exclusive competence of the EU, Member States have lost the prerogative to organise their own independent trade policies and be involved autonomously in the negotiations of trade agreements. In the same vein, the Member States of the EU participate in the WTO under the umbrella of the EU and take part in negotiations and the majority of internal meetings through delegates of the European Commission. The picture is, however, more complex than it would appear from the mere observation of EU treaties. In fact trade agreements can include clauses on subjects that do not fall under the exclusive competence of the EU, or do not fall under the competence of the EU at all. It is also possible that trade agreements may regulate issues that rely on competences that are difficult to allocate between the EU and Member States. These issues have produced the relevant consequence that EU Member States maintain a presence during the negotiation of free trade agreements and, so far, it is common that they sign the resulting treaties. This phenomenon—called 'mixity'—produces a variety of legal consequences the most important of which is that the resulting treaty requires the ratification of all Member States to enter into force.[9] All the free trade agreements between the EU and developing countries considered in the case studies were concluded as mixed agreements. This landscape is likely, however, to change in the future since the CJEU's Opinion 2/15 confirmed that the EU can conclude EU-only agreements covering most of the issues which are now included in free trade agreements with third countries.

D. How the EU Influences International Trade Law

Amending international trade law is a complex legal and political process, happening through lengthy negotiations between the EU and third countries, where agreeing on modifications of existing agreements is an extremely

[9] Mixed agreements and mixity are one of the most complex areas of the law of external relations of the European Union and a classic of the case law of the European Court of Justice. For an introduction to mixed-agreements, see P Eeckout, *External Relations of the European Union* (Oxford University Press, 2009) 190–225; P Koutrakos, *EU International Relations* Law (Hart Publishing, 2006) 359; R Leal-Arcas, 'The European Community and mixed agreements' (2001) 6 *European Foreign Affairs Review* 483. For a more detailed analysis see C Hillion and P Koutrakos, *Mixed Agreements Revisited: The EU and its Member States in the World* (Hart Publishing, 2010); M Cremona, 'External Relations of the EU and the Member States: Competence, Mixed Agreements, International Responsibility, and Effects of International Law' EUI Working Paper LAW No. 2006/22; E Steinberger, 'The WTO Treaty as a mixed agreement: problems with the EC's and EC Member States' membership of the WTO' (2006) 17 *European Journal of International Law* 837.

complex endeavour. For instance, the Uruguay Round of negotiations that brought about the creation of the WTO and shaped present multilateral trade law lasted eight years. The new round of multilateral trade negotiations, begun at Doha, has been going on since 2001 and is encountering significant obstacles in reaching any kind of agreement on a revision of existing treaties.[10] An alternative to multilateral trade negotiations is the conclusion of bilateral and plurilateral free trade agreements. These agreements are allowed by Article XXIV GATT and are easier to conclude since fewer states take part in the negotiations. Free trade agreements were not the preferred source of international trade law until 2000 but increased in number since the difficulties of concluding the Doha Round of negotiations became apparent.[11] Today, free trade agreements are a common instrument by which countries contribute to the evolution of international trade law. The effect on the multilateral trading system of these agreements is disputed, since instead of modifying multilateral trade rules through a mutually agreed solution, free trade agreements introduce an alternative to WTO law that is fragmented into a kaleidoscope of trade agreements.[12]

The EU takes part in both the Doha Round and the negotiations of free trade agreements and is a major player in modifying international trade law. Since international commerce is one of its exclusive competences, the EU takes part in the negotiations as a united trading block and is highly influential in shaping the final result of the negotiations. In fact, the centralisation of the trading influence of 28 countries into a single supranational entity created a powerful actor that has emerged as a major global economic player. Accordingly, the EU Common Commercial policy is a fundamental force in providing future directions to international trade law.[13]

[10] On the stalemate of the Doha Round see E Van Der Marel, 'Polly wants a Doha deal: what does the trade community think?' (2011) 10 *World Trade Review* 551. See also A Bouet and D Laborde, 'Assessing the potential cost of a failed Doha Round' (2010) 9 *World Trade Review* 319.

[11] Even if the trend of substituting multilateral trade law with bilateral or plurilateral trade agreements is evident, countries are contributing to the process to different extents. The European Union is heavily involved in the conclusion of PTAs and the US and China are following suit; however, other countries have been less keen on using preferential trade agreements beyond regionalism. For an updated map of Preferential Trade Agreements existing in the world see WTO, Participation in Regional Trade Agreements, available at http://www.wto.org/english/tratop_e/region_e/rta_participation_map_e.htm. For an overview of the legal issues of the conclusion of Preferential Trade Agreements see L Bartels and F Ortino (eds), *Regional trade agreements and the WTO legal system* (Oxford University Press, 2006).

[12] J Bhagwati, *Termites in the Trading System: How Preferential Agreements Undermine Free Trade* (Oxford University Press, 2008).

[13] On the directions of the EU external trade policy, see the Communication from the Commission, 'Global Europe competing in the world' and Communication from the Commission, 'Trade for All, Towards a more responsible trade and investment policy', available at <http://trade.ec.europa.eu/doclib/cfm/doclib results.cfm?docid=153846> accessed 27 December 2017.

The EU takes part in the creation and modification of international trade law in four ways. First, the EU is an influential member of the WTO and participates in the Doha Round of multilateral trade negotiations. This round of negotiations has the objective of modifying numerous aspects of existing regulation including the norms relevant for the international trade of food. Second, the EU negotiates protocols of accession to the WTO with countries that wish to become members of the organisation. Often, these protocols include norms on import and export policies that differ from the regulation provided in general WTO law. For instance, when China and Russia negotiated their accession protocols, they accepted additional constraints on export restrictions. Third, the EU is one of the most active users of the WTO Dispute Settlement System. Bringing cases based on existing treaties, the EU prompts the WTO Panel and the WTO Appellate Body to clarify their legal content. Finally, the EU pursues a policy of conclusion of free trade agreements outside the WTO framework and is negotiating, or has already concluded, free trade agreements with more than 100 countries.[14] The EU aims to conclude free trade agreements with developed countries, emerging economies and developing countries alike. In particular, the EU has fully embedded free trade agreements in its development policy and negotiates free trade agreements with all the members of the African, Caribbean and Pacific group of states,[15] a group of 77 developing countries including some of the weakest economies of the world. Since all these treaties include clauses on import and export of food, the strategy will profoundly modify existing international law.[16]

III. THE EU TRADE STRATEGY

A. Overview of the Policy

The Lisbon Strategy contained a chapter on external trade that underlined the importance for the EU to find new markets for its products and services.

[14] The website of the European Commission provides regular updates on the status of the negotiations: <http://ec.europa.eu/trade/creating-opportunities/bilateral-relations/agreements/>.

[15] Case studies concerning the Caribbean and African states are included in Chapter 6 and Chapter 7.

[16] For an overview of the relation between the EU and former European colonies, see L Bartels, 'The Trade and Development Policy of the European Union' in M Cremona (ed), *New Developments in the EU's External Relations Law* (Oxford University Press, 2008); A Voiculescu, 'Unorthodox human rights instruments: the ACP-EU development co-operation from the Lomé Conventions to the Cotonou Agreement' (2006) 4 *Journal of Commonwealth Law and Legal Education* 85; S Bartelt, 'ACP-EU development cooperation at a crossroads? One year after the second revision of the Cotonou Agreement' (2012) 17 *European Foreign Affairs Review* 1.

In terms of trade policy this meant taking suitable action in the international arena to create an international trading system supportive of EU economic development. In this way the external trade strategy was directly linked with the main objective of the Lisbon Strategy of making the EU 'the most competitive and dynamic knowledge-based economy in the world capable of sustainable economic growth with more and better jobs and greater social cohesion'. The Strategy was revised in 2005 and 2015;[17] the link between internal economic policies and external trade was deepened as a consequence of the need to supporting the achievement of the Lisbon economic and employment targets.[18] This prompted the Directorate General for Trade of the European Commission to publish a Communication in 2006 titled 'Global Europe: Competing in the World.'[19] The Communication outlined the policy objectives of the EU Common Commercial Policy for the following years, presenting an ambitious plan to make existing international trade law more supportive of the goals of the Lisbon Strategy. The Communication took stock of recent global economic developments and maintained that it is a priority for the EU to open third country markets to EU exports, negotiating the elimination of import barriers on EU products. This meant first of all achieving better trade deals in order to lower the tariffs imposed on EU exports by third countries beyond what was achieved in the Uruguay Round. In addition, the Communication identified the objective of tackling export restrictions by third countries that limit the access of the EU 'to resources such as energy, metals and scrap, primary raw materials including certain agricultural materials, hides and skins'. The Communication maintained that third countries should eliminate export restrictions on such products whenever not justified by environmental or security reasons. The Communication was the foundation for a wide strategy of opposition to trade barriers posed by third countries when conflicting with European economic development. The strategy was extended in the subsequent years and developed into several sub-policies dealing with specific aspects of international trade law. The following two paragraphs elucidate the goals of the EU Common Commercial Policy with regard to the instruments that are the object of this research: import tariffs and export restrictions.

[17] Communication from the Commission, 'Trade for All, Towards a more responsible trade and investment policy', available at <http://trade.ec.europa.eu/doclib/cfm/doclib_results.cfm?docid=153846> accessed 27 December 2017.

[18] Presidency Conclusions, Lisbon European Council, 23 and 24 March 2000.

[19] Communication from the Commission, 'Global Europe: Competing in the world. A contribution to the EU's Growth and Jobs Strategy' COM(567) final; Communication from the Commission, 'Trade for All, Towards a more responsible trade and investment policy', available at <http://trade.ec.europa.eu/doclib/cfm/doclib_results.cfm?docid=153846> accessed 27 December 2017.

B. Tariffs and the Market Access Strategy

A trade tariff is a tax on imported goods used by countries to limit the quantity of a certain good imported from a third country. When third countries impose a tariff on an EU export they make it less marketable on their domestic markets and thereby directly affect European businesses involved in the production, marketing and exportation of the product as well as downstream producers. Accordingly, every tariff imposed by a third country on European exports can be translated into a loss of economic revenues and jobs in the EU. In the Uruguay Round countries agreed maximum tariffs applicable on EU products but every country retained a certain level of freedom to limit imports from the EU. The maximum tariff applicable on the EU export depends on the country and the product, since different countries negotiated different obligations and bound their tariffs on EU exports at different levels in the WTO tariff schedule. One of the key objectives of the EU strategy is tackling the import tariffs levied on EU exports that WTO law still allows. This action augments the presence of EU businesses in third country markets and should provide a positive contribution to the European economy and support the creation of new jobs. This dimension of the Global Europe strategy developed into a sub-policy called 'Market Access Strategy'.

The strategy was explained in 2007 through a set of Communications and is the latest revision of one of the core branches of the EU Common Commercial Policy.[20] In the policy documents the EU Commission identifies a list of 10 barriers to EU exports that should be opposed in the WTO and through bilateral and plurilateral trade agreements. Of these barriers traditional instruments such as tariffs and customs procedures are recognised as one of the main challenges to tackle.

Notably, one of the core components of the Market Access Strategy, called the Market Access Partnership, provides a platform for exchange of information on existing trade barriers, linking the Commission directly with Member State officials and European businesses. The Partnership allows the Commission to have first-hand knowledge from economic operators of the challenges that EU products face when trying to access third-country markets. The Commission then draws on this wealth of information during trade negotiations within and outside the WTO and to plan its legal actions in the WTO Dispute Settlement System. The Partnership has a steering committee bringing together the Commission, Member States and business representatives to exchange information and develop strategies on

[20] Communication from the Commission 'Global Europe: a stronger partnership to deliver market access for European exporters' COM(2007) 183 final.

how to remove barriers. There are then several working groups for specific products. The two working groups dealing with barriers on food products are the oldest ones, they have been active since 2005 and representatives of the European food industry have participated regularly since June 2008.[21] The Partnership also uses a Market Access Database that classifies existing trade barriers to EU exports and helps the Commission study the regulatory instruments to tackle them.[22]

C. Export Restrictions and the Raw Materials Initiative

Export restrictions are measures with which countries put an artificial ceiling or tariff on the export of goods. The main objective of these instruments is limiting the quantity of a certain good exported to third countries. The main EU policy on international regulation of export restrictions is included in the so-called 'EU Raw Materials Initiative' an economic policy stemming from the Global Europe Strategy and having the main objective of ensuring the supply of raw materials to European processing industries. The policy responds to the need to ensure that tight commodity markets, due to the rise of emerging economies, do not hamper European economic development. The policy proposes several actions, the first of which is the pursuit of a 'raw materials diplomacy' with a view to securing access to raw materials lacking in the EU. This part of the policy is highly relevant for the objectives that the EU pursues during the negotiation of international trade agreements and is influential on the EU's attitude with regard to modifications of international trade law. As the 2008 EU Commission Communication 'The raw materials initiative—meeting our critical needs for growth and jobs in Europe' clarifies, access to primary and secondary raw materials is a priority in EU international trade regulatory policy. In particular, the policy provides that the EU should work towards the elimination of trade-distorting measures taken by third countries in all areas relevant to access to raw materials. The Communication states that:

> The EU will take vigorous action to challenge measures which violate WTO or bilateral rules, using all mechanisms and instruments available, including enforcement through the use of dispute settlement. More generally, the EU will act against the protectionist use of export restrictions by third countries. In determining its actions, the EU will take as priority those export restrictions that pose the greatest

[21] European Commission, Active working groups under the Market Access Partnership—March 2011, available at <http://trade.ec.europa.eu/doclib/docs/2011/march/tradoc_147653.pdf> accessed 15 October 2015.

[22] See European Commission, Market Access Database User Guide, available at <http://madb.europa.eu/userguide/EN_def.pdf> accessed 15 October 2015.

> problems for EU user industries or give their domestic downstream industries an unfair competitive advantage on international markets.[23]

The 2011 Communication on volatility of commodities prices consolidates this policy goal, contextualising it within the ongoing multilateral and regional trade negotiations. The Communication considers the regulation of export restrictions a matter falling within the purview of the raw materials policy, and states that the EU should: 'further embed raw materials issues, such as export restrictions ... in ongoing and future EU trade negotiations in bilateral, plurilateral and multilateral frameworks.'[24]

The EU Raw Materials Initiative has been influential on the position taken by the EU in the WTO Dispute Settlement System, in the Doha Round and in the negotiations of regional trade agreements. In all these three contexts the EU contributed to the modification of international trade law on export restrictions and supported an approach to export restrictions much more restrictive than the one contained in Article XI GATT and Article 12 of the WTO Agreement on Agriculture. In the WTO Dispute Settlement System the EU participated in the landmark cases *China—Raw Materials* and *China—Rare Earths*[25] that contested several export restrictions imposed by China on raw materials critical for EU industries. The cases, based on Article XI GATT and China's WTO Accession Protocol, resulted in a clarification of the multilateral discipline and in a restrictive interpretation of the legal requirements of the exceptions to Article XI GATT.[26] In the Doha Round, the EU supports the revision of Article XI GATT and its exceptions in order to limit the recourse to export restrictions on both food and raw materials.[27] In addition, when new states desire to become members of the WTO, the EU negotiates with them obligations on export restrictions going beyond the existing WTO framework. This happened most notably with China and Russia and a handful of other countries.[28] Finally, when negotiating free

[23] Communication from the Commission, 'The raw materials initiative—meeting our critical needs for growth and jobs in Europe' COM(2008) 699 final; G Gruni, 'Going from one extreme to the other: food security and export restrictions in the EU–CARIFORUM Economic Partnership Agreement' (2013) 19 *European Law Journal* 864.

[24] Communication from the Commission, 'Tackling the challenges in commodity market and on raw materials' COM(2011) 025 final.

[25] *China—Measures related to the exportation of various raw materials*, WT/DS395/AB/R; *China—Measures related to the exportation of rare earths, tungsten and molybdenum*, WT/DS/431/AB/R.

[26] J Peng and N Cunningham, 'WTO case analysis, suggestions and impacts: China—Measures Related to the Exportation of Various Raw Materials' (2012) 7 *Global Trade and Customs Journal* 27.

[27] S-A Mildner and G Lauster, 'Settling Trade disputes over Natural Resources: Limitations of International Trade Law to Tackle Export Restrictions' (2011) 3 *Gottingen Journal of International Law* 251.

[28] This is so because countries wishing to join the WTO have to provide additional trade advantages to existing members in order to achieve the consensus on their accession.

trade agreements outside the WTO framework the EU supports restrictive clauses on export restrictions. Free trade agreements concluded by the EU since 2005 have often included clauses on export restrictions that are more restrictive than multilateral trade law.[29]

D. The Role of Free Trade Agreements in the EU Trade Strategy

A distinctive quality of the Global Europe Strategy is the fact that the European Commission proposed to intervene in multilateral trade law not only through WTO negotiations and the WTO Dispute Settlement System but also through the conclusion of free trade agreements under Article XXIV GATT.[30] By 2005 the EU had already concluded several free trade agreements. For instance, the conclusion of a free trade agreement is a step towards accession of new Members and is a common feature of its relationship with neighbouring countries in Eastern Europe and Northern Africa. However, these agreements dealt with more limited issues than WTO law and were concluded only with countries having a special relationship with the EU.[31] A novelty of the 2006 Communication was that the EU Commission planned to conclude free trade agreements much more liberally with countries and on issues that were generally dealt with through the WTO system. There are several reasons for this choice that are both internal to EU institutions and linked with the wider economic context.[32] The fact that the Doha Round of negotiations was struggling to deliver results was one of the main drivers of the decision of EU policy-makers to find alternative ways to liberalise trade. In fact, in July 2008 the trade negotiations in

[29] Gruni G, 'Going from one extreme to the other: food security and export restrictions in the EU–CARIFORUM Economic Partnership Agreement' (2013) 19 *European Law Journal* 864.

[30] We will deal with this issue at length in Chapter 5 of this book.

[31] See PJ Cardwell, 'EuroMed, European neighbourhood policy and the Union for the Mediterranean: overlapping frames in the EU's governance of the Mediterranean' (2011) 49 *Journal of Common Market Studies* 219.

[32] On the political dimension of the decision of complementing the EU multilateral trade strategy with the conclusion of free trade agreements, see the Communication 'Global Europe' above. In addition see the declarations of Peter Mandelson (at the time EU Commissioner for external trade), for instance, European Commission, 'Mandelson argues for bilateral agreements that boost global free trade', London, 9 October 2006, available at <http://trade.ec.europa.eu/doclib/docs/2006/october/tradoc_130517.pdf> accessed 15 October 2016; H Mahony, 'Mandelson Defends Third-World Free Trade', *Bloomberg Businessweek*, 16 October 2006, available at <http://www.businessweek.com/stories/2006-10-16/mandelson-defends-third-world-free-trade> accessed 15 October 2016; P Mandelson, 'Free trade is our only way forward', *The Telegraph*, 6 July 2008, available at <http://www.telegraph.co.uk/comment/personal-view/3560228/Free-trade-is-our-only-way-forward.html> accessed 15 October 2015.

the Doha Round collapsed because of a sharp disagreement between India and developed countries on a special mechanism to protect farmers from food products originating in developed countries.[33]

In this context, free trade agreements appeared to be the only legal instrument having a chance to advance trade liberalisation and remove barriers to EU trade within a relatively short amount of time. This is also because Article XXIV GATT obliges the parties to free trade agreements to liberalise 'substantially all the trade' between them. This means that while negotiations in the WTO do not necessarily achieve substantial liberalisation, the conclusion of a free trade agreement always achieves at least the objective of eliminating 80 per cent of customs tariffs on goods traded between the parties.[34]

The 2006 Communication 'Global Europe' was carefully drafted to announce the decision to use free trade agreements to regulate international trade, reassuring partners about the strong commitment of the EU to the multilateral trading system. In particular, the Communication declared that 'the EU's priority will be to ensure that any new FTAs, including our own, serve as a stepping stone, not a stumbling block for trade liberalisation'. In addition, the Commission maintained that free trade agreements must be 'approached with care' because there is a real risk to 'complicate trade, erode the principle of non-discrimination and exclude the weakest economies'. The Communication, however, already hinted that free trade agreements were going to play a major role in EU trade action and that they were going to extend the purview of international trade law on issues not already regulated by existing WTO regulation. In 2012, six years after the publication of the Global Europe Strategy the EU was negotiating, or had already concluded, free trade agreements with more than 100 countries. Negotiations involved developed and developing countries alike, major global economies such as China, India and South American countries as well as small countries and least-developed countries. At the time of writing the EU has already concluded several agreements under the Global Europe Strategy. If the Strategy achieves all its objectives it will produce a major shift in international trade law and the EU will be regulating the majority of its trade relations through free trade agreements instead of WTO law.[35]

[33] See F Ismail, 'An assessment of the WTO Doha Round July–December 2008 collapse' (2009) 8 *World Trade Review* 579.

[34] See below Chapter 5 of this book.

[35] Whether free trade agreements are a complement to WTO law or rather an alternative to it is a controversial issue. See G Marceau and J Wyatt, 'Dispute settlement regimes intermingled: Regional trade agreements and the WTO' (2010) 1 *Journal of International Dispute Settlement* 67; J Bhagwati, *Termites in the Trading System: How Preferential Agreements Undermine Free Trade* (Oxford University Press, 2008); WTO, *The WTO and preferential trade agreements:*

IV. THE RIGHT TO FOOD IN THE EXTERNAL RELATIONS OF THE EU

A. Competences

The realisation of the right to food is a complex issue requiring the intervention of states in numerous policy areas. This paragraph clarifies the legal bases for actions at EU level which are relevant for the realisation of the right to food through international co-operation: the regulation of international trade of food; and the provision of food aid to vulnerable countries in case of food shortages.

Because international trade of food falls within the Common Commercial Policy the EU has exclusive competence on the subject. This means that the policymaking on international trade of food happens at EU level and the EU is competent to conclude relevant international agreements. The explicit exclusive external competence means that Member States cannot contribute to the evolution of the international rules on trade of food autonomously, and take part in this process through the procedures provided in EU Treaties. This applies to all areas of international policymaking relevant for international commerce of food, be it the Doha Round, the WTO Dispute Settlement Body or free trade agreements. Therefore, the EU has exclusive competence for the negotiations on the revision of the WTO Agreement on Agriculture and the clauses of multilateral trade law relevant for the realisation of the right to food. The EU also has exclusive competence to start a legal action against other countries in the WTO Dispute Settlement System when it deems that its partners are not respecting their obligations on the international trade of food. In the same vein, it is the EU that negotiates the clauses regulating trade of food products in free trade agreements.

The picture is more complex with regard to the provision of food aid during a food crisis in a third country. Member States have been reluctant to provide the EU with an external power in this regard. These disputes over competences on the direct provision of food to vulnerable individuals in third countries mirror a disagreement on the existence of a domestic EU competence to provide food to European citizens in need. Recently, these differences brought Germany to dispute the legality of the EU Food

From co-existence to coherence, World Trade Report 2011, available at <https://www.wto.org/english/res_e/booksp_e/anrep_e/world_trade_report11_e.pdf> accessed 15 October 2015; M Matsushita and YS Lee, 'Proliferation of Free Trade Agreements and Some Systemic Issues—In Relation to the WTO Disciplines and Development Perspectives' (2008) 1 *The Law and Development Review* 23; LE Trakman, 'The Proliferation of Free Trade Agreements: Bane or Beauty?' (2008) 42 *Journal of World Trade* 367.

Distribution Programme for the Most Deprived Persons[36] (a programme dispensing food to around 18 million people) and the European Court of Justice to declare that the EU has no internal competence to provide food to people in need.[37] However, whereas the Lisbon Treaty did not provide a solution to the lack of domestic competence it extended EU *external* powers, specifically providing at Article 214 TFEU the EU with the competence to offer humanitarian aid to third countries. In addition, food aid during food crises can be provided through development co-operation, an external competence based on Articles 208, 209, 210 and 211 of the Treaty on the Functioning of the European Union. Under this competence the EU has developed several external funds that can be activated during a food crisis to provide aid to vulnerable countries. Therefore, the Lisbon Treaty created a situation where the EU external competence on direct provision of food to vulnerable individuals is stronger than the one the EU has domestically. This allowed the EU to establish external instruments to intervene in case of food shortages in third countries whereas it does not have the same powers at domestic level.

The nature of the competences to provide development co-operation and humanitarian aid is different from that of the one the EU has in external trade. The Treaties in fact expressly clarify that the two policy areas are complementary to the action of Member States in the same fields. In doing so, the Treaties codified previous case law of the European Court of Justice where the Court had developed the doctrine of 'parallel competences', namely areas of EU action where the exercise of the competence by the EU does not prohibit the action of Member States in the same field. Therefore, Member States are entitled to develop their own food aid policies beside the one carried out by the EU through the procedures defined in the Treaties. In the same vein, they can conclude treaties with third countries that work as a framework to development co-operation and humanitarian aid alongside the one concluded by the EU.[38]

[36] See the page of the programme on the website of the Directorate General for Agriculture and Rural Development of the EU Commission <http://ec.europa.eu/agriculture/most-deprived-persons/index_en.htm>. On the legal dispute around the EU competence to run the programme and the attempts of the EU Commission to maintain it, see European Commission, Press Release, 'European Commission puts new amendments on the table to overcome deadlock for the Deprived Scheme', 3 October 2011, available at <http://europa.eu/rapid/press-release_IP-11-1148_en.htm?locale=en> accessed 15 October 2012; 'EU Observer, EU to cut food aid for the poor', 21 October 2011, available at <http://euobserver.com/social/114013> accessed 15 October 2015.

[37] Case T-576/08 *Federal Republic of Germany v. European Commission*, ECJ, 13 April 2011.

[38] For a taxonomy of EU external competences and the definition of parallel external competences, see P Eeckout, *EU External Relations Law* (Oxford University Press, 2011); A Ward, 'Community Development Aid and the Evolution of the Inter-institutional Law of the European Union' in A Dashwood and C Hillion (eds), *The General Law of EC External Relations* (Sweet & Maxwell, 2000) 160.

B. The EU External Food Security Policy

Since the EU and Member States have shared competence in the field of development co-operation, there is the risk that the EU and its Members will implement policies that are in contradiction between each other. This issue has been present since the first EU development programmes and was the source of disputes before the European Court of Justice. In 2005 the EU and Member States decided to give their efforts in development co-operation a common framework in order to define the main policy objectives and coordinate their activities. The framework took the form of a Joint statement by the Council and the representatives of the governments of the Member States meeting within the Council, the European Commission and the European Parliament titled 'European Consensus on Development'.[39] The document identifies shared values, goals, principles and commitments that EU institutions and Member States will implement in their respective development policies. The Consensus on Development highlights the intention of the EU and its Member States to collaborate with multilateral institutions towards the common objective of reducing poverty, fighting hunger and supporting social development. The Consensus has a wide scope involving numerous aspects of development co-operation including democratic governance, political, economic and social reforms, conflict prevention, social justice, human rights promotion, equitable access to public services, education, culture and health. The Consensus also refers to respect for human rights, fundamental freedoms, peace, good governance, gender equality, rule of law, solidarity, justice, and commitment to multilateralism as common values to be promoted in the relationship between Europe and third countries.

It is within this framework that the EU renewed its development strategies and created a set of policies specifically directed to the fight against global hunger. The European Commission then extended and clarified the policy framework through a set of Communications and other internal policy documents.[40] In particular, the EU contributes to the fight against hunger

[39] Joint statement by the Council and the representatives of the governments of the Member States meeting within the Council, the European Parliament and the Commission on European Union Development Policy: 'The European Consensus', [2006] OJ C46/1.

[40] See Communication from the Commission, 'The EU approach to resilience: learning from food security crises' COM(2012) 586 final; Communication from the Commission, 'An EU policy framework to assist developing countries in addressing food security challenges' COM(2010) 127 final; Communication from the Commission, 'A thematic strategy for Food Security—Advancing the food security agenda to achieve the MDGs' COM(2006) 21 final; Communication from the Commission, 'Evaluation and future orientation of Council Regulation (EC) No. 1292/96 on Food Aid Policy and Food Aid Management and Special Operations in Support of Food Security' COM(2001) 473 final.

through five policy instruments. First, the EU has several external structural funds, such as the EU Development Fund and the EU Development Co-operation Instrument, to which developing countries can apply to receive economic support. These funds have a structure similar to the domestic European Social Fund and have financial chapters dedicated to the promotion of food security.[41] Second, the Food Security Thematic Programme provides a policy umbrella to numerous development programmes organised by the EU in vulnerable countries.[42] Third, in the aftermath of the 2007–2008 food crisis the EU created an additional external fund called Food Facility, endowed with one billion euros and having an expedited bureaucratic structure. The fund pursues the objectives of encouraging producers to increase food supply, it provides safety nets to local populations affected by volatile food prices and improves food management in the longer term.[43] Fourth, the EU provides food directly to populations in need at the occurrence of extreme food shortages and famines, through its humanitarian aid programmes.[44] Finally, the EU coordinates its efforts with multilateral institutions and concludes ad hoc agreements with the Food and Agriculture Organization, the World Food Programme and the United Nations. These agreements provide the framework for the development of additional policies.[45] All these policies are coordinated by the Directorate General for

[41] See Communication from the Commission, 'Towards the full integration of co-operation with ACP countries in the EU budget', COM(2003) 590 final.

[42] The Programme is based on the Development Co-Operation Instrument. See Regulation (EC) No. 1905/2006 of the European Parliament and of the Council of 18 December 2006 establishing a financing instrument for development cooperation, [2006] OJ L378. The Regulation is amended regularly: see Commission Regulation (EC) No. 960/2009 of 14 October 2009 amending Regulation (EC) No. 1905/2006 of the European Parliament and of the Council establishing a financing instrument for development cooperation, [2009] OJ L270; Regulation (EU) No. 233/2014 of the European Parliament and of the Council of 11 March 2014.

[43] Regulation (EC) No. 1337/2008 of the European Parliament and of the Council of 16 December 2008 establishing a facility for rapid response to soaring food prices in developing countries, [2008] OJ L354/62; Commission Decision of 30 March 2009 for implementing the facility for rapid response to soaring food prices in developing countries to be financed ..., [2009] OJ L354/62; European Commission, EuropeAid, *The Food Facility A rapid response from the European Union*, available at <http://ec.europa.eu/europeaid/infopoint/publications/europeaid/documents/184a_foodfacility_en.pdf> accessed 15 October 2015.

[44] The legal base for this kind of intervention is the Instrument for Humanitarian Aid, Council Regulation (EC) No. 1257/96 of 20 June 1996 concerning humanitarian aid. The last amendment of the Regulation is Regulation (EC) No. 219/2009 of the European Parliament and of the Council of 11 March 2009, [2009] OJ L87.

[45] Memorandum of Understanding Concerning the establishment of a Strategic Partnership between the Food and Agriculture Organization and the European Commission of the European Communities in the field of development and humanitarian affairs, available at <http://ec.europa.eu/development/icenter/repository/MoU_EC_FAO_signed_en.pdf> accessed 15 October 2012> accessed 15 October 2015; Memorandum of Understanding Concerning the establishment of a strategic partnership between the World Food Programme and the Commission of the European Communities in the field of humanitarian and recovery assistance in developing countries, available at <http://ec.europa.eu/development/icenter/repository/MoU_EC_WFPsigned_en.pdf> accessed 15 October 2012.

Development Co-operation of the European Commission, the Directorate General for Humanitarian Aid and the EU External Action Service.

V. FOOD SECURITY IN THE NEGOTIATIONS OF FREE TRADE AGREEMENTS

The Lisbon Treaty included several articles on the general objectives of the external action of the EU which explicitly mandate the EU to include objectives such as sustainable development, human rights and development co-operation in all areas of external policies. The Court of Justice of the EU interpreted this mandate in Opinion 2/15 as an 'obligation' falling on the EU to include such interests in the Common Commercial Policy when negotiating a free trade agreement with a third country. As the rest of the research shows, however, it is not always clear how the Commission intends to pursue these non-trade objectives when concluding a free trade agreement with a third country, especially with regard to the economic sections of the free trade agreement such as import and export of food products. An early attempt to pursue this direction is the initiative called Policy Coherence for Development.

The Policy Coherence for Development is a policy review programme aiming to progressively embed development objectives within other external policies.[46] In particular, the Consensus on Development stressed that the policies in which the EU has exclusive competence such as trade should contribute to the attainment of the Millennium Development Goals,[47] now Sustainable Development Goals,[48] and other development objectives set

[46] See Communication from the Commission, 'Policy Coherence for Development—Establishing the policy framework for a whole-of-the-Union approach' COM(2009) 458 final; Commission Staff Working Document, 'Policy Coherence for Development Work Programme 2010–2013' SEC(2010) 421 final; Communication from the Commission, 'A twelve-point EU action plan in support of Millennium Development Goals' COM(2010) 159 final; Commission Staff Working Paper, 'EU 2011 Report on Policy Coherence for Development' SEC(2011) 1627 final; Report from the Commission, 'EU 2009 Report on Policy Coherence for Development' SEC(2009) 1137 final.

[47] For an introduction to Millennium Development Goals and their relation with human rights see C Doyle, 'Millennium development goals and human rights: in common cause or uneasy partners?' (2009) 13 *International Journal of Human Rights* 5; E Dominguez Redondo, 'The Millennium Development Goals and the human rights based approach: reflecting on structural chasm with the United Nations system' (2009) 13 *International Journal of Human Rights* 29; G Schmidt-Traub, 'The Millennium Development Goals and human rights-based approaches: moving towards a shared approach' (2009) 13 *International Journal of Human Rights* 72.

[48] See 'The New European Consensus on Development, Joint Statement by the Council and the Representatives of the Governments of the Member States Meeting within the Council, the European Parliament and the European Commission', available at <https://ec.europa.eu/europeaid/sites/devco/files/european-consensus-on-development-final-20170626 en.pdf> accessed 19 December 2017 at 52.

at EU level. Since in the EU, and often in Member States, policymaking is fragmented, the Consensus highlights that at all levels new instruments, procedures and mechanisms need to be devised in order to promote the inclusion of development objectives within other policy areas. Within this context the Consensus defines specific objectives to be pursued within the WTO and through the negotiations of free trade agreements with developing countries. In particular, the EU in the 2005 version of the Consensus, supported 'rapid, ambitious and pro-poor completion of the Doha Round and EU–ACP Economic Partnership Agreements'.[49]

The 2005 Consensus was followed by a Communication of the European Commission that elaborated further these general policy goals. The Communication identified a long list of trade objectives and modifications of international trade law that the Commission considered necessary in order to align international trade regulation with the pursuit of the Millennium Development Goals.[50] Seven of them are particularly relevant for the object of this research. First, the Commission maintained that the Doha Round should provide improved market access for agricultural goods produced across the developing world. Second, the results of the Doha Round should provide the necessary differential treatment for developing countries, in particular least-developed countries and vulnerable economies. Third, the EU commits itself to full elimination of all remaining tariff escalation, high tariffs and tariff peaks, bringing duties on products produced by vulnerable countries as close as possible to zero.[51] Fourth, the EU is committed to ensuring a development-friendly and sustainable outcome of the EU–ACP Economic Partnership Agreements. This means that promotion of South–South trade and the strengthening of local markets are the prime objectives of the process. Fifth, the EU is committed to protecting developing countries from trade liberalisation of agricultural imports from the EU, ensuring that market openings will be asymmetrical and progressive. Sixth, the EU will extend its Generalised System of Preferences, targeting the countries most in need and making it simpler, more transparent and stable.[52] Finally, the EU is committed to prevent its trade agreements from producing an erosion of tariff preferences of most vulnerable countries.

The European Consensus on Development and the Policy Coherence for Development have provided several guidelines at the time of the negotiation of free trade agreements with developing countries to include in the EU

[49] European Consensus on Development, December 2005, para 34, 14820/05.

[50] Communication from the Commission, 'Policy Coherence for Development Accelerating progress towards attaining the Millennium Development Goals' COM(2005) 134 final.

[51] For a thorough explanation of these trade instruments and their impact on the right to food see Chapter 5 of this book.

[52] Ibid.

Common Commercial Policy objectives that do not respond to immediate EU economic necessities. From these objectives emerges a deep commitment by the EU to differential treatment for developing countries. In addition, the EU Commission appears aware of the need to differentiate between different developing countries and protecting the most vulnerable from the competition of more developed trade partners. The EU Commission is also committed to targeting specific trade mechanisms, such as tariff escalation, that produce negative effects on vulnerable individuals in the developing world. All these pledges and commitments, if put into practice, would modify the landscape of international trade law and produce an international system of trade of food products more supportive of the realisation of the right to food. Even if the policy documents of the European Commission made the choice of not using a human rights language,[53] the policies listed above go in the direction of correcting some the deficiencies of the present international trade system, providing immediate support to the individuals for whom the right to food is not realised.

VI. CONCLUSIONS

The chapter has taken into account the institutional dimension of the external action of the EU with regard to international trade of food. The chapter has highlighted that the Member States of the EU have lost the prerogative of organising their commercial policy and the EU is competent for the planning of the policy, the conclusion of international trade agreements and the participation in trade-related international organisations. All the organs of the EU are involved in the policy and take part in the evolution of international trade law through the procedures contained in the Treaty on the European Union and the Treaty on the Functioning of the European Union. The EU during the last decade has developed an extensive policy having the objective of influencing the development of international trade law on the basis of European economic necessities. The policy reaches numerous areas of international trade regulation including the law on import and export of food products. The bulk of policymaking happens in the Directorate General for External Trade of the European Commission.

The EU also has an external policy to fight global hunger based on explicit competences given to the Union by the Lisbon Treaty. The policy

[53] On the relation between human rights and development co-operation, see P Alston and M Robinson (eds), *Human Rights and Development* (Oxford University Press, 2005); G De Beco, 'The interplay between human rights and development the other way round: the emerging use of quantitative tools for measuring the progressive realisation of economic, social and cultural rights' (2010) 4 *Human Rights and International Legal Discourse* 265.

uses several external instruments to provide food and economic aid to vulnerable countries and funds programmes against hunger on the territory of numerous countries exposed to food shortages. The policy is run in close co-operation with Member States, since in this area the EU does not have exclusive competence. The present structure of the EU action to promote food security in third countries is based on a political document titled 'European Consensus on Development'. In the 2005 version the Union and its Member States defined common objectives in the field of development cooperation which also include the fight against global hunger. The policy was extended and clarified through several political statements and policy documents and was reinforced after the 2007–2008 global food crisis through an additional external fund dedicated to the support of countries affected by food shortages and endowed with one billion euros. The bulk of the policymaking on the EU food security policy happens in the Directorate General for Development Co-operation and in the Directorate General for Humanitarian Aid of the European Commission. The policy is linked with the multilateral food security framework and is connected with the activities of the EU, the World Food Programme and the United Nations programme on Millennium Development Goals.

Through an administrative programme called Policy Coherence for Development, the EU external food security policy should go beyond the areas of development co-operation and humanitarian aid and inspire other areas of EU policymaking and especially the ones where the EU has exclusive competence. Accordingly, the European Consensus for Development mandates that the external trade policy of the EU should intervene in existing international trade law to create a system more supportive of global food security and the pursuit of Millennium Development Goals. This policy objective was reiterated in the most recent version of the Consensus in 2017.[54] Within this framework the European Commission identified at the time of negotiating the Economic Partnership Agreements, specific areas of international trade law that should be modified in order to support the progress towards universal food security. In the list the EU Commission included several major shortcomings of the multilateral system, including tariff escalation and the exposure of vulnerable countries to import surges. The policy papers also recognised the need to provide vulnerable countries with special and differential treatment and sufficient policy space to organise external trade policies on the basis of their development needs.

[54] Joint Statement by the Council, and the Representatives of the Governments of the Member States meeting with the Council, the European Parliament and the European Commission, 'The new European Consensus on Development Our World Our Dignity Our Future' available at <https://ec.europa.eu/europeaid/sites/devco/files/european-consensus-on-development-final-20170626_en.pdf> accessed 28 December 2017.

From this chapter, three preliminary conclusions can be drawn. First, the Lisbon Treaty in Article 21 TEU provided the Union with a general mandate to inspire its external action in all areas to the promotion of human rights, defined as civil and political rights and economic and social rights. In addition, the Lisbon Treaty provided that the EU external trade policy should be driven in a spirit of international co-operation with third countries. Accordingly, the EU Treaties explicitly provide the legal foundations for a holistic vision of the Common Commercial Policy rooted in the respect and promotion of economic and social rights in third countries. This more comprehensive approach to trade policy, which also includes non-economic objectives, is also emerging in the case law of the Court of Justice of the European Union. In Opinion 2/15 on EU competences to conclude free trade agreements, the Court in fact refers to an obligation to include sustainable development in its Common Commercial Policy based on Article 21 TEU.

Second, within the EU, the policymaking on international law of import and export policies of food is fragmented between different policies and administrative apparatuses. The Directorate General for Trade of the European Commission develops the economic part of the policy which responds mainly to the necessity of supporting European development and the creation of new jobs in the EU. At the same time, the part of the policy aiming to make international trade law an instrument to support the fight against global hunger is more fragmented and is based on an internal administrative policy called Policy Coherence for Development, having the objective to allow the use of the EU external trade policy to pursue non-trade objectives such as food security in vulnerable countries. The existence of this policy manifests the awareness of EU organs, EU bureaucracy and EU Member States of the shortcomings of the present international trading system in terms of promotion of food security. Besides this, the policy demonstrates the capacity of the EU to develop plans of action to correct these shortcomings and contribute to the creation of an international trading system that is fully supportive of food security in vulnerable countries.

Finally, even if the Lisbon Treaty frames the EU external action in terms of promotion of universality and indivisibility of human rights, a policy language based on human rights has rarely filtered into EU external policymaking. In fact, the policy documents on the EU external food security policy generally avoid the use of a normative language and do not mention the human right to food. The European Consensus on Development and the instruments of intervention in case of food crises use alternative concepts such as food security and 'development goals'. This attitude shows that the EU did not fully incorporate economic and social rights in its external action and there is still reticence to define the EU action to fight global hunger in terms of progressive realisation of individual entitlements to an adequate amount of food. After the adoption of the Lisbon Treaty, however, there is no legal limit to reframe the EU external food security policy in terms of promotion of the human right to food. Actually, there is an obligation to consider human rights in all areas of EU external action. Notwithstanding the reticence to use the human right to food as a general policy framework, the EU at least on one occasion used economic and social rights to provide legal structure to its relationship with third countries. This is Article 9 of the Cotonou Agreement where the EU undertook to 'promote and protect all fundamental freedoms and human rights, be they civil and political, or economic, social and cultural'. Accordingly, the EU, its 28 Member States and the 77 Countries of the African, Caribbean and Pacific regions that signed the Agreement included the realisation of the right to food within the objectives of their relationship.[55]

The chapter has showed the composite picture of an evolving institutional setting with clearer external competences provided by the Lisbon Treaty and new policies being developed. It has also showed a strong potential of the EU to become a driving force in the use of regional and multilateral trade regulation to pursue the realisation of global food security. In fact, if the priorities identified in the Policy Coherence for Development initiative influence trade negotiations the EU could provide a substantial contribution to the creation of an international regulation of trade of food products that is fully supportive of the realisation of the right. This depends on the capacity of the EU Commission, Council and Parliament as well as EU Member States to put these policy objectives at the forefront of the negotiations and promote their crystallisation into international norms. In doing so the EU has to respect existing legal obligations under WTO law. For this reason before entering into the details of the trade agreements between the EU and countries vulnerable to food shortages it is necessary to assess the policy space left to the EU to modulate import and export policies and negotiate new rules on international trade of food. The following chapter provides this analysis, considering the norms in WTO agreements applicable to the import and export of food between the EU and vulnerable countries.

[55] For a more extensive analysis of human rights obligations stemming from EU international agreements, see Chapter 2 of this book. See also L Bartels, 'Human rights provisions in Economic Partnership Agreements in light of the expiry of the Cotonou Agreement in 2020', European Parliament EP/EXPO/B/DEVE/FWC/2013-08/Lot5/11.

5

The Right to Food in the WTO

I. INTRODUCTION

IN THE ANALYSIS carried out in the previous chapters we showed how the European Union has, after the Lisbon Treaty, obligations under Article 21 TEU to consider human rights in all areas of its external action, including the Common Commercial Policy. Additional obligations on the EU and its Member States stem from international human rights law and human rights clauses included in the Cotonou Agreement and in free trade agreements with third countries.[1] Chapter three showed how the action of the EU in this area should also be inspired by the awareness of the limits of the international food market as an instrument to ensure access to food, in view of its instability and the structure of the market which promotes higher concentrations of market power.

As the previous chapter showed, the EU is manifesting the intention to develop policies to include human rights and development co-operation objectives in trade agreements with vulnerable states. However, it remains often unclear from the policy documents what exactly the EU means by a world trade law that includes such non-economic concerns. In particular it remains open to interpretation how international law on the import and export of food should be drafted in order to also achieve the objectives of human rights protection and development co-operation the EU is setting for itself. This chapter delves into the law of the WTO on the import and export of food products, highlighting the steps which have been taken to protect the categories which are particularly exposed to hunger and malnutrition.

The WTO is central to this research for four main reasons. First, it provides the general international law on the trade of food products which the EU has to respect when exporting and importing food to and from third countries. Second, the rounds of negotiations in the GATT and WTO developed most of the legal know-how of international trade law we use today.

[1] Besides Chapter 2 of this book, see L Bartels, 'Human rights provisions in Economic Partnership Agreements in light of the expiry of the Cotonou Agreement in 2020', European Parliament, EX/EXPO/B/DEVE/FWC/2013-08/Lot5/11.

Accordingly, the instruments and concepts developed in the context of the WTO are the basis for all trade agreements, including the Economic Partnership Agreements the EU concluded with the Caribbean and sub-Saharan Africa. Third, the WTO puts limits on what the EU can do when negotiating free trade agreements with third countries. Therefore, WTO obligations have an influence on the content of the free trade agreements that are the object of the case studies. Finally, the WTO remains the place where countries settle their disputes on international trade law, and the interpretation of WTO treaties given by the Appellate Body is highly influential on developments in international trade law.

From this chapter will emerge a picture of an institution which was designed to deal with the liberalisation of international trade without being bound by or considering other areas of international law or food security concerns. Yet, there are some instruments embedded in the WTO which already take some small steps in the direction of protecting some of the categories which are particularly exposed to hunger and malnutrition. Accordingly, there is space for the EU to build on these instruments to develop a system of international trade of food which protects the most vulnerable countries and is fully aware of the limits of the international food market as an instrument to promote access to food. This is a challenge for trade lawyers who will have to design solutions to balance trade liberalisation with other objectives of international cooperation that have been so far excluded from the system. This is also a challenge for human rights and food security specialists, who are called upon to redesign the role of their areas of expertise so that it fits economic concepts and rules, such as trade liberalisation or comparative advantage, which have been fully accepted by the international community. As this chapter will show, there is ample space to design rules of the international food market which protect food security without undermining the conceptual premises of international trade law.

The following sections will focus on the instruments used in the WTO to regulate the import and export of food products. Section II concentrates on tariffs, section III on safeguards, section IV on the special safeguard mechanism for agriculture and section V on export restrictions. Section VI concludes.

II. IMPORT RESTRICTIONS

The two main instruments that countries use to regulate import flows are tariffs and quantitative import restrictions. Since the GATT, the regulation of tariffs and quantitative import restrictions constitutes the core content of international trade agreements on goods that maintained the main objective to prevent the import policies of one country from producing discriminatory negative economic effects on its trade partners. In the WTO the Agreement on Agriculture is the main instrument to regulate import restrictions on food products. The Agreement on Agriculture defined three main obligations on member countries. First it required them to eliminate all non-tariff import restrictions and convert them into tariffs (the so-called tariffication process).[2] Secondly, it obliged developed countries to lower their tariffs on average by 36 per cent over six years with a minimum of 15 per cent per tariff line. Being granted differential treatment, developing countries were allowed to lower them on average by 24 per cent with a minimum reduction of 10 per cent per tariff line.[3] Least-developed countries were exempted from reduction commitments. Finally, the Agreement on Agriculture obliged member countries to bind their tariffs to a WTO tariff schedule.[4]

The Agreement on Agriculture is the result of the Uruguay Round, which started with the aspiration of revolutionising how agriculture goods were traded in the world. However, many developed countries used legal loopholes and escamotages to avoid opening their markets to producers in the developing world. In fact, through 'dirty tariffication',[5] lax interpretation of reduction commitments[6] and the use of tariff escalation,[7] more influential

[2] Article 4.2, WTO Agreement on Agriculture.

[3] World Trade Organization, 'Reduction methods', available at <https://www.wto.org/english/tratop_e/agric_e/agnegs_swissformula_e.htm> accessed 29 December 2017; M Daly and H Kuwahara, 'The impact of the Uruguay Round on Tariff and non-Tariff Barriers to Trade in the Quad' (1998) 21 *The World Economy* 207.

[4] Ibid. S Joseph, *Blame it on the WTO?* (Oxford University Press, 2017) 181.

[5] K Mechlem, 'Harmonizing Trade in Agriculture and Human Rights: Options for the Integration of the Right to Food into the Agreement on Agriculture' (2006) 10 *Max Planck UNYB* 127, 145; I Goldin and D van de Mensbrugghe, 'Assessing agricultural tarrification under the Uruguay Round' in W Martin and L Alan Winters, *The Uruguay Round and Developing Countries* (Cambridge University Press, 1996); MD Ingco, 'Tariffication in the Uruguay Round: How Much Liberalisation?' (1996) 19 *The World Economy* 425; MD Ingco, 'Agricultural Trade Liberalization in the Uruguay Round. One Step Forward, One Step Back?', World Bank, Policy Research Working Paper 1500, August 1995; JJ Nogues, 'Comment to "Trade, Growth, and Poverty—A Selective Survey" by A Berg and A Krueger, and "Doha and the World Poverty Target" by L Alan Winters'. Commentary presented at the Annual World Bank Conference on Development Economics, 10–11 May 2002, Brussels; WTO, *From GATT to the WTO: the multilateral trading system at the Millennium* (Kluwer Law International, 2000) 14; E Hathaway and MD Ingco, 'Agricultural liberalization and the Uruguay Round' in *The Uruguay Round and the developing countries* (World Bank, 1996).

[6] K Mechlem, 'Harmonizing Trade in Agriculture and Human Rights: Options for the Integration of the Right to Food into the Agreement on Agriculture' (2006) 10 *Max Planck UNYB* 127, 143; The World Bank, *Global Economic Prospects 2004*, 117–119.

[7] On the negative effect of tariff escalation there is extensive literature. See J Stiglitz, *Making globalization work* (Penguin Books, 2006) 87–88; F Cheng, 'Tariff Escalation in world Agricultural Trade' in P Pinstrup-Andersen, and F Cheng (eds), *Case studies in food policy for developing countries Volume III Institutions and International Trade Policies* (Cornell University Press, 2009); FAO, *The state of food insecurity in the world 2003*, 20; MA Aksoy, 'Global Agricultural Trade Policies' in MA Aksoy and JC Beghin (eds), *Global Agricultural Trade and Developing Countries* 37, 48; J Lindland, 'The impact of the Uruguay Round on tariff escalation in agricultural products' (1997) 22 *Food Policy* 487.

WTO Members failed to meet many of the promises on agriculture made in the so-called Uruguay Round 'grand bargaining', on the basis of which developing countries would open their markets in processed goods in exchange for less protection on agricultural and textile products by developed countries.

Within the Agreement on Agriculture developing countries were given differential treatment through the clause in paragraph 14 of the Agreement on Modalities.[8] The clause allowed them to avoid reduction commitments on tariffs that had not been bound in previous trade negotiations, using so-called 'ceiling bindings'. Because the large majority of agricultural tariffs in developing countries were unbound before the Uruguay Round, this option allowed them to pick very high tariff bindings unrelated to the effective level of protection they had. As a consequence, developing countries maintained considerable policy space to increase tariffs as they wish and avoided the 24 per cent reduction commitment. In addition, the Agreement on Agriculture provided additional flexibilities for developing countries and least-developed countries.[9]

After the conclusion of the Uruguay Round further attempts at trade liberalisation through the WTO proved extremely controversial and the following round of negotiations, the Doha Round, never produced substantial results. In fact trade in food and in agricultural products has been one of the most controversial issues in the round and one of the reasons for its failure. The Doha Round had started with a specific focus on developing countries and the explicit mandate to correct some of the imbalances of the system emerging from the Uruguay Round. Notably, in the Doha Round new Modalities were proposed on the basis of which commitments of tariff reductions would also be based on the status of country, with least-developed countries making no cuts, and on a classification of goods. In fact in the Doha Round an attempt was being made to create lists of sensitive and special products which would be subject to a lower degree of liberalisation. Special products are products which are particularly relevant for developing countries which would be subject to smaller cuts or to full exemptions. With the Doha Round in a stalemate the main achievements of negotiations on agriculture were the Bali package of 2013 and the Nairobi package of 2015.

[8] K Mechlem, 'Harmonizing Trade in Agriculture and Human Rights: Options for the Integration of the Right to Food into the Agreement on Agriculture' (2006) 10 *Max Planck UNYB* 127.

[9] Exceptions are contained in Annex 5 to the Agreement on Agriculture, and the most relevant for the right to food is the one allowing developing countries to maintain non-tariff barriers with regard to primary agricultural products that are the predominant staple in the traditional diet: see K Mechlem, 'Harmonizing Trade in Agriculture and Human Rights: Options for the Integration of the Right to Food into the Agreement on Agriculture' (2006) 10 *Max Planck UNYB* 127, 143.

These two packages, however, avoided more controversial issues relative to import restrictions and focused mainly on public stockholding for food security and elimination of export subsidies.

III. SAFEGUARDS

Safeguard measures are instruments of trade defence that a country can apply temporarily to prevent its economy or domestic producers from suffering serious harm from imports or trade concessions.[10] The most common kind of safeguard is the imposition of an additional tariff on imported goods when the quantity or the price of the imported goods is injuring domestic producers. Article XIX GATT and the Safeguards Agreement, one of the agreements concluded in the Uruguay Round, contain the regime of general multilateral safeguards applicable to all products. In addition, the Agreement on Agriculture identifies a special safeguard applicable in certain cases to imports of agricultural goods. The two regimes are considerably different and define distinctive options that countries can utilise to protect their agricultural producers from foreign imports, depending on the circumstances.

The General Safeguards of Article XIX GATT and the Agreement on Safeguards are based on a burdensome administrative procedure which requires the demonstration of several substantive requirements. In fact the WTO Member wishing to impose a safeguard has to demonstrate the existence of a sudden increase of imports based on unforeseen developments, causing serious harm.[11] There are additional procedural elements to be respected and the WTO Member needs to demonstrate a causal link between the import surge and the injury. In addition, the use of safeguards creates a duty to compensate other WTO Members. All these legal requirements made the general safeguard particularly unfit to deal with instability of the international food market, which requires a quick policy response to prevent market instability from affecting local producers.

Considering all the elements above, several shortcomings appear particularly evident for the use of general safeguards to protect food security.

First, the regime emerging from the GATT and the Agreement on Safeguards does not take into account the fact that import surges are more

[10] P Van den Bossche and W Zdouc, *The Law and Policy of the World Trade Organization* (Cambridge University Press, 2013) 606.

[11] For an overview of the legal issues and case law related to WTO safeguards, see AO Sykes, *The WTO Agreement on Safeguards: a Commentary* (Oxford University Press, 2006); PM Rodriguez, 'Safeguards in the World Trade Organization ten years after: a dissociated state of the law?' (2007) 41 *Journal of World Trade* 159.

dangerous for certain vulnerable countries, and does not consider their administrative fragility. The asymmetry in the food security consequences of the surges is not reflected in substantial special and differential treatment for developing countries. Countries particularly vulnerable to food insecurity did not receive any particular facilitation with regard to the burdensome substantive requirements or the administrative procedure. Besides, the law of safeguards does not take into account the urgency of implementing the defensive measure when national food security is at stake. In fact, the present legal framework implies that the state is able to monitor the effects of its trade policy on its domestic market. This is often not the case in a vulnerable country; with a weak administrative apparatus this information is difficult to collect. Even when the data is available, the establishment of the causal link between the surge and the injury to domestic producers requires advanced analytical capability, not always available in developing countries. After the causal link is established and the provisional safeguards have been adopted, the investigation to make them permanent needs to fulfil the other substantive requirements, for which the same shortcomings in data collection and analysis will prove a burden difficult to overcome.

Secondly, safeguard measures are not cost-free. Their adoption has to be accompanied by the compensation of the exporting country. Even when the developing country has fulfilled all the obligations of WTO law it may still not be able to pay compensation. The requirement of compensation was agreed with influential traders in mind, but the approach is detrimental to small and vulnerable developing countries which, without having any impact on international trade, are subjected to the same rules as developed countries and big exporters such as Brazil and China. Compensation creates a further disincentive for vulnerable countries that cannot expose themselves to the risk of paying compensation or of retaliation.

Finally, Article 9 of the Agreement on Safeguards provides limited protection to vulnerable states from safeguards used by more influential traders for substantive reasons and lack of implementation. The article states that:

> safeguard measures shall not be applied against a product originating in a developing country Member as long as its share of imports of the product concerned in the importing Member does not exceed 3 per cent, provided that developing country Members with less than 3 per cent import share collectively account for not more than 9 per cent of total imports of the product concerned.

The Appellate Body highlighted its intention to enforce Article 9 exceptions in the case *United States—Line Pipe Safeguards* where it maintained that developed countries must take 'all reasonable steps' to comply. However, the exclusion works only when developing countries together account for less than nine per cent of total imports in the developed country, so excluding from its application key products produced by vulnerable farmers in tropical countries. In addition, the nine per cent threshold is calculated without distinguishing between middle-income developing countries and countries particularly vulnerable to food shortages. There is no apparent justification to exclude from protection against safeguards by developed countries all developing countries including those most exposed to malnutrition, when only some of them are leading traders of a certain product. Another objectionable element is that WTO Members, which are all obliged to notify to the WTO the safeguard measures they adopt, do not have to notify their compliance with Article 9. This leaves the enforcement of an important clause on differential treatment entirely to the WTO adjudicatory bodies. The fact that there are no examples of vulnerable countries responding to unfair safeguards through the WTO adjudicatory bodies may signal that scarcity of resources in the developing world is hampering the implementation of the clause. In addition, the case law on the issue shows that developed countries have paid scarce attention to the implementation of Article 9.[12]

For all the reasons above the debate on food security and safeguards has concentrated on the other instrument provided by the Agreement on Agriculture: the Special Safeguard which attempts to overcome some of burdensome administrative and substantive requirements of the general safeguard. This instrument is considered in the following section.

IV. THE SPECIAL SAFEGUARDS (SSG)

During the Uruguay Round several countries negotiated a transitional mechanism, in the form of a Special Safeguard, enabling countries to adopt tariff increases when certain conditions, indicating a threat to their local producers, are fulfilled.[13] In the Uruguay Round the system was made available to every country for the agricultural products subject to tariffication. Furthermore, to be able to use the system, the country interested had to

[12] See paragraph 134 of the case *US—Line Pipe Safeguards*: 'As the Panel emphasized, too, the available documents reveal no effort whatsoever by the United States—apart from the claimed "automatic" structure of the measure itself—to make certain that *de minimis* imports from developing countries were excluded from the application of the measure. Whatever the "expectations" of the United States, we are not persuaded by the facts before us that the United States took all reasonable steps that it could and, thus, should have taken to exclude developing countries exporting less than the *de minimis* levels in Article 9.1 from the scope and, therefore, the application of the supplemental duty.'

[13] See TP Stewart, *The GATT Uruguay Round. A Negotiating History, Volume IV: The End Game* (Kluwer, 1999) 18; JM Finger, 'A special safeguard mechanism for agricultural imports: what experience with other GATT/WTO safeguards tells us about what might work' (2010) 9 *World Trade Review* 289; J-J Hallaert, *Special Agriculture Safeguards: Virtual Benefits and Real Costs—Lessons for the Doha Round* (International Monetary Fund, 2005); S Rai, *Recognition and Regulation of Safeguards Measurer Under GATT/WTO* (Routledge, 2011).

include the acronym SSG beside the tariff line in the WTO tariff schedule. Countries were obliged to use this opportunity at the moment of negotiating their tariff bindings, and accession to the SSG was not left open after the conclusion of the negotiations. The conditions of implementing the SSG are based on two alternative triggers, one based on import volumes and one based on the price of the imported good. The price trigger allows the importing country to charge an additional duty when the price of the commodity is below a reference price, calculated as the average of the price of the good between 1986 and 1988.[14] The volume trigger allows the WTO Member to compare each year's imports with the average of imports over the previous three years. Whenever the volume of imports attains the reference volume of a percentage defined in the Agreement on Agriculture, the importer can add an additional duty. The reference level is calculated through a complex formula provided in paragraph 4 of Article 5. These requirements are applicable directly without judicial or administrative assessment and should produce the effect of raising the price on the domestic market, protecting national producers.[15] The SSG works automatically on the basis of the two alternative triggers. No investigation is required and countries can impose the additional SSG duty whenever one of the two conditions is fulfilled. The administrative procedure needed to implement the SSG is negligible but there are numerous additional technical requirements attached to the trigger conditions. Such requirements oblige the country to assess a range of economic variables to define when the trigger has been effectively met or to define the additional duty allowed or the maximum period of implementation.

The SSG has been, since the beginning of the Doha negotiations, at the very centre of the debate and had great responsibility for the collapse of the negotiations.[16] In 2004 WTO Members reached an agreement on the continuation of the mechanism after the end of the reform programme and by 2005 there was general agreement that both price and volume triggers should be maintained. However, the detail of the regulation to be adopted proved highly contentious. When India proposed a system based on the protection of food security and smallholder livelihoods, the negotiations stalled and major exporters abandoned the negotiating table.[17] In 2008 Pascal Lamy proposed a compromise blurring the distinction between price

[14] WTO, *Handbook on Notification Requirements Under the Agreement on Agriculture* (WTO, 2015) 29.

[15] Ibid, 22.

[16] R Baldwin, 'Resolving the conflict leading to the collapse of the Doha Round', VOX, CEPR's Policy Portal, available at <http://voxeu.org/article/how-resolve-doha-stalemate-better-agricultural-safeguard-trigger> accessed 2 January 2016.

[17] R Wolfe, 'The special safeguard fiasco in the WTO: the perils of inadequate analysis and negotiation' (2009) 4 *World Trade Review* 517.

trigger and volume trigger and making the SSG available in most of the cases only when both requirements are fulfilled.[18] Because of the fear that deepening the discussion on the SSG would lead to another stalemate, limitations to the instrument flourished.[19] In 2015, as a part of the Nairobi package, Ministers adopted a Decision on the Special Safeguard Mechanism for Developing Countries (SSM), allowing developing countries to increase tariffs on agricultural products in case of import surges or price declines. The Decision, however, does not go beyond the agreement on pursuing negotiations on the issue and there is still disagreement on the details.[20]

Because, of the 39 countries reserving the right to use the SSG, 22 are developed countries, the instrument remained unavailable to the majority of countries vulnerable to food shortages.[21] Moreover, because in this case the necessity of protection is concentrated in certain vulnerable countries and the use of SSG by developed countries damages fragile agricultural economies, an asymmetrical system would be fairer. By contrast, a clause similar to Article 9 of the Safeguards Agreement, forbidding tariff increases against developing countries, is absent from the SSG regime. Embedding special and differential treatment in the SSG would avoid the present situation where, de facto, the SSG is an additional trade burden on developing country exports towards developed countries, especially Europe. In fact, statistics show that the developed countries that have access to the SSG have used it extensively. The consequence has been that developing countries that have access to the SSG showed that it was used in less than one per cent of the cases in which it was available.[22] In sub-Saharan Africa where numerous malnourished people live, only South Africa, Swaziland, Botswana and Namibia have adopted SSG measures. In South America, only Mexico and Venezuela have used the SSG, and in the Caribbean, only Barbados.[23] Because there is no qualitative requirement, countries can adopt the SSG without regard to the fact that restricting access for certain products bears consequences for the realisation of the right to food in the exporting country.[24]

[18] WTO News, 'Negotiations can find compromise on the safeguard issue—Lamy', 13.12.2008, available at <https://www.wto.org/english/news_e/sppl_e/sppl98_e.htm> accessed 29 December 2017.

[19] See S Joseph, *Blame it on the WTO? A human rights critique* (Oxford University Press, 2011).

[20] WTO, Special Safeguards Mechanism for Developing Countries, WT/MIN(15)/43—WT/L/978.

[21] K Mechlem, 'Harmonizing Trade in Agriculture and Human Rights: Options for the Integration of the Right to Food into the Agreement on Agriculture' (2006) 10 *Max Planck UNYB* 127, 145.

[22] Ibid, 146.

[23] R Sharma, 'Effective special safeguards mechanism' in JR Deep Ford, C dell'Aquila and P Conforti, *Agricultural trade policy and food security in the Caribbean* (FAO, 2007) 160.

[24] S Singham, *A General Theory of Trade and Competition: Trade Liberalisation and Competitive Markets* (Cameron May, 2007) 182; OECD, The Uruguay Round Agreement on Agriculture. An Evaluation of its Implementation in OECD Countries (2001) 32.

An additional shortcoming is that even though procedural requirements are negligible, technical conditions make the SSG difficult to implement, often to the detriment of most vulnerable Members of the WTO. If the SSG is adopted on the basis of the price trigger, the allowed additional duty is proportional to how much the import price has fallen below the 1986–1988 reference price. The Food and Agriculture Organization noted that this system, fixed on prices of more than 30 years ago, is too rigid because often international prices today bear no relation to the situation in the '80s. This weakens considerably the SSG because the price trigger might not reflect the current level below which local producers are threatened. When the price set in the '80s is too low it might be reached only when the surge has already caused great distress to local producers. The SSG could have provided for regular revisions of the price trigger to ensure effective protection.[25]

Analogous issues affect the volume trigger. The SSG obliges the countries using the volume trigger to calculate consumption changes and the degree of market penetration. Both variables require advanced data collection capability that might not be present in vulnerable countries. Besides, the complex formula emerging from the Agreement on Agriculture raises the trigger whenever there is an increase in consumption in the previous years. However, as the Food and Agriculture Organization observes, consumption is likely to be flat or even decreasing in developed countries while is generally on the rise even in the poorest developing countries. This by no means signifies that developing countries are more equipped to absorb trade shocks. In fact, the consumption mechanism may work against the development tide, making food security more difficult to realise as long as consumption increases.[26] Finally, the SSG in its present form does not take into account the capacity of the country to adjust to import surges. Adjusting to import surges or to a period of price depression is easier for countries providing domestic support to their farmers.[27] Besides, domestic support and export subsidies, concentrated in developed or transitional economies, make import surges in the developing world potentially more harmful.

The SSG, to be an effective instrument of protection of food security in the developing world, should take these differences between countries into

[25] FAO, *Institutional requirements for the implementation of Special Safeguard Mechanism*, FAO Brief on Import Surges No. 5, available at <ftp://ftp.fao.org/docrep/fao/009/ah490e/ah490e00.pdf> accessed 8 January 2015.

[26] Ibid.

[27] See FAO, 'Trade Policy Technical Notes on issues related to the WTO negotiations on Agriculture—A special safeguard mechanism for developing countries, Technical Note No. 9', available at <ftp://ftp.fao.org/docrep/fao/008/j5425e/j5425e00.pdf> accessed 8 January 2015.

account. Accordingly, an automatic safeguard should be widely available across the countries particularly vulnerable to hunger and malnutrition and progressively restricted as long as the country is more capable of ensuring domestic availability of food.

V. THE ENABLING CLAUSE, WAIVERS AND FREE TRADE AGREEMENTS

What has been described so far is the general discipline of tariffs and quantitative restrictions resulting from the Uruguay Round. This discipline applies to every WTO Member on the basis of the agreed tariff schedule. EU Member States do not have independent tariff schedules and the results of the Uruguay Round apply directly to the EU common external tariffs. The tariffs negotiated under the framework of the Agreement on Agriculture have to be applied in a non-discriminatory way, respecting the most favoured nation principle. Whenever a WTO Member lowers a tariff towards another WTO Member it has to do so vis-à-vis every other member of the Organization. Otherwise, the tariff reduction is actionable and can result in a complaint filed to the WTO Dispute Settlement Body.[28] This principle applies to agriculture as well, including goods that are sensitive for the realisation of the right to food in vulnerable countries. However, WTO law provides exceptions to this rule that developed countries can use also to correct the results of the Uruguay Round with regard to those countries that are prone to food shortages. The EU and other developed countries could use exceptions to the most favoured nation rule to grant them a minimum amount of exports, raise their income, and improve economic accessibility to an adequate amount of food. The use of special and differential treatment as an instrument to promote development and poverty reduction has been much debated and there is disagreement on its usefulness and effectiveness.[29] However, exceptions to the most favoured nation rule remain the only

[28] M Matsushita, TJ Schoenbaum and PC Mavroidis, *The World Trade Organization. Law, Practice, and Policy* (Oxford University Press, 2006) 202.

[29] Tariff preferences received numerous critical accounts, especially from liberal economists. See J Bhagwati, D Greenway and A Panagariya, 'Trading Preferentially: Theory and Policy' (1998) 108 *Economic Journal* 1128; C Ozden and Eric Reinhardt, 'The Perversity of Preferences: The Generalized System of Preferences and Developing Country Trade Policies, 1976–2000', Policy Research Working Paper 2955 (World Bank, 2003); I Borchert, 'Trade diversion under Selective Preferential Market Access' (2009) 42 *Canadian Journal of Economics* 1390; G Grossman and A Sykes, 'A Preference for Development: The Law and Economics of GSP' (2005) 4 *World Trade Review* 41; C Michalopoulos, 'The Role of Special and Differential Treatment for Developing Countries in GATT and the World Trade Organization', Policy Research Working Paper 2388 (World Bank, 2000).

instruments available under WTO law to correct the results of the Uruguay Round without renegotiating WTO agreements. As a consequence, they have gained considerable attention within the academic debate on how to use trade law to promote development. From the perspective of the right to food, they could be crucial to interrupting the vicious cycle that excludes farmers in the developing world from global trade, especially in vulnerable countries, locks them into poverty and hampers their economic access to an adequate amount of food.[30] Special and differential treatment of vulnerable countries can be granted through three legal instruments: the WTO enabling clause; special waivers voted for by two thirds of WTO membership; and preferential trade agreements under Article XXIV GATT. The following three sub-sections go through the three exceptions to the most favoured nation rule. A fourth evaluates the present arrangement in the light of the right to food.

A. The Enabling Clause

The enabling clause is part of the WTO system through Article 1(b)(iv) of GATT 1994, which included in the GATT all the Decisions adopted by contracting parties before the creation of the WTO.[31] It allows developed countries to derogate from the most favoured nation principle to provide preferential access to developing countries. Developing countries, however, differ considerably among each other, and WTO law generally does not take into account these differences and does not provide any agreed classification of developing countries. For this reason, the definition of developing country commonly used during trade negotiations includes a variety of states, from extremely poor ones up to middle-income OECD countries such as South Korea or emerging global powers such as China. This situation led to the problem of defining the legality of differential treatment between countries classified as developing countries but having different characteristics. Accordingly, recent WTO case law has had to define to what

[30] J Stiglitz goes as far as proposing to substitute the most favoured nation principle with a system where richer countries open up their markets to poorer ones whilst poorer countries maintain their trade barriers towards richer countries. Stiglitz maintains that middle-income countries should eliminate trade barriers towards poorer partners but be allowed to maintain tariff protection vis-à-vis developed countries. See J Stiglitz, *Making globalization work* (Penguin Books, 2007) 83.

[31] For a general overview of the legal issues concerning the enabling clause, see L Bartels, 'The WTO Enabling Clause' in B Remiche and H Ruiz-Fabri (eds), *Le commerce international entre bi et multilatéralisme* (Larcier, 2010) 249; L Bartels, 'The WTO enabling clause and positive conditionality in the European Community's GSP programme' (2003) 6 *Journal of International Economic Law* 507.

extent developed countries can discriminate between developing countries when they grant them preferential access under a Generalised System of Preferences (GSP). This problem emerged when the EU developed several programmes granting additional tariff preferences to countries that had ratified pre-determined lists of international conventions. The practice became contentious with the developing countries that had not received preferential treatment, and a complaint was filed to the WTO Dispute Settlement Body. This gave the opportunity to the WTO courts to clarify the enabling clause in the landmark judgment *European Communities—Conditions for the Granting of Tariff Preferences to Developing Countries*. The Appellate Body, reversing the Panel's judgment, maintained that, because development needs are not equal among all developing countries, developed countries can discriminate between them as long as they 'ensure that identical treatment is available to all similarly-situated GSP beneficiaries, that is, to all GSP beneficiaries that have the development, financial and trade needs to which the treatment in question is intended to respond'.[32]

The case gave considerable policy space to developed countries in the way they design their preferential arrangements. However, it also obliged them not to discriminate in an unpredictable way between developing countries. This means that preferential arrangements based on a closed list of beneficiaries are not consistent with WTO law. GSP schemes must clarify the criteria to be eligible for them and must be opened to applications from all developing countries.

The GSP schemes have several shortcomings which are well identified in literature. For instance the GSP schemes do not appear to solve the imbalances which persist in the system since the conclusion of the Uruguay Round.[33] In addition, the voluntary character of tariff preferences makes them prone to abuses from developed countries that can use them as an instrument of political pressure. Moreover, the fact that tariff preferences can be cancelled at any time makes them a weak instrument of income promotion because economic operators need security and investments cannot rely on ever-changing preferential tariffs.[34]

[32] *European Communities—Conditions for the Granting of Tariff Preferences to Developing Countries* (WT/DS246/AB/R).

[33] UN Conference on Trade and Development (UNCTAD), *Trade Preferences for LCDs: an Early Assessment of Benefits and Possible Improvements*, 2004, available at <http://unctad.org/en/pages/PublicationArchive.aspx?publicationid=1063>.

[34] Lorand Bartels and Christian Haberli proposed to solve this issue through a complex procedure under GATT Article II. See L Bartels and C Haberli, 'Binding Tariff Preferences for Developing Countries under Article II GATT' (2010) 13 *Journal of International Economic Law* 969.

B. Waivers

Article IX of the Agreement Establishing the WTO contains a residual procedure enabling contracting parties to waive obligations whenever the decision is approved by three quarters of WTO Members. The waiver must be limited in time and the decision adopting it has to state the exceptional circumstances justifying the decision. This procedure has been used for a variety of purposes including that of allowing developed countries to provide preferential treatment to some developing countries in derogation of the most favoured nation principle when this would not be allowed by WTO legislation. Because waivers are temporary, they offer limited reliability and their expiry makes trade preferences suddenly inconsistent with WTO law. A notable example of the use of waivers is that adopted to make compatible with WTO law the Cotonou Agreement between the EU and the African, Caribbean and Pacific (ACP) group of states. The Cotonou Agreement is an instrument of development cooperation that included a substantial trade component giving the EU access to goods produced in ACP countries duty free or with a tariff considerably below the one offered through the EU GSP. The waiver expired in 2007, forcing the contracting parties to the Cotonou Agreement to review their relationship. The expiration of the waiver had major consequences for ACP countries that found themselves in the position of having to conclude preferential trade agreements with the EU in order to preserve their tariff preferences. As it will be seen in the case studies, this came at a cost in both economic and human rights terms.[35]

C. Free Trade Agreements

Article XXIV GATT allows Member States to conclude preferential trade agreements.[36] To make them compatible with WTO law the most favoured nation principle does not apply to the parties to a preferential trade agreement in their relation with each other. This exception to the GATT is the legal basis for a plethora of free trade areas and allows the EU to pursue its widespread strategy of conclusion of free trade agreements with third countries outside the WTO. To be consistent with multilateral trade law, preferential trade agreements have to respect numerous conditions, the most important of which is that the agreement has to liberalise 'substantially all

[35] See Chapters 6 and 7 of this book.

[36] See paragraph 5 of Article XXIV GATT: 'Accordingly, the provisions of this Agreement shall not prevent, as between the territories of contracting parties, the formation of a customs union or of a free-trade area or the adoption of an interim agreement necessary for the formation of a customs union or of a free-trade area'.

the trade' between the contracting parties.[37] This means that a free trade agreement, to be compatible with WTO law, should provide at least of 80 per cent liberalisation of trade in goods.[38] The requirement has to be met within 10 years from the conclusion of the agreement. The EU uses free trade agreements widely to give preferential access to its common market to neighbouring countries and, increasingly, to its trade partners around the world.[39]

D. Free Trade Agreements and Food Security

The use of preferential trade agreements to support the income of vulnerable categories in developing countries, giving them preferential access to the market of a developed country, is a contentious matter. Whereas the enabling clause and waivers allow developed countries to offer non-reciprocal access to their markets to developing states, Article XXIV GATT obliges the parties to a preferential trade agreement to eliminate tariffs substantially on both sides. This means that while the developing country gains access to the developed country's market, also the developed country gains almost complete market access to the developing country. The WTO Panel clarified the point in the case *EC—Bananas II*,[40] where it stated that the Lomé Convention, the predecessor of the Cotonou Agreement, could not be justified under Article XXIV GATT because it offered non-reciprocal preferential access to the developing countries taking part in the Convention. These countries had preferential access to the EU market but were able to maintain trade barriers on imports coming from Europe. In other words, the principle of non-reciprocity included in Part IV of the GATT, which should inspire multilateral trade law, cannot be applied in the context of preferential trade negotiations. This legal requirement limits considerably the policy space the EU and developing countries have when they negotiate a

[37] See paragraph 8 of Article XXIV GATT: 'A free-trade area shall be understood to mean a group of two or more customs territories in which the duties and other restrictive regulations of commerce … are eliminated on substantially all the trade between the constituent territories in products originating in such territories.' This obligation does not exist on countries when they negotiate multilateral trade agreements.

[38] It is, however, unclear how the 80 per cent threshold should be calculated: see El Hadji Abdourahmane Diouf, 'The ACP Advantage: Interpreting GATT Article XXIV and Market Access Implications for EPAs, Trade Negotiations Insights', 14.09.2009, available at <https://www.ictsd.org/bridges-news/trade-negotiations-insights/news/the-acp-advantage-interpreting-gatt-article-xxiv-and> accessed 29 December 2017.

[39] See Chapter 4 of this book on the centrality of free trade agreements in the EU Common Commercial Policy.

[40] *EEC Import Regime for Bananas*, Report of the Panel (DS38/R), 11 February 1994, unadopted (*EC—Bananas II*). See also *European Communities—Regime for the Importation, Sale and Distribution of Bananas*. Report of the Appellate Body (DS27/AB/R), 9 September 1997 (*EC—Bananas III*).

preferential trade agreement among themselves. In particular, Article XXIV makes the EU unable to agree on clauses affording substantial protection of developing countries from its agricultural exports. This condition makes preferential trade agreements unsuitable to promote the income of vulnerable groups in developing countries because such agreements expose them to the competition of producers in the developed world.[41] Exposing vulnerable categories to the full force of European competition, preferential trade agreements have the potential to produce widespread negative effects on the realisation of the right to food.

E. Preferential Treatment and Food Security: The State of Play

Human rights literature has devoted scant attention to the interplay between the law of preferential treatment in the WTO and the realisation of the right to food. This part of legislation is, however, crucial for correcting the imbalances of the Uruguay Round and ensuring access by vulnerable countries to high-value markets. Looking at these norms from the perspective of human rights, it is inappropriate that market access to developed countries, so fundamental for the realisation of economic and social rights, is left to the unrestricted will of more developed states. The importance of eliminating trade barriers to the exports of developing countries is also recognised in the first commitment of Article XXXVII of the fourth part of the GATT. This norm, however, remained aspirational and was never duly implemented. The voluntary character of the instrument made tariff preferences a double-edged sword prone to abuses and political utilisations. In fact, by conceding or revoking preferences developed countries can influence the share of wealth each vulnerable country obtains from international trade and the income of exporters and producers in the developing world. An additional problem is that the revocation of tariff preferences bears consequences for food security that WTO law does not oblige its Members to consider. The end of a preferential scheme affects the economic access to adequate food of those producers in the developing world who relied on the scheme for their livelihood. In other cases WTO law prescribes the obligation to compensate partners for changes in trade policies producing adverse effects, but not in this case.[42] WTO law could also have required binding of tariff preferences in order to provide more security and avoid abuses of donor countries.[43]

[41] Abou Abass, 'The Cotonou Trade Regime and the WTO' (2004) 10 *European Law Journal* 439.

[42] Such as Article 8 of the Agreement on Safeguards, see M Matsushita, TJ Schoenbaum and PC Mavroidis, *The World Trade Organization. Law, Practice, and Policy* (Oxford University Press, 2006) 458.

[43] See above n. 34.

In addition, some of the norms used for preferential treatment are outdated and do not reflect or regulate the use of them which is made today. This includes Article XXIV GATT, which was drafted decades ago but is now widely used to produce new international legislation including the North–South preferential agreements that are the object of this research. The Uruguay Round missed the opportunity to amend Article XXIV, acknowledging its new function and allowing non-reciprocal liberalisation when vulnerable countries are involved in the agreement. Under the rules resulting from the Round a country exposed to hunger and malnutrition has to eliminate its tariffs on trade in goods almost completely whenever it enters a preferential trade agreement. This is so even when the trade partner is a developed country able to affect the livelihoods of farmers through its agricultural exports. In contrast, the corresponding article of Article XXIV GATT in the General Agreement on Trade in Services (GATS) provided that whenever a preferential agreement liberalises trade in services and developing countries are parties, 'flexibility should be provided … in accordance with the level of development of the countries concerned'.[44] It would have been enough for the Uruguay Round to introduce the same clause in Article XXIV GATT to make it more conducive to the realisation of the right to food. The Doha Declaration recognised this necessity at paragraph 29 where it stipulates: 'We also agree to negotiations aimed at clarifying and improving disciplines and procedures under the existing WTO provisions applying to regional trade agreements. The negotiations shall take into account the developmental aspects of regional trade agreements'.

The prohibition of non-reciprocal liberalisation of trade in goods in preferential trade agreements also led to the problem of possible abuses by developed countries with regard to the different forms of preferential treatment available under WTO law. Because all three forms are voluntary (GSP, waivers, preferential trade agreements) and have different consequences for the vulnerable partner of the relationship, more regulation would have been needed on the prerogative of developed countries to pick one form or the other. In fact, the result of the Uruguay Round leaves open the possibility that developed countries use tariff preferences to pressure developing countries in the direction of preferential trade agreements in order to obtain access to their internal markets. This practice would be dangerous for the

[44] The reference here is to Article 5, paragraph 3.a of the General Agreement on Trade in Services. See L Bartels, 'The trade and development policy of the European Union' (2007) 18 *Journal of International Economic Law* 715, 754; R Adlung and M Molinuevo, 'Bilateralism in services trade: is there fire behind the (BIT-) smoke?' (2008) 11 *Journal of International Economic Law* 365; R Lang, 'Renegotiating GATT Article XXIV—a priority for African countries engaged in North-South trade agreements', United Nations Economic Commission for Africa African Trade Policy Centre, Work in Progress No. 33.

right to food because it exposes groups vulnerable to food shortages almost to the full force of the competition of the more developed partner.[45]

VI. EXPORT RESTRICTIONS

Export restrictions are measures with which countries put an artificial ceiling or a tariff barrier to the export of goods. The most relevant of them are export bans, export quotas, export taxes and export licences. Export bans forbid the export of a certain good, temporarily or indefinitely, so that producers have to sell it exclusively on the domestic national market. Through export quotas countries define the quantity of a certain good that can be exported abroad, reserving the exceeding production for the national market. Export taxes are duties levied on exports. Export taxes have been widely used to increase public revenues and, depending on their amount, they can also affect the quantity exported. In fact, very high export taxes can produce effects comparable to export quotas and bans. Export licences are administrative certifications with which a country grants to certain exporters the right to export determined goods to determined countries.[46] The objective of export restrictions is limiting the quantity of a certain good exported abroad or producing tax revenues from the activity of exporters, and for centuries countries have controlled their export regime in order to satisfy domestic needs.

The interplay between export restrictions and food security is threefold and changes depending on the characteristics of the country implementing them. First, at the occurrence of food crises in vulnerable countries, export restrictions can be used to create or refill buffer stocks and direct national food production to satisfy domestic food security. Certain developing countries widely used this strategy, for instance, when natural disasters affected the quantity of food available on their territory. More generally export restrictions can be used when national food production is directed too heavily towards third countries without regard to the needs of local populations. Secondly, when export restrictions take the form of export taxes they generate revenues that can be directed to the realisation of

[45] For a very critical account of the attitude of the European Union towards tariff preferences, see Oxfam, *Weighing the options*, Briefing note prepared for the Pacific Trade Ministerial, Port Vila, Vanuatu, 31 July–1 August 2007, available at <http://www.acp-eu-trade.org/library/files/Oxfam_EN_310707_Oxfam_Weighing-the-options.pdf> accessed 7 January 2012.

[46] For an overview of export quotas in WTO law, see M Matsushita, TJ Schoenbaum and PC Mavroidis, *The World Trade Organization. Law, Practice, and Policy* (Oxford University Press, 2006) 259; J Kim, *Recent Trends in Export Restrictions*, OECD Trade Policy Working Papers, available at <http://www.oecd-ilibrary.org/docserver/download/fulltext/5kmbjx63sl27.pdf?expires=1326112273&id=id&accname=guest&checksum=1950BFC3DD46E666F4CD102AF1AB6848> accessed 9 January 2012.

economic and social rights, including the right to food. This means that the elimination of export taxes has the potential to affect public expenditure directed towards the realisation of the right to food whenever tariff cuts are not replaced by other sources of public income. Finally, export restrictions can produce negative effects on food security because they limit the amount of food available on the international market. Reducing global food supply, export restrictions tighten market conditions on countries dependent on foreign imports to realise the right to food of their citizens.[47] This is particularly so when export restrictions are implemented by major exporters of products that are central for the realisation of the right, such as wheat, rice and other basic food staples. When major exporters reduce food exports, export restrictions are particularly detrimental for vulnerable countries and net food importers.

Because the implementation of export restrictions can be both positive and negative for the realisation of the right to food, it is extremely challenging to design an international regulation that works for every country. Ultimately, the compatibility of export restrictions with the realisation of the right to food depends on the characteristics of the implementing country, its vulnerability to food shortages and the importance of their exports for global food supply. For instance, export restrictions on wheat by the EU, Russia, the US or Canada would have extremely severe consequences on the realisation of the right in net food-importing countries. By contrast, export restrictions by minor exporters could be justified from a human rights perspective when they are necessary to secure the realisation of the right to food at domestic level.

A. Export Restrictions in the GATT

For the normative prescriptions of the law of comparative advantage, export restrictions and taxes are protectionist measures that should be eliminated. These instruments in fact create market distortions and shelter inefficient producers. This creates a loss of efficiency and diminishes the global amount of wealth that the system is able to create. Notwithstanding their status in classical economic theory, international trade rounds have always been incapable of regulating the practice because countries are reluctant to give away their sovereignty on export policy. The GATT was heavily influenced by US export legislation, which made extensive use of export restrictions to avoid shortages of raw materials and as instruments of proactive

[47] See Chapter 3 of this book for the definition of net food-importing countries.

international action.[48] The unwillingness to impose international obligations on export policies resulted in a deep asymmetry in GATT and WTO law between regulation of imports and regulation of exports. While the former reached an advanced level of complexity, the latter remains embryonic and unsubstantial.

As far as export quotas and bans are concerned, Article XI GATT contains a general prohibition of quantitative restrictions. Notwithstanding this general prohibition, GATT identifies numerous exceptions applicable to export quotas, making the provision fragile and open to the interpretation of WTO Members. In fact, Article XI contains an extensive exception allowing temporary export bans or quotas to prevent or relieve critical shortages of foodstuffs or other products essential to the exporting contracting party. Making limitations on export quotas even less substantial, Article XX containing GATT general exceptions includes two paragraphs to ensure that GATT Members can adopt any kind of export restrictions to serve particular national interests. Paragraph (h) allows GATT Members to conclude international commodity agreements to limit the quantity of a certain commodity delivered to the international market. In this case the export limitations that the commodity agreement prescribes can be implemented by the state without conflicting with the GATT. In addition, GATT Members are free to adopt all kinds of export restrictions when implementing a governmental stabilisation plan to hold the price of domestic materials below the world price when this is necessary to ensure essential quantities of such materials.

WTO law is even more lenient towards export taxes. In fact, no substantial limitation was put on the practice. The only restraint implied during the Uruguay Round was that export taxes could not be so high as to be a quantitative restriction in disguise. The breadth of the exceptions, and the fact that no constraints were put on export taxes left GATT Members considerable freedom to design export policies. For instance, in the '70s Brazil applied export taxes on coffee beans, leaving export of processed coffee tax-free in order to favour the development of Brazilian coffee processing industries.[49] After the creation of the WTO, the Dispute Settlement Body stressed that quantitative restrictions are a particularly opaque form of trade barrier, but no substantial case law arose from the body. Controversies were generally settled through ad hoc international agreements regulating exported quantities on the basis of agreed quotas.[50]

[48] M Matsushita, TJ Schoenbaum and PC Mavroidis, *The World Trade Organization. Law, Practice, and Policy* (Oxford University Press, 2006) 259.

[49] LS Jarvis, 'The rise and decline of rent-seeking activity in the Brazilian coffee sector: Lessons from the imposition and removal of coffee export quotas' (2005) 33 *World Development* 1881.

[50] M Matsushita, TJ Schoenbaum and PC Mavroidis, *The World Trade Organization. Law, Practice, and Policy* (Oxford University Press, 2006) 259.

B. Export Restrictions in the Agreement on Agriculture

Because the GATT de facto did not manage to put export quotas and taxes under control, the Uruguay Round had to deal with the problem such practices created for vulnerable Members. In fact, when large exporters limit the quantity of sensitive goods available on the international market they can affect the availability of those goods in importing countries. This mechanism is particularly dangerous with regard to agricultural products because export restraints by exporters can cause or intensify food shortages in net food-importing countries. The Uruguay Round dealt with the issue in Article 12 of the Agreement on Agriculture, which has the objective of tackling some of the shortcomings of the GATT regulating the conditions under which export restrictions of farm products can be adopted. The article does so by providing for differential treatment between developed and developing countries and requiring that any consequences for net food-importing countries are considered before the adoption of export restrictions on foodstuffs.[51] Article 12 applies only to developed countries and net food-exporting developing countries when they use the exception to Article XI GATT allowing import restrictions to deal with food shortages. The article provides that before the institution of an export ban or quota the WTO Member shall give due consideration to the effects of such prohibition or restriction on importing Members' food security. In addition the country adopting the export prohibition or restriction must inform the WTO Committee on Agriculture in writing and seek consultation with any other WTO Member that the measure might affect. The Member adopting the measure is responsible for giving any necessary information to the importing Member.[52]

C. Direction of the Doha Round

Negotiations on Agriculture, which started one year before Doha, prioritised tariff reduction and the decrease of export subsidies and domestic support. The Doha Declaration does not contain specific reference to export restrictions even if it includes a statement on deepening the discussion on non-trade concerns such as food security and the environment. The 2004 negotiating framework states that regulation of export restraints has to be

[51] See Chapter 3 of this book.

[52] G Gruni, 'Going from one extreme to the other: food security and export restrictions in the EU–CARIFORUM Economic Partnership Agreement' (2013) 19 *European Law Journal* 864.

strengthened and that this is an issue of interest. The historical asymmetry between regulation of imports and regulation of exports is certainly present in the Doha Round, and even though there is general awareness of the necessity of regulating export restrictions, political support is weak. When the global food crisis deflagrated in 2007 and 2008 following a price spike, the role of a lack of regulation on export restrictions in exacerbating the crisis became evident.[53] As a consequence, several international agencies, including the Food and Agriculture Organization, and numerous governments maintained that export restrictions needed to be discussed urgently within the Doha framework. So far, however, progress on the issue has remained unsubstantial.

D. Export Restrictions and the Right to Food

The lax approach of the GATT with regard to export restrictions, both quantitative and tax-based, resulted in widespread use of such instruments across the board and, besides developed countries, export restrictions flourished in the developing world.[54] Transitional economies desiring to use their riches of raw materials to boost industrial development can adopt escalating export restrictions, discouraging export of primary commodities and facilitating export of processed goods. Developing countries also used export taxes to fund government programmes in the absence of solid systems of domestic taxation.[55] The present GATT regime of export restrictions, which amounts to the substantial absence of regulation of the practice, is unable to

[53] See, FAO, 'The Breakdown of the Doha Round Negotiations. What Does it Mean for Dealing with Soaring Food Prices?', Economic and Social Perspectives, Policy Brief No. 3, August 2008, available at <ftp://ftp.fao.org/docrep/fao/011/aj221e/aj221e.pdf> accessed 9 January 2012.

[54] The most reliable instrument to monitor the use of export restrictions in the world is the Trade Policy Review mechanism of the WTO. For an overview of the use of export restrictions in the world trading system, see J Bonarriva, M Koscielski and E Wilson, 'Export controls: an overview of their use, economic effects and treatment in the global trading system', US International Trade Commission, Office of Industries Working Paper No. ID-23, available at <http://www.usitc.gov/publications/332/working_papers/ID-23.pdf> accessed 9 January 2015.

[55] For an overview of the relation between trade and public revenues see L Bartels, 'Trade and Human Rights', *Max Planck Encyclopedia of Public International Law* (August 2011 edn) <http://www.mpepil.com/subscriber_article?script=yes&id=/epil/entries/law-9780199231690-e1550&recno=1&searchType=Quick&query=trade+and+human+rights> accessed 17 January 2012; H-J Chang, *Bad Samaritans* (Bloomsbury Press, 2008) 69; J Stiglitz, *Making Globalization Work* (Penguin Books, 2007) 66; United Nations Economic Commission for Africa, African Trade Policy Centre, 'Fiscal Implications of Trade Liberalization on African Countries', Work in Progress No. 5, available at <http://www.uneca.org/atpc/Work%20in%20progress/5.pdf> accessed 16 January 2015.

avoid dangerous market behaviour from large exporters. Under the GATT regime large exporters are free to cause or exacerbate price spikes, reducing the quantity of food available on the international market and affecting food availability and economic accessibility of food in countries relying on food imports for their domestic food security. Besides, the Uruguay Round did not take substantial steps to prevent the adoption of export restrictions from distressing vulnerable WTO Members. Whenever a state adopts an export restriction it does not have to discriminate between importing countries able to cope with the restrictions and countries unable to do so. In particular, there is no obligation to protect net food-importing countries. As a consequence, the present regime, when export restraints are adopted, is unable to shelter the food security of vulnerable countries and avoid an evident cause of instability of the food marketplace. Besides, the actual regime of export restrictions gives disproportionate market and political power to large exporters which are able to affect food security anywhere in the world and especially in net food-importing countries.

The lack of regulation of export restrictions means also that GATT leaves WTO Members, including vulnerable ones, free to adopt emergency measures to deal with food shortages. By leaving states the necessary amount of sovereignty to use their own food production to bring down prices on the national market or directly provide food staples to their population, GATT allows state intervention in case of food emergencies. Future modifications of the GATT need to maintain this exception to be compatible with the obligations of GATT Members under international human rights law. However, more efforts are needed during trade negotiations to strike the balance between the necessity to ensure supply on the national market and the need to prevent market volatility and price escalations.

The food security clause in the Agreement on Agriculture does not change the general picture drawn by the GATT. Article 12 only creates a mild form of differential treatment on notification obligations, which does not limit the prerogative of developed countries and net food-exporting countries to adopt export restrictions in such a way that is detrimental to countries prone to food shortages. The article does not even oblige the exporter to exclude least-developed countries from the measure. In addition, the small number of notifications received so far suggests that the large majority of WTO Members did not inform the WTO of their export restrictions and that the information that has to be included in the notification is minimal.[56] Finally, Article 12 does not provide for any emergency mechanism avoiding

[56] G Gruni, 'Going from one extreme to the other: food security and export restrictions in the EU–CARIFORUM Economic Partnership Agreement' (2013) 19 *European Law Journal* 864.

panic market behaviour at the occurrence of sudden price spikes. From the analysis of the notified export restrictions, it is evident that the contribution of export restrictions to major human rights violations such as the 2008 global food crisis was not a priority for the Agricultural Committee. Article 12 is an important recognition of the potential effects of export restrictions on the right to food. However, binding obligations are needed to avoid at least the most evident cases of violations of the right to food caused through the adoption of export restrictions.

VII. CONCLUSIONS

The chapter has assessed the multilateral norms relevant for the import and export of food from the perspective of the realisation of the human right to food. This chapter is a necessary premise to the assessment of the recent trade agreements concluded by the EU with the Caribbean and Africa carried out in Chapter six and Chapter seven. The EU, in fact, in designing its policies with vulnerable countries, has to respect the prescriptions of multilateral trade law. Accordingly, any attempt to evaluate the EU external action towards countries vulnerable to food shortages cannot disregard the fact that pre-existing international treaties already regulate this action.

The chapter has taken into account the most relevant trade instruments that states use to control imports and exports of food. The analysis clarified that these instruments always produce a multiplicity of effects and that generally their utilisation requires attentive weighing of the characteristics of the countries involved. Often, trade measures produce effects both within the implementing countries and in all the other countries importing or exporting the food staple involved in the measure. Whenever import or export policies have consequences for the access to food of individuals, they must be handled with care and in accordance with the human rights obligations of the implementing country. Otherwise, trade instruments can produce unintended consequences and work against the realisation of the right to food in vulnerable countries. It is common that the same trade instrument can have both positive and negative consequences, depending on the characteristics of the countries involved and on the ways it is implemented.

As far as tariffs and other import restrictions are concerned, the Uruguay Round did not manage to produce a positive impact on the income of vulnerable countries and missed the opportunity to ban tariff practices, such as tariff escalation, that explicitly work against the realisation of the right. More generally, flawed design, legal loopholes and misapplication did not improve the participation of vulnerable countries and producers in the world economy. Notably, it is the GATT itself that recognises the importance of market access for vulnerable producers in its inspirational, but unimplemented, Article XXXVII. In this regard, preferential access for developing countries constitutes a crucial area of debate which, however, so far, has not been able to change the main outcome of the Round. Throughout the regulation of tariffs WTO law has often been interpreted to the detriment of market access of vulnerable producers, and the importance of certain key products for the realisation of the right to food was not taken into account during the negotiations. With the Doha Round struggling to change this picture, free trade agreements have become central for the evolution of this area of international trade law.

Similar shortcomings affect the regulation of safeguards as well, with key products and vulnerable countries excluded or discouraged from applying implemented measures no matter what the consequences of rising imports for the realisation of the right to food at domestic level. The Special Safeguard in the Agreement on Agriculture remains conceptually the best example of reconciliation between trade objectives and human rights duties, but in its current form it is of no use for the large majority of vulnerable countries.

The regulation of export restrictions is unsubstantial and WTO law does not create particular restrictions on countries. The freedom to reduce or block exports of food to third countries can be a threat to the right to food whenever this practice reduces access to food by individuals in net food-importing countries or other vulnerable states. The Agreement on Agriculture does not take this problem into account and provides only an extremely lax system of notifications of export restrictions that is ineffective and scarcely implemented. This lack of obligations also means that vulnerable countries are free to adopt export restrictions to protect national food security. It is important that future negotiations duly take into account this necessity when regulating export restrictions.

The way WTO law regulates preferential trade agreements is crucial for the way the EU interacts with vulnerable countries because it limits the extent to which the EU can modify tariffs agreed at multilateral level. Most notably, WTO law requires substantial liberalisation of trade of goods whenever a preferential trade agreement is concluded. Elimination of tariffs is required no matter what the characteristics of the countries involved in the process are, and also when vulnerable countries are parties to the agreement. The obligation is highly influential on the way the EU relates to vulnerable countries whenever it has a preferential trade agreement with them. The norm is potentially detrimental to the right to food because it obliges vulnerable countries to expose themselves to the full force of competition from developed countries whenever they enter a trade agreement with them. This problem requires attention by the EU whenever it concludes a trade agreement with vulnerable countries. As we will see in the case studies, the fact that Article XXIV GATT requires Members to liberalise 'substantially all the trade' produces major consequences for vulnerable countries involved in recent Economic Partnership Agreements with the EU.

There are some clear efforts to go beyond traditional trade policy in the Doha Round, and the Bali and Nairobi packages are examples of actions in favour of food security that the WTO has achieved in some specific areas. However, there is an evident impasse within the Doha Round, with the WTO still struggling to fully incorporate the Doha spirit of using the Organization to improve support to more vulnerable Members. Policy directions which would solve some of the issues above—such as the identification of special and sensitive goods to be exempted from liberalisation or the development of an improved special safeguard mechanism—remain controversial and far from adoption. On all these issues a clear stance by the EU in support of the reform programme would be necessary, but probably not sufficient to achieve the objective of incorporating food security objectives in the WTO. In addition, cooperation between the WTO and food security organisations such as the FAO remains limited. For instance, the indices of countries vulnerable to food shortages do not play a role at the moment in shaping the obligations on tariffs, safeguards and export restrictions. Overall the WTO at the moment is failing to diversify legal and policy approaches on the basis of the vulnerability of its Members to food shortages.

In conclusion, WTO law has produced mixed results on the policy space that countries have to use trade instruments to facilitate the realisation of the right to food domestically and in third countries. In certain cases such as preferential trade agreements, WTO law is incisive and creates severe limitations; in others, like export restrictions it leaves extensive space. Accordingly, the EU should do its best to prevent the shortcomings of the multilateral system from being mirrored in its own external action and to use all the leeway the WTO leaves to facilitate the realisation of the right to food. This dimension is particularly important when the EU negotiates preferential trade agreements with vulnerable countries. In this regard, the EU could exploit all the leeway WTO leaves to create preferential agreements that are conducive to the realisation of the right to food. This is certainly possible, for instance, with regard to export restrictions for which WTO law does not pose any substantial obligation on its Members. The same can be done with safeguards, where there is considerable space to invent more efficient instruments specifically designed to protect vulnerable countries from the vagaries of the international food market. In the areas where WTO law creates a straitjacket that does not allow the EU to pursue its external action according to food security objectives, the issue can be flagged in the WTO and the necessary amendments can become a priority of the EU's action in the Organization. In fact, even though the evolution of multilateral trade law also depends on the other WTO Members, the EU is highly influential and has unrivalled practical experience in achieving its external trade objectives. A robust action towards a reform of the WTO in the direction of the inclusion of food security would leave a mark. For instance, this applies to Article XXIV GATT, which appears to expose vulnerable countries to food insecurity when they enter a preferential trade agreement with developed countries.

The allocation of these priorities in the EU external action is not an easy task. EU external policies are highly fragmented and institutional incentives to take into account human rights or food security in external trade might not always be present. The consequences of the EU action to embed food security within international trade law can be evaluated only by taking into account the details of the clauses of the resulting international trade treaties. The following chapters will do so with regard to seven recent free trade agreements concluded between the EU and developing countries vulnerable to food shortages. Chapter six concentrates on the free trade agreement between the EU and the Caribbean, and Chapter seven, on the six free trade agreements the EU has concluded in sub-Saharan Africa. These chapters will ascertain whether the free trade agreements incorporate the priorities that the EU Commission identified through the Policy Coherence for Development initiative, that coincide with the ones defined in this chapter, namely: increased access to the EU market for vulnerable producers; elimination of tariff escalation; protection of vulnerable countries from import surges; preservation of policy space on external trade by vulnerable countries; and differential treatment for countries exposed to food shortages. In addition, the next chapter will consider to what extent the EU is building on the few achievements of the Doha Round and the Bali and Nairobi packages with regard to the inclusion of food security in world trade law. As the two chapters will show, the EU was not able to do so and the text of the free trade agreements distance themselves not only from EU human rights obligations but also from the Doha Round's attempts to include food security in trade agreements. In doing so the EU appears to resist the Doha Round spirit of inclusion of development concerns in world trade law.

6

The EU–CARIFORUM Economic Partnership Agreement

I. INTRODUCTION

THE PREVIOUS CHAPTER elucidated the aspects of the law of the WTO relevant for the import and export of food across national borders. That chapter also clarified that this body of norms limits the space of the EU when it negotiates trade deals with partner countries. In addition, Chapter five made clear the major challenges posed by the present WTO legislation on import and export policies for the realisation of the right to food. The chapter concluded that the legislation often remains lax and leaves space to WTO Members to design their own external trade policies. This is so with regard to import policies but it is especially true as far as export restrictions are concerned. There, WTO law imposes very few obligations and, when it does, exceptions provide wide policy space with regard to the export of food. The chapter suggested that the future WTO negotiations could build upon these existing clauses in order to make the multilateral trading system more supportive of the realisation of the right to food.

This chapter examines the details of one of the trade agreements that the EU concluded with a group of small developing countries in the Caribbean region. The agreement is part of the EU trade strategy introduced in Chapter four, and since its adoption it regulates the trade flows of food between the EU and the Caribbean. Of all the agreements that the EU concluded with developing countries this research starts from the study of this particular agreement for four reasons. First, Caribbean countries that concluded the trade agreement with the EU are countries particularly exposed to food shortages because of their level of development, their size and their exposure to natural disasters. At the same time, Caribbean countries, because of their dimension and economic structure, cannot influence the international price of food.[1] These characteristics make Caribbean countries

[1] Together, Caribbean countries account for the 0.3% of world agricultural exports: see JR Deep Ford, C dell'Aquila and P Conforti, *Agricultural trade policy and food security in the Caribbean* (FAO, 2007).

significantly exposed to the conditions of the international food market that can have an impact on their food security and level of poverty.[2] Second, the EU–Caribbean Economic Partnership Agreement is an expression of both the EU external trade policy and the EU external development and human rights policies. Accordingly, it is the perfect case on which to test the capacity of the EU and its 'Policy Coherence for Development' initiative to include human rights objectives in free trade agreements. Third, the agreement with the Caribbean was the first of a batch of agreements that the European Commission proposed to conclude between the EU and some of the poorest countries of the world, including sub-Saharan Africa. Accordingly, the analysis of this agreement provides the background for the examination of the EU agenda in sub-Saharan Africa performed in the following chapter. Finally, since the Agreement was concluded under Article XXIV GATT and substitutes WTO law in the relationship between the EU and the Caribbean, it shows a glimpse of the wider effects of the EU external action on the development of international trade law.

This chapter follows the structure of the previous chapter on the WTO and is divided into four further sections. Section II introduces the free trade agreement between the EU and the Caribbean by highlighting its general objectives. Section III examines the regulation of import restrictions included in the free trade agreement. The fourth section presents the regulation of trade safeguards applicable to food imported into the Caribbean from the EU and shows to what extent they protect the right to food from import surges of food. The fifth section provides the analysis of the new regulation of export restrictions included in the EU–Caribbean agreement in the light of the role that export restrictions on food play at the occurrence of major food crisis. The chapter concludes with a general assessment of the import and export regulation of the EU–Caribbean Economic Partnership Agreement in the light of the right to food.

II. THE EU–CARIFORUM ECONOMIC PARTNERSHIP AGREEMENT

The Economic Partnership Agreement between the CARIFORUM States and the European Community and its Member States ('the Caribbean EPA') is a mixed agreement concluded in 2008 between the EU, its Member States and 15 Caribbean countries.[3] Since the Caribbean EPA is part of both the

[2] Ibid.

[3] The parties to the Agreement are the EU, its Member States and CARIFORUM countries, a group of countries including: Antigua and Barbuda, the Bahamas, Barbados, Belize, Dominica, The Dominican Republic, Grenada, the Republic of Guyana, Haiti, Jamaica, Saint Christopher and Nevis, Saint Lucia, Saint Vincent and the Grenadines, the Republic of Suriname, and the Republic of Trinidad and Tobago.

EU trade policy and the EU development policy, it was presented as an instrument to support the development of Caribbean countries and the improvement of human rights in the area. Accordingly, the first objective of the Caribbean EPA, stated in its Article 1, is 'Contributing to the reduction and eventual eradication of poverty through the establishment of a trade partnership consistent with the objective of sustainable development, the Millennium Development Goals and the Cotonou Agreement'. In addition, the Agreement contains a clause referring to sustainable development and the commitment of the parties to 'fully take into account the human, cultural, economic, social, health and environmental best interests of their respective population and of future generations'.

From a human rights perspective, the Agreement includes a general human rights clause in its preamble and refers to the human rights commitments of the Cotonou Agreement between the EU and developing countries that include core international human rights instruments such as the International Covenant on Economic, Social and Cultural Rights.[4] Even if the agreement never mentions explicitly the right to food it refers to food security, since the parties acknowledged the vulnerability of Caribbean countries and 'recognise[d] the need to avoid major disruption of markets for agricultural, food and fish products in CARIFORUM States'.[5] The fact that the EU agreed to these clauses can be considered an expression of the EU's external human rights and development policies as well as the principles of Article 21 of the Treaty on the European Union and the other EU human rights commitments identified in Chapter four. More generally, the Caribbean EPA is part of the EU action towards African Caribbean and Pacific (ACP) countries which, as seen above, has the central objective to support their economic development and to promote the realisation of human rights on their territory. This objective extends to all the parts of the Agreement including the ones regulating import and export of food.

From a trade law perspective, the Caribbean EPA is a free trade agreement, concluded under Article XXIV of the GATT, which has the main trade objective of liberalising 'substantially all the trade' between the parties.[6]

[4] For a brief introduction to human rights clauses applicable to the EU external action, see Chapter 2 of this book.

[5] Article 37.

[6] For a thorough introduction to Article XXIV GATT and its meaning for the realisation of the right to food, see Chapter 5 of this book. In addition, on Article XXIV GATT and free trade agreements between the EU and developing countries, see C Milton and O Ochieng, 'The EU-ACP economic partnership agreements and the "development question": constraints and opportunities imposed by Article XXIV and special and differential treatment provisions of the WTO' (2007) 10 *Journal of International Economic Law* 363. For a general analysis of Article XXIV GATT and the meaning of the expression 'substantially all the trade', see M Matsushita, 'Regionalism and the disciplines of the WTO: analysis of some legal aspects under Article XXIV of the GATT' (2005) 13 *Journal of International Economic Law* 191.

The agreement includes law on numerous areas such as import and export barriers, intellectual property, investment and core labour standards. The Caribbean EPA contains innovative rules on import restrictions, safeguards and export restrictions that are considerably different from what exists in WTO law. The following sections present the EPA discipline of the three trade instruments that are the object of this research (import restrictions, safeguards and export restrictions) and consider whether this new development of international trade law can be considered a positive step towards the progressive realisation of the right to food.

III. IMPORT RESTRICTIONS

The Caribbean EPA contains a detailed regulation of import restrictions that substitutes the previous conditions to which the EU and the Caribbean were subject under WTO law. This new regulation applies to the flows of all goods, including agricultural products and other food products, between the EU and the Caribbean.

A. The EPA Regime on Import Restrictions

The regulation of import restrictions is the part of the Caribbean EPA that was influenced the most by WTO law. This is so because the obligation to liberalise 'substantially all the trade' when concluding a free trade agreement under Article XXIV GATT applies primarily to import restrictions such as import quotas and taxes. This condition is subject to interpretation but there is agreement that WTO law obliges WTO Members to eliminate at least 80 per cent of all import tariffs when they enter a trade agreement between each other. As we pointed out in the previous chapters, this condition limits considerably the space of the negotiators of a trade agreement to include trade conditions favourable to the most vulnerable members of the treaty. Accordingly, the principle of differential treatment, as stated in Article XXXVI: 8 GATT, finds very limited application to free trade agreements such as the Caribbean EPA.[7] The legal obligation to liberalise 'substantially all the trade' was a driving force during the negotiations of the Caribbean EPA and is responsible for the elimination of the majority of import restrictions that were still allowed under WTO law. As happens in WTO law, obligations under the EPA are not the same for developed

[7] On special and differential treatment in WTO law and the right to food, see Chapter 5 of this book.

countries (the EU), and for developing ones (the Caribbean). Accordingly, this section first takes into account the obligations that the Caribbean EPA creates on the EU and then the obligations applicable to Caribbean countries. The final part of the section provides the analysis of the new legal scenario in the light of the human rights duties to realise the right to food.

(i) Regime Applied to the European Union

Under the Caribbean EPA the EU agreed to eliminate all import restrictions on the flow of goods originated in the Caribbean. However, several exceptions are contained in Annex II, which allows the EU to apply import tariffs and quotas on a limited list of products that are principal exports of the Caribbean region. In particular, the Caribbean EPA allows the EU to protect its internal market from imports of sugar and sugar products originating in the Caribbean within the limits contained in the Annex. Annex II also deals with the phasing out of the preferences that certain Caribbean countries had on their sugar imports since the colonial period. These countries had preferential quotas and prices that afforded them substantial preferential treatment when entering the European market.[8] These preferences assured that vulnerable producers of sugar and bananas in the Caribbean region maintained a stable income without regard to market conditions. Under the new EPA the Caribbean lost these preferences and will now have to compete with other exporters to sell their products in the EU common market.

(ii) Regime Applied to the Caribbean

The regime applicable to Caribbean import tariffs on goods originating in the EU is more complex. In fact, since the negotiators recognised the vulnerability of Caribbean countries they attempted to stretch the 'substantially all the trade' principle of Article XXIV GATT to provide a certain level of differential treatment to Caribbean countries, allowing them to maintain import tariffs on sensitive products.[9] In addition, the EPA allows Caribbean

[8] On the preferences provided to Caribbean countries before the EPA, see L Bartels, 'The Trade and Development Policy of the European Union' in M Cremona (ed), *New Developments in the EU's External Relations Law, Collected Courses of the Academy of European Law* (Oxford University Press, 2008) 128.

[9] This was done, however, by the EU giving an interpretation of Article XXIV that some commentators consider more favourable to gaining market access in the developing world. See El Hadji Abdourahmane Diouf, 'The ACP Advantage: Interpreting GATT Article XXIV and Market Access Implications for EPAs, Trade Negotiations Insights', 14.09.2009, available at <https://www.ictsd.org/bridges-news/trade-negotiations-insights/news/the-acp-advantage-interpreting-gatt-article-xxiv-and> accessed 29 December 2017.

countries to phase out tariffs on certain products through a step-by-step process, terminating in 2033 at the latest. This decision taken during the negotiations resulted in the attachment to the main body of the Treaty of a schedule of around 1500 pages containing a classification of the goods traded between the EU and the Caribbean and their respective tariffs from 2009 to 2033. In the EPA the 2033 tariff is considered the point of arrival of the process of liberalisation and is the maximum tariff that Caribbean countries should maintain in their relationship with the EU indefinitely. In any case, the imposition of tariffs higher than the ones included in the tariff schedule requires the re-negotiation of the Caribbean EPA.

From the analysis of the schedule, five trends can be identified. First, since the Caribbean EPA is subject to Article XXIV GATT, negotiators could not exempt from the tariff reduction more than around 20 per cent of the products included in the schedule. This is so because otherwise other WTO Members could dispute that the Caribbean EPA reaches the liberalisation that Article XXIV GATT requires. Accordingly, the large majority of EU products will enter the Caribbean market duty-free from 2033 at the latest. However, the Caribbean EPA liberalised numerous tariff lines immediately or will do so by 2020, which means that the EPA produces effects on the tariffs applicable to EU imports into the Caribbean also in the short term.

Second, in order to avoid import surges, several agricultural products and other food products are exempted from the process of liberalisation. For the exempted products the Caribbean EPA does not regulate the applicable tariff, which means that the import of the product remains regulated by WTO law. For instance, most Caribbean countries do not have obligations to eliminate import tariffs on milk and dairy products, wheat flour, rice and maize and certain kinds of meat. Tariff protection of the Caribbean market is often maintained also for certain processed products such as canned food and pasta.

Third, even if numerous sensitive food products were excluded from the process of liberalisation, overall, the EPA will still eliminate a large part of import tariffs on food by 2033. This is so because, as any other product, food is subject to the obligation under Article XXIV GATT of liberalising 'substantially all the trade' when concluding a free trade agreement.

Finally, since the maintenance of tariff protection on certain food products that are crucial for Caribbean welfare was considered a priority, the rest of the tariff lines regarding non-food products had to be liberalised beyond the threshold of Article XXIV GATT. This is so because GATT does not distinguish between food products and other products when obliging countries to pursue substantial liberalisation in trade agreements. Accordingly, in order to concentrate tariff protection on food, Caribbean countries had to remain more exposed on other product categories. For instance, under the EU–Caribbean EPA, Caribbean countries will lose the prerogative to impose tariffs on most European industrial products by 2033.

B. The Caribbean EPA Regime and the Right to Food

Since from its conclusion the Caribbean EPA takes the place of WTO import regulation between the countries involved, the Caribbean EPA has produced considerable change to the conditions applicable to the trade of food between the EU and Caribbean countries. In particular, the Caribbean EPA modified the maximum tariffs applicable to food products that the EU and Caribbean countries are allowed to charge. In particular, the Caribbean EPA eliminated the large majority of import tariffs, going well beyond what WTO law provides. The driving force of this change is Article XXIV GATT, which obliges WTO Members to liberalise 'substantially all the trade' when concluding a free trade agreement. The vast process of trade liberalisation triggered by the Caribbean EPA applies to the trade of products that are relevant for the realisation of the right to food in Caribbean countries. The effects of the Caribbean EPA on the right to food depend on three main outcomes of the agreement. First, the Caribbean EPA obliges the EU to open up its market to the large majority of products produced in the Caribbean. Second, the Caribbean EPA obliges Caribbean countries to import a large variety of goods duty-free from the EU. Third, the Caribbean EPA reduces the amount of public revenues that Caribbean countries are able to raise through import tariffs. In all these three aspects the Caribbean EPA departs from WTO law. This section provides the evaluation of the new situation from the perspective of the realisation of the right to food.

(i) Caribbean Food Imports to the EU

The effect of Caribbean imports on the EU internal market is likely to be negligible due to the scant variety of Caribbean exports and the extremely limited role that these products play in the EU economy. In contrast, the modification of European obligations with regard to tariffs on Caribbean goods can have consequences on the realisation of the right to food in the Caribbean because Europe is a prominent export market for Caribbean products. In this regard, the phasing out of EU preferential treatment for certain Caribbean countries on imported sugar and bananas is likely to harm Caribbean local producers. Accordingly, in the absence of social safety nets, the EPA could produce significant pressure on two of the few export industries of the region. This is particularly so since the phasing out of the preferences will happen under the Caribbean EPA in a period of less than 10 years, which might not be sufficient for Caribbean local producers to adjust to the new conditions. If this happens, the EPA, reducing the income of already vulnerable individuals, could impact their economic access to sufficient food.

On the other hand, the Caribbean EPA could also support the realisation of the right to food as long as it corrects the deficiencies of the WTO system with regard to the access of the Caribbean to the EU market. Since the Caribbean EPA obliges the EU to eliminate any tariff on Caribbean products, practices such as 'dirty tariffication' and tariff peaks that flourished under the WTO system[10] will be no longer possible under the Caribbean EPA. This modification of international trade law could be a positive step but with two caveats. First, the fact that the EU cannot apply any import quota or tariff on Caribbean exports should favour these countries in their access to the EU market. However, this advantage will last only if the EU does not conclude free trade agreements with other trade partners. In fact, when the EU strategy to conclude free trade agreements is concluded the Caribbean will receive import conditions similar to all the other countries included in the strategy. For instance, since Mexico and South Korea have concluded free trade agreements with the EU, under the EPA the Caribbean receives similar tax-free conditions to those received by these countries under their free trade agreements with the EU.[11] This means that even though the Caribbean states obtained duty-free access to the EU market the EPA erodes considerably the preferential treatment of Caribbean countries because more competitive countries will receive similar conditions through other trade agreements concluded by the EU. In the absence of economic policies supporting the competitiveness of Caribbean producers it is possible that Caribbean countries will not in practice be able to benefit from improved access to the EU market.

The second caveat is that Annex II of the Caribbean EPA allows the EU to impose import restrictions on several sectors where Caribbean countries have a competitive edge on the international market. Accordingly, Annex II limits the beneficial effects of the Caribbean EPA for Caribbean farmers. These two aspects of the EPA could reduce considerably the contribution of the EPA to Caribbean food security.

To sum up, regulation of tariffs in developed countries is crucial for the realisation of the right to food because it influences the income of farmers in the developing world—a sector of society where there is a high concentration of malnourished people. In the previous chapter we showed how the WTO has done very little to solve this problem and WTO law still allows numerous trade mechanisms that limit the access of vulnerable states to the markets of rich countries. From the analysis of EU obligations under the Caribbean EPA emerges a mixed scenario where there is no guarantee that Caribbean countries will benefit from increased access to the EU market. In fact, whereas the Caribbean EPA eliminates immediately several preferences granted to Caribbean countries since the colonial period, improved access to the EU market will depend on market conditions and the capacity

[10] See above Chapter 5 of this book.
[11] For the introduction to the Global Europe Strategy, see Chapter 4 of this book.

of Caribbean countries to compete with other exporters. In other words, the negative effects of the EPA are inevitable and immediate,[12] while the positive effects are possible but not at all sure. The risk is that the increased access to the EU market granted to Caribbean countries remains on paper while more competitive emerging economies erode the market shares that the EU granted to Caribbean countries before the EPA.

(ii) EU Food Imports to the Caribbean

When there is a process of tariff reduction on the scale of the Caribbean EPA the main risk for the right to food comes from import surges, as explained at length in the previous chapters. Since with tariff reduction imported goods become cheaper, local producers can go out of business. Accordingly, cheap imports of food can create economic distress to local farmers, who in developing countries are a social group particularly affected by food insecurity. For these reasons tariff reduction has to be dealt with carefully in order to avoid any negative effect on already fragile agricultural economies.[13]

The risk of increased imports of key food products from Europe to the Caribbean was manifest to negotiators when the countries decided to conclude a free trade agreement including the elimination of import tariffs on food products, since it was flagged in the Sustainability Impact Assessment.[14] To avoid this problem the Caribbean EPA contains some special and differential treatment allowing Caribbean countries to protect their national markets from EU exports of certain food products. This attempt to ensure differential treatment for Caribbean countries, allowing certain import tariffs on sensitive food products, however, clashed with the obligation stemming from Article XXIV GATT. The result is that even though some efforts were made to protect Caribbean producers from EU exports, the Caribbean EPA reduces considerably the capacity of Caribbean countries to raise import tariffs to protect their domestic markets. Since the large majority of food products will be imported from the EU duty-free by 2033, it is likely that some of these new imports will displace local producers in some sensitive sectors. Since the Caribbean EPA could not provide protection

[12] On the consequences of the phasing out of the Sugar and Banana protocols, see B Ahmed, 'The impact of Globalization on the Caribbean Sugar and Banana Industries', The Society for Caribbean Studies Annual Conference Papers vol. 2 (2001) <http://www.caribbeanstudies.org.uk/papers/2001/olv2p1.pdf> accessed 29 March 2011, and R Lapper, 'A bitter harvest: the Caribbean faces the prospect of a life without sugar', *Financial Times* (15 August 2005) <http://www.ft.com/cms/s/0/97801242-0d28-11da-ba02-00000e2511c8.html#axzz1G1M0B0r4> accessed 29 March 2011.

[13] See the studies on import surges of the Food and Agriculture Organization, cited above in Chapter 5 of this book.

[14] See the 'Sustainability Impact Assessment of the EU–CARIFORUM Economic Partnership Agreement', n. 23 below.

to all vulnerable sectors allowing Caribbean governments to utilise import tariffs, alternative instruments are needed to avoid consequences for the realisation of the right to food. These could be the use of import safeguards or public policies such as investment in agriculture or the creation of social safety nets.[15]

To recapitulate, in the previous chapter we highlighted that the obligation to liberalise 'substantially all the trade' of Article XXIV GATT could pose real problems to the right to food if developed countries conclude free trade agreements with developing states. This is so because Article XXIV GATT de facto forbids special and differential treatment for vulnerable countries in free trade agreements. This means that free trade agreements erode the, already limited, mechanisms supporting the developing world that were put in place by the WTO.[16] With the Caribbean EPA this limitation of Article XXIV GATT manifests its consequences in the regulation of Caribbean import tariffs. Even though some efforts were made to provide Caribbean producers with tariff protection the large majority of EU products will be imported into the Caribbean duty-free. This will increase the risk of import surges, diminish the capacity of Caribbean countries to react to them and augment the dependency of Caribbean consumers on the EU export business.

(iii) Reduction of Trade Revenues in Caribbean Countries

Another challenge to the right to food that the EPA creates is that it diminishes the public revenues of the countries taking part in the agreement.[17] For the EU the impact is negligible because Caribbean countries are minor trade partners but for the Caribbean the impact could be important. In fact, a study issued by the European Parliament shows that in several Caribbean countries trade taxes constitute more than 20 per cent of the national

[15] On the necessity to allow trade measures to cope with food insecurity, see Chapter 3 of this book.

[16] For a more general analysis of the consequences of EU free trade agreements on WTO special and differential treatment, see C Milton and O Ochieng, 'The EU-ACP economic partnership agreements and the "development question": constraints and opportunities imposed by Article XXIV and special and differential treatment provisions of the WTO' (2007) 10 *Journal of International Economic Law* 363.

[17] For an overview of the relation between trade and public revenues see L Bartels, 'Trade and Human Rights', *Max Planck Encyclopedia of Public International Law* (August 2011 edn), http://www.mpepil.com/subscriber_article?script=yes&id=/epil/entries/law-9780199231690-e1550&recno=1&searchType=Quick&query=trade+and+human+rights> accessed 17 January 2015. H-J Chang, *Bad Samaritans* (Bloomsbury Press, 2008) 69; J Stiglitz, *Making Globalization Work* (Penguin Books 2007) 66; United Nations Economic Commission for Africa, African Trade Policy Centre, 'Fiscal Implications of Trade Liberalization on African Countries', Work in Progress No. 5, available at <http://www.uneca.org/atpc/Work%20in%20progress/5.pdf> accessed 16 January 2015.

budget. Overall, the impact of the EPA is not negligible in the Caribbean, since certain countries could lose up to 2.5 per cent of their overall public revenues.[18] This is so because in the Caribbean trade revenues mainly come from import duties and taxes on the export of natural resources. Since the Caribbean EPA eliminates a large part of existing import tariffs it reduces the amount of revenues available to Caribbean countries. A sensitive reduction in public revenues could reduce the capacity of Caribbean countries to intervene in the case of sudden food shortages due to global price spikes or environmental disasters.[19] In other words, if Caribbean countries do not recoup the revenues lost through the EPA their capacity to intervene to protect and fulfil the right to food would be weakened.

However, substituting trade revenues with alternative instruments of domestic taxation is not a straightforward process in developing countries, and recent research highlights that alternative instruments of taxation could be too expensive in low-income countries.[20] This is so because in states with a weak administrative apparatus it is more effective to levy trade taxes than to enforce a tax on consumption. A study of the International Monetary Fund, for instance, examining loss of trade revenues between 1975 and 2000, provided evidence that high-income countries recovered them straightforwardly, middle-income countries recouped only 35–55 per cent of revenues, whereas low-income countries recovered 30 cents for each lost dollar at best.[21] For these reasons development literature notes that in history numerous developed countries have relied on trade revenues until improved tax collection allowed transition to a different system.[22]

This new challenge was also identified in the Sustainability Impact Assessment conducted by the EU during the negotiation of the Agreement. The study highlights that

> a crucial element the negotiators have to take into account during the trade negotiations is the implementation of mechanisms to mitigate the negative impact of a fall in government revenues and the development of other revenue creating activities in order to be less dependent on trade taxes.[23]

[18] European Parliament, *The CARIFORUM-EU Economic Partnership Agreement: the development component* (2009) 27 <http://www.europarl.europa.eu/thinktank/en/document.html?reference=EXPO-DEVE_ET(2009)406994>.

[19] In addition to this immediate effect on the economic capacity to protect food security, additional negative effects may stem from the diminished capacity of developing countries to invest in their economic development. See, for instance, Stiglitz's infant economy argument, J Stiglitz, *Making Globalization Work* (Penguin Books, 2007) 70.

[20] H-J Chang, *Bad Samaritans* (Bloomsbury Press, 2008) 69; Joseph Stiglitz, *Making Globalization Work* (Penguin Books, 2007) 66.

[21] T Baunsgaard and M Keen, 'Trade Revenue and (or?) Trade Liberalization', International Monetary Fund Working Paper WP/05/112, June 2005.

[22] H-J Chang, *23 Things They Don't Tell You About Capitalism* (Bloomsbury Press, 2008) 62.

[23] PricewaterhouseCoopers, 'Sustainability Impact Assessment (SIA) of the EU-ACP Economic Partnership Agreements. Regional SIA: Caribbean ACP Countries', 30 January 2004 http://trade.ec.europa.eu/doclib/docs/2005/january/tradoc_121202.pdf.

For these reasons the Food and Agriculture Organization, in its policy briefs on international trade law, prefers regulatory options that do not limit excessively the revenues of developing countries that trade taxes generate.[24]

IV. SAFEGUARDS

The previous chapter presented the limits of safeguards in WTO law with regard to the protection of the right to food from import surges. That chapter argued that the procedural and substantive requirements of WTO general safeguards are not designed to provide effective protection in case of import surges of food in vulnerable countries. In particular, the human rights implications of import surges do not appear in the regulation; the procedure is too burdensome for developing countries and special and differential treatment for vulnerable countries is almost non-existent. The preceding chapter also discussed the WTO Special Safeguard, concluding that even though this automatic mechanism is highly inefficient it is conceptually more promising, and if amended could become an effective instrument of protection of vulnerable countries. This is so because the Special Safeguard works automatically and through a system of triggers that activate import tariffs as soon as the signs of import surges are present on the international market.

This section presents the EPA safeguards, evaluating them in the light of the protection of the right to food. It will emerge that the safeguards of the Caribbean EPA suffer from the same shortcomings as WTO safeguards, and that no efforts were made to design innovative instruments of protection of vulnerable countries. This is so even though the process of liberalisation triggered by the Caribbean EPA is much more radical than the one implemented in the Uruguay Round, and the risk of import surges more significant.

A. Substantive Requirements

The regulation of EPA safeguards is contained in Articles 25 and 40 of the Treaty. Drafting the regulation of the Caribbean EPA safeguards, negotiators drew inspiration from Article XIX GATT and the WTO Safeguards Agreement,[25] but widened the conditions for recourse to the instrument.

[24] See, for instance, how the FAO proposes to regulate export taxes, a trade instrument with a much less evident impact on public revenues than tariffs. R Sharma, 'Food Export Restrictions: Review of the 2007–2010 Experience and Considerations for Disciplining Restrictive Measures', FAO Commodity and Trade Policy Research Working Paper no. 32 (FAO, 2010).

[25] See above Chapter 5 of this book.

In fact, besides the classical case of 'serious injury to a domestic industry', Article 25 refers to 'disturbances in a sector of the economy', 'major social problems' and 'deterioration in the economic situation of the importing party'. Safeguards are also available when a surge of imports causes or threatens to cause 'disturbances in the markets of like or directly competitive agricultural products or in the mechanisms regulating those markets'.

The rules on the duration of the safeguards grant some differential treatment to Caribbean countries. In fact, whereas the EU can adopt safeguards for two years and extend them up to four years, Caribbean countries can do so for four years and confirm them up to eight. In special circumstances, the time limit can reach 10 years if the safeguard protects 'infant industries'. In any case, the safeguard has to contain clear elements progressively leading to their elimination. In addition, no safeguard can be applied to the import of a product that has previously been subject to such a measure for a period of at least one year.

Finally, acknowledging the gap in development and competitiveness between the parties, and with a view to preventing negative effects on food security, Article 40 of the EPA provides that:

> Where compliance with the provisions of this Agreement leads to problems with the availability of, or access to foodstuffs or other products essential to ensure food security of a Signatory CARIFORUM State and where this situation gives rise or is likely to give rise to major difficulties for such a State, that Signatory CARIFORUM State may take appropriate measures in accordance with the procedures laid down …

B. Procedure

A major difference between the general WTO safeguards and the EPA safeguards is that in the EPA there is a structured system of supranational supervision. Accordingly, the parties to the Caribbean EPA have lost the prerogative to implement safeguards autonomously even at the occurrence of substantive conditions justifying their utilisation. This is so also when safeguards would be justified by a food crisis triggered in the Caribbean by import surges. In fact, the CARIFORUM–EU Trade and Development Committee (TDC), a common intergovernmental body, supervises the entire process of adoption of the EPA safeguards. Safeguards are an instrument of last resort, available only if the TDC does not issue a recommendation on how to remedy the circumstances or if, within 30 days of the matter being referred to the TDC, no other satisfactory solution has been reached. The TDC can be bypassed only in exceptional circumstances and for a limited amount of time of 180 for the EU and 200 days for the Caribbean.

C. Evaluation in the Light of the Right to Food

The EPA regulation of safeguards is inspired by the WTO general safeguards even though it introduces the innovation of a supranational body, the TDC, supervising the entire process of adoption. With regard to the protection of the right to food, this arrangement incorporates in the EPA the shortcomings of WTO law. Furthermore, the decision not to include a Special Safeguard mechanism fully dedicated to the avoidance of import surges makes the EPA safeguards a particularly weak mechanism for protection of the right to food. This section enumerates four clear inadequacies of the EPA safeguards.

First, the EPA contains only general safeguards inspired by the GATT and the WTO Agreement on Safeguards that are based on substantive requirements that have already proved difficult to apply at the occurrence of food security emergencies. In fact, as shown in the previous chapter, general safeguards are technically difficult to implement when import surges are caused by sudden modifications of market conditions. Furthermore, the EPA does not include any automatic mechanism based on the Special Safeguard of the WTO Agreement on Agriculture. This would have allowed an automatic response to the conditions of the international market when they constitute a risk for Caribbean food security. The decision not to include a form of Special Safeguard in the EPA constitutes a substantial handicap in terms of protection of food security of Caribbean countries. This is particularly unfortunate since the Food and Agriculture Organization, at the time the EPA was negotiated, had already developed proposals for special food security safeguards that could have been incorporated in the Agreement.[26] The EU itself included innovative special food security safeguards in other trade agreements.[27] The absence of an automatic mechanism for protection of food security makes the Caribbean EPA a step back also with respect to WTO law.

Second, in terms of sovereignty, the EPA entails a more extensive transfer of powers to supranational institutions than what happens in WTO law. In fact, the choice of putting safeguards under the control of a supranational body is a departure from the model of the WTO Safeguard Agreement, where the adoption of multilateral safeguards follows a national investigation and notification to the WTO has to be done only at the end of the procedure. With the EPA, CARIFORUM States have subjected the prerogative of adopting safeguards to the assessment of the TDC. As a consequence, the effectiveness of safeguards implemented in case of import surges of food rely on the interpretation that the TDC will give of the conditions of Article 25

[26] See above Chapter 5 of this book.
[27] See for instance the Free Trade Agreement between the EU and Central America.

and Article 40 and on the TDC's awareness of the social effects of the EPA. The composition of the TDC, the attitude of its members with regard to food security issues, and the absence of internal divisions are crucial for the success of the use of the safeguard clause as an instrument of protection of food security. In the absence of research facilities at the disposal of the TDC it is up to Caribbean states themselves to identify negative effects, associate them with the liberalisation schedule of the EPA and advocate the necessity of a safeguard during a TDC meeting.[28] Moreover, the decision to centralise the control over EPA safeguards in the TDC, an intergovernmental body with no specialisation in food security issues, creates a burdensome supranational mechanism that slows down the adoption of safeguards and makes them subject to diplomatic bargaining. In addition, since all members of the EPA are represented in the TDC and the adoption of the safeguard requires majority voting, the safeguard can be adopted only with the agreement of countries in which the import surge might not have manifested. Furthermore, in this system the EU has to provide its consent in the TDC to the adoption of a safeguard on the import of food into the Caribbean. This aspect of the regulation is likely to slow down even more the adoption of the safeguard and put EU export business in the position of providing an informal opinion on the decision.[29] The EPA could have at least facilitated the adoption of emergency food security safeguards by keeping the procedure at national level where the effects of import surges are more evident. The fact that the TDC does not have any research facility which can draw a picture of the consequences of the EPA on food security suggests that it is especially unlikely that the TDC will facilitate the adoption of safeguards if the effects of import surges are felt only in one Caribbean country or only in a region of a Caribbean country. Even if it was already evident from the Uruguay Round experience that trade safeguards have to be implemented quickly to be an effective instrument of protection of food security, the Caribbean EPA introduces a procedure that is potentially even slower than the one provided by WTO law.

Third, Article 40, which is the only one explicitly referring to food security, is a mere rhetorical expedient that does not make the safeguards of the Caribbean EPA a more efficient protective mechanism. In fact, Article 40 does not create a Special Safeguard but only adds an extra case to the triggers contained in Article 25. Article 40 relies entirely on the general discipline of Article 25 for the procedure of application and the nature of safeguards available to Caribbean countries. Common side-effects on food

[28] For this reason, the CARICOM intends to implement *rapid-response mechanisms* to identify and examine deleterious effects of the implementation of the EPA on consumers and domestic agricultural, food and fisheries sectors.

[29] On the participation of European food business to the EU external action see above Chapter 4 of this book.

security caused by trade adjustment shocks or price fluctuations seem to find a place already in the general safeguard clause under the label 'major social problems'. If Article 40 has any function, it is to avoid restrictive interpretations that could leave food security out of reach. However, because Article 40 does not extend the room for application of the general discipline on safeguards the reference to food security appears rhetorical. Moreover, Article 40 provides that also in case of import surges on food the only applicable safeguards are those of Article 25 that require the very burdensome procedure supervised by the TDC. Article 40 would have made more sense if linked with an automatic protective mechanism similar to the WTO Special Safeguard of the WTO Agreement on Agriculture.

Finally, because of the potential risks of the EPA for food security in the Caribbean and the negligible impact of the EPA on the EU, the reconciliation of trade liberalisation and the protection of the right to food would have required more asymmetry. It is particularly surprising that no distinction is made between agricultural and industrial goods and that for both categories, both the EU and the Caribbean can adopt import safeguards. As showed above, a positive aspect of the EPA is that it eliminates tariff barriers for Caribbean exports to the EU. The safeguard regime, however, could reintroduce tariff escalation by the backdoor, allowing the EU to temporarily restrict imports from the Caribbean whenever they gain access to the EU market. More generally, the special and differential treatment provisions of the EPA safeguards do not reflect the difference in market power of the EU and Caribbean countries. The fact that the maximum duration of the safeguards is longer for Caribbean countries is a mild form of differential treatment that is even weaker than what is provided in WTO law. In fact, Article 9 of the WTO Agreement on Agriculture obliges developed countries to exonerate developing countries from trade safeguards in the presence of certain conditions.[30] Since this, already weak, norm is not reproduced in the EPA, Caribbean countries remain exposed to EU safeguards irrespectively of their level of development and the consequences of the EU safeguards for their domestic markets. The negotiators of the EPA could have used Article 9 of the WTO Agreement on Agriculture as a model to give Caribbean countries more protection from EU safeguards.

In addition, the EPA could have been the occasion to provide Caribbean countries with protection also from EU safeguards implemented under the GATT and the WTO Agreement on Safeguards. This would have amended one of the shortcomings of WTO law that still allows developed countries to use safeguards against vulnerable states. However, the EPA clause that forbids the EU to adopt WTO safeguards against the Caribbean expires

[30] On Article 9 of the WTO Agreement on Agriculture, see Chapter 5 of this book.

in 2019. This means that by 2019 the EU will be allowed to temporarily raise its tariff protection against Caribbean countries even beyond the WTO tariff bindings.

V. EXPORT RESTRICTIONS

The previous chapter clarified that export restrictions are a particularly weak area of WTO law and that all WTO Members have preserved extensive policy space to restrict the export of food towards third countries. The preceding chapter also pointed out that Article XXIV GATT (contrary to what happens with import restrictions) does not oblige WTO Members to eliminate export restrictions when concluding a free trade agreement. This means that in the Caribbean EPA negotiators had the liberty to preserve WTO law on export restrictions without producing any substantial modification of the pre-existing framework. In particular, the parties to the agreement where free to maintain Article XI GATT and the exception of Article XI.2(a) GATT, allowing export restrictions on food to prevent or relieve food shortages. Although WTO law did not require any specific intervention on export restrictions, the parties to the Caribbean EPA made the choice of including an extremely restrictive regulation of the trade practice. In fact, the Caribbean EPA forbids export restrictions on any product including food, producing a profound change in the regulation of food exports between the EU and the Caribbean. This section presents the articles on export restrictions of the Caribbean EPA and reflects on the consequences this decision might have for the realisation of the right to food.

A. Export Restrictions in the Caribbean EPA

The Caribbean EPA contains a thorough regulation of export restrictions that will be applied instead of Article XI GATT in the relationship between the parties. The new regulation is contained in Articles 14 and 26 of the Agreement and introduces a complete ban on export restrictions that is unprecedented in international trade treaties concluded by the EU. Article 26 refers to quantitative restrictions and provides that:

> no … export prohibitions … or export restrictions on originating exports other than customs duties and taxes and fees … whether made effective through quotas, import or export licences or other measures, shall be maintained … No new such measures shall be introduced.[31]

[31] EU–CARIFORUM Economic Partnership Agreement, Article 26.

Notably, the clause not only prohibits the parties from adopting any form of quantitative restriction on exports, it also obliges them to dismantle any existing restriction. The regulation is made more restrictive by Article 14, which refers to the imposition of taxes on exports. In fact, the Article extends the ban to export taxes providing that: 'customs duties on exports shall not be applicable to goods originating in the CARIFORUM State and imported into the EC and vice versa'.[32]

The differences between the regulation of export restrictions contained in the EPA and WTO law are substantial. First, quantitative restrictions are forbidden without exceptions. In fact, Article 26 of the EPA provides a harsher version of Article XI GATT which eliminates all the exceptions to its second paragraph including that of Article XI.2(a) allowing the use of quantitative restrictions to prevent or relieve critical food shortages.

Second, the EPA includes an innovative regulation on export taxes, prohibiting the practice altogether. Article 14 is unprecedented in EU trade practice and there is nothing similar in WTO law. The options being discussed in the Doha Round never go as far as Article 14 and include exceptions allowing a certain margin for adoption of export taxes by WTO Member States. For instance, a paper circulated by Japan proposes to bind export taxes through a WTO schedule similar to the one used for import taxes. This would put a ceiling on export taxes, leaving margins to Member States to use the policy.[33]

Finally, the EPA does not reproduce several general exceptions to the GATT which in multilateral trade law increase the space of WTO members to use export restrictions. In particular the EPA does not replicate the exceptions of Article XX(g), Article XX(i) and Article XX(j). The three exceptions allow certain restrictions of international trade, including export restrictions when the action is related to the 'the conservation of natural resources', the provision of materials to domestic processing industries and the 'acquisition or distribution of products in general or local short supply'. The choice not to include these exceptions in the EPA rules out the use of export restrictions as an instrument of intervention in case of shortages of a certain good on the territory of the parties to the agreement.

To sum up, the EPA between the EU and the Caribbean includes an innovative regulation of export restrictions that prohibits the practice altogether. This regulation, that applies only to trade relationships between the EU and the Caribbean, shifts from multilateral trade law towards the complete

[32] EU–CARIFORUM Economic Partnership Agreement, Article 14.

[33] See the Negotiating proposal by Japan on WTO Agricultural Negotiations, available at <http://docsonline.wto.org/imrd/directdoc.asp?DDFDocuments/t/G/AG/NGW91.doc> accessed 23 December 2015.

elimination of any kind of quantitative and tax-based export restriction. This extremely restrictive regulation applies without discriminating between products, and includes food and agricultural products.

B. Evaluation in the Light of the Right to Food

The main problem of WTO law on export restrictions from the perspective of the right to food is that it allows too much space to influential exporters to implement export restrictions also with regard to vulnerable countries. This excessive freedom afforded to influential exporters exposes vulnerable countries, and especially net food importers, to food shortages caused by export restrictions imposed by third countries. Since numerous countries vulnerable to food shortages are also net food importers, WTO law should prevent the situation in which sudden interruptions of exports of food by a WTO Member trigger food shortages in other countries. Chapter three showed how only a very limited number of countries have enough market power to influence the realisation of the right to food in third countries by implementing export restrictions. Accordingly, it is on these countries that international trade law should concentrate when regulating export restrictions.

As noted in the previous chapter, the positive aspect of WTO law is that the lax attitude on export restrictions allows countries exposed to food shortages but with no influence on the international food market to intervene on their export flows at the occurrence of a food crisis. Under WTO law, for instance, it was common practice by Caribbean countries to utilise export restrictions on basic food products at the occurrence of food shortages on their territories. The preceding chapter concluded that a reform of international trade law supportive of the right to food should protect vulnerable countries from export restrictions by large exporters while still allowing countries exposed to food shortages to intervene on their export flows at the occurrence of a food crisis. In other words, international trade law should afford special and differential treatment to countries vulnerable to food shortages and limit the capacity of large influential exporters of food to implement export restrictions.

This is not what happens with Articles 14 and 26 of the Caribbean EPA, where negotiators opted for a general abolition of export restrictions applicable both to the EU and to Caribbean countries. With this choice Caribbean countries have lost the prerogative to impose export restrictions on food even at the occurrence of a major food crisis caused by market instability or natural disasters. This aspect represents the main human rights deficit of the regulation of export restrictions of the Caribbean EPA, and deserves a brief comment.

(i) Export Restrictions as Short-term Response to a Food Crisis

The role that export restrictions have played during international price spikes brought several governments and international organisations to call for their regulation. However, the studies conducted so far did not reach the point of suggesting a general ban on export restrictions. This is so because in certain limited situations export restrictions can be an instrument to deal with the negative effects of global price spikes, especially in developing countries that lack solid social safety nets. In fact, when prices are high on the international market domestic traders tend to export the food they purchase at the expense of local customers.[34] To avoid this practice several developing countries implement export restrictions during global food crises. The policy has helped several vulnerable countries to drive local prices down and supply food to the weakest parts of their societies. When large exporters of food implement export restrictions their policy produces effects on third countries that can be particularly distressful if the importer is a developing country or a net food importer. However, when the country implementing the policy is a small exporter with no influence on the international price of food there is no immediate risk for the international community. In this case, export restrictions are a legitimate instrument of intervention to fight supply shortages and high prices at local level.[35] For this reason the proposals appearing in the Food and Agriculture Organization policy briefs to regulate export restrictions in the context of the Doha Round do not propose to ban export restrictions altogether but go in the direction of making the practice more predictable and less distressful on global prices and net food importers. This could be done for instance, by including tax-rate quotas or defining limits to export restrictions in international agreements. This would allow countries to use the policy when prices on the international market hamper their domestic food security but in a predictable way and within agreed limits that do not foster panic behaviour and food shortages in other countries.[36] The proposals appearing so far in the Doha Round also try to find a balance between different priorities and do not go in the direction of eliminating export restrictions altogether.[37]

[34] FAO, 'Responding to the food crisis: synthesis of medium-term measures proposed in inter-agency assessment' (FAO, 2009).

[35] On the domestic role of export restrictions during food crisis see FAO, *The State of Food Insecurity in the World: How does international price volatility affect domestic economies and food security?* (FAO, 2011), 24.

[36] See Sharma, 'Food Export Restrictions', n 24 above, at fn 9.

[37] See, WTO Agriculture Negotiations Backgrounder, Export restrictions and taxes, available at <http://www.wto.org/english/tratop_e/agric_e/negs_bkgrnd09_taxes_e.htm> accessed 23 November 2016.

By contrast, the radical approach to export restrictions of the free trade agreement between the EU and the Caribbean produces the consequence of depriving Caribbean countries of a policy response in case of a food emergency in the region. Since the two articles make no distinction between different kinds of goods, the regulation applies equally to industrial products, raw materials and food. Accordingly, the regulation produces a shift in international trade law towards the elimination of the practice from the spectrum of international trade policies that countries can implement. Articles 14 and 26 mean, for instance, that state parties are forbidden from limiting the export of their natural resources or taxing them to produce public revenues. The new regulation also forbids any kind of emergency mechanism that uses export restrictions to increase the quantity of a certain good or material on the territory of the state. This implies that the parties to the agreement cannot limit their exports to the other parties in order to supply certain products or materials to domestic industries. In a similar vein they cannot apply restrictions on food exports in order to supply the domestic market at the occurrence of food shortages. Because the contribution of the Caribbean to the global food supply is irrelevant[38] the clause limits the space for intervention of Caribbean countries without having any positive impact on global food security. This is so because restrictions on export of food to the EU implemented by Caribbean countries would produce effects only at domestic level without affecting the international price of food.[39] During the 2007–2008 food crisis, for instance, Guyana and Suriname imposed restrictions on the export of certain rice products in order to ensure adequate supply to the domestic market.[40] If the EPA is applied to the letter, Caribbean countries will be stopped from implementing such actions and will have to keep exporting food to the EU even in the wake of a major food crisis.

This problem creates a new challenge to food security which does not exist in WTO law. In WTO law, export restrictions are regulated lightly and WTO Members maintained extensive policy space to implement export restrictions on food in an unpredictable fashion both through quotas and export taxes. This lack of regulation produced an excessive use of export restrictions by large exporters that compromised food security in importing

[38] In 1998 the contribution of the Caribbean to global supply of agricultural products was 2% and it declined to 0.3% in 2004. See Caribbean Agribusiness website <http://174.123.68.234/primary-dropdown/agribusiness-organisations-country>.

[39] JR Deep Ford, C dell'Aquila and P Conforti, 'Caribbean Countries as small and vulnerable economies' in JR Deep Ford, C dell'Aquila and P Conforti, *Agricultural trade policy and food security in the Caribbean* (FAO, 2007).

[40] FAO, *The response of Latin American and the Caribbean to higher and volatile food prices and opportunities for regional cooperation*, http://174.123.68.234/primary-dropdown/agribusiness-organisations-country.

countries. In contrast, in the EPA, negotiators went too far and by eliminating export taxes and quotas altogether, have stripped a group of countries vulnerable to food shortages of an instrument of intervention in case of food crisis.

VI. CONCLUSIONS

The EU concluded the Caribbean EPA in 2008 with the objective of supporting Caribbean development and the realisation of human rights, including economic and social rights. The EPA intervenes in international trade law by introducing a *lex specialis* that applies only to the trade between the EU and the Caribbean. The Caribbean EPA innovates considerably from WTO law in all the trade instruments taken into account in this research: import restrictions, safeguards and export restrictions.

The analysis of this innovative regulation under the light of the right to food has elucidated that the Caribbean EPA does not solve many of the problems of WTO law and often creates new challenges for the realisation of the right to food in the Caribbean. First, with regard to import restrictions, the Caribbean EPA limits the capacity to intervene of Caribbean countries at the occurrence of import surges and increases their exposure to the vagaries of the international market. In addition, increased access for Caribbean producers might not make much difference from the existing framework, since at the same time the Caribbean EPA erodes the preferential treatment provisions provided by WTO law and previous arrangements between the EU and the Caribbean.

Second, even though the clauses on import restrictions limit severely the capacity to intervene on import surges of Caribbean countries, the EPA does not contain any automatic Special Safeguard mechanism. Without Special Safeguards Caribbean countries have no efficient mechanism of protection at their disposal on the occurrence of import surges of food from the EU. In fact, the general safeguards the Caribbean EPA provides are very burdensome to apply and it is unlikely that they will provide Caribbean vulnerable producers with efficient protection.

Finally, the Caribbean EPA forbids any form of export restrictions, limiting the capacity of Caribbean countries to intervene at the occurrence of food shortages due to market instability or natural disasters. This means that if the Caribbean EPA is applied to the letter, the Caribbean will have to keep exporting food to the EU even at the occurrence of major food shortages.

Whenever the Caribbean EPA forbids the prompt intervention of Caribbean Governments to protect their citizens from hunger and malnutrition it forbids the exercise of the human rights duties required by the

International Covenant of Economic, Social and Cultural Rights. In particular, the Caribbean EPA does not provide sufficient emergency mechanisms that would have allowed Caribbean countries to shelter their citizens when market instability increases food insecurity. The absence of efficient safeguards and the prohibition to use export restrictions even at the occurrence of a major food crisis constitute a particularly evident human rights deficit.

The case study also highlighted that some of the human rights deficits of the Caribbean EPA depend on pre-existing WTO law while others were the consequence of deliberate policy decisions of the negotiating parties. In particular, the regulation of import restrictions was deeply affected by the obligation to liberalise 'substantially all the trade' in Article XXIV GATT. In this part of the Caribbean EPA the EU and its partner countries made some efforts to protect vulnerable states from excessive exposure to the international food market and to EU exports. However, WTO law did not allow a free trade agreement based on the principle of non-reciprocity[41] that would have granted full protection of Caribbean producers from EU competition. Accordingly, a regulation of import restrictions that is fully respectful of human rights duties can be achieved only within the WTO through a modification of Article XXIV GATT or the adoption of a waiver for developing countries.[42]

The situation is different with regard to safeguards and export restrictions. In both cases, the EU and Caribbean countries were free under WTO law to create protective mechanisms allowing the intervention of Caribbean countries on their trade flows of food at the occurrence of import surges or food shortages. Accordingly, the human rights deficit of the Caribbean EPA in these policy areas depends on a decision of the EU and Caribbean countries. This means also that with regard to safeguards and export restrictions the Caribbean EPA could be re-negotiated to make it more supportive of the realisation of the right to food.

[41] The previous chapter discusses the WTO principle of non-reciprocity at length.
[42] See Chapter 5 on special and differential treatment.

7

The Economic Partnership Agreements between the EU and Sub-Saharan Africa

I. INTRODUCTION

THE PREVIOUS CHAPTER examined the import and export regulation of food in the trade agreement between the EU and the Caribbean. The chapter concluded that with regard to the realisation of the right to food, the agreement does not solve the problems in WTO law and creates new challenges for the realisation of the right. The EU-Caribbean trade agreement was the first comprehensive agreement concluded under the umbrella of the Global Europe Strategy with a group of developing countries vulnerable to food shortages. As shown in Chapter four, the Caribbean trade agreement is only a fraction of a wider project by the EU to conclude free trade agreements with the entire developing world. At the end of the process the EU will be regulating its trade relationships with vulnerable countries through free trade agreements instead of WTO law. This operation could have a serious impact on the realisation of the right to food if the deficiencies that emerged from the Caribbean free trade agreement are reproduced in other treaties.

Of the areas of the world where the EU is negotiating free trade agreements, sub-Saharan Africa is among the most sensitive in terms of realisation of the right to food. In fact, sub-Saharan Africa is the home to around 230 million malnourished people and is characterised by economic fragility and exposure to natural disasters.[1] Notwithstanding this extremely disadvantaged economic setting, since 2006 the European Union has been attempting to conclude free trade agreements with every African country. This study considers six agreements, involving 16 sub-Saharan countries.[2]

[1] FAO, *Food security and agricultural development in sub-Saharan Africa* (FAO, 2006); J Ziegler, 'Peasant Farmers and the Right to Food a History of Discrimination and Exploitation', Requests Addressed to the advisory committee stemming from human rights council resolutions: right to food, A/HRC/AC/3/CRP.5.

[2] See European Commission, Overview of EPA, available at <http://trade.ec.europa.eu/doclib/docs/2009/september/tradoc_144912.pdf> accessed 4 July 2017.

This chapter takes into account the clauses on the import and export of food of the six free trade agreements the EU has concluded with sub-Saharan countries. This chapter has the main objective of assessing whether the deficiencies of the Caribbean agreement are present also in the treaties concluded so far with African countries. The chapter is divided into six sections plus this introduction. In the second section we present the free trade agreements between the EU and sub-Saharan countries, summarising the state of the negotiations and the economic setting of the EU action. The third section stresses the vulnerability of African countries and the special status some of them have in WTO law. In the fourth section we consider the regulation of import tariffs. The fifth section assesses the regulation of safeguards on food products imported into African countries from the EU. In this section we answer the question whether the treaties provide African countries with a quick and efficient mechanism to protect their citizens from import surges of food from the EU. Section VI looks at the clauses on export restrictions, assessing to what extent the treaties allow African countries to use this instrument at the occurrence of food shortages on their territory. Section VII concludes.

The chapter shows that also the EU–Africa free trade agreements limit the capacity of vulnerable states to realise the right to food. This is so even though the African legal and economic settings are different from the Caribbean one and would have required particular attention to the effects of the treaties on the realisation of the right to food. In fact, in sub-Saharan Africa there are numerous least-developed countries that are particularly vulnerable to food shortages.

II. THE STATE OF NEGOTIATIONS BETWEEN THE EU AND AFRICA

As explained at length in Chapter four the European Union aims to conclude free trade agreements with more than 100 countries across the world. This strategy includes also all sub-Saharan countries and these countries have been involved in close negotiations with the EU since 2006. In order to smooth the conclusion of the trade agreements the European Commission divided sub-Saharan Africa into five zones: West,[3] Central,[4] Eastern and Southern,[5]

[3] This group includes: Benin, Burkina Faso, Cape Verde, Ivory Coast [Côte d'Ivoire], Gambia, Ghana, Guinea, Guinea-Bissau, Liberia, Mali, Mauritania, Niger, Nigeria, Senegal, Sierra Leone, Togo.

[4] This group includes: Cameroon, Central African Republic, Chad, Republic of Congo, Democratic Republic of Congo, Equatorial Guinea, Gabon, and São Tomé and Príncipe.

[5] This group includes: Comoros, Djibouti, Eritrea, Ethiopia, Madagascar, Mauritius, Malawi, Seychelles, Sudan, Zambia and Zimbabwe.

Eastern African Community[6] and South African Development Community.[7] Each group of countries constitutes a separate platform to negotiate and conclude free trade agreements with the EU.[8]

The objective of the Global Europe Strategy in sub-Saharan Africa is to achieve five comprehensive free trade agreements, one for each area. The agreements will replace most of existing WTO law in the relationship between the EU and the countries involved.

The negotiations with the five groups of African countries started in 2006 at the same time as the negotiations with Caribbean countries. The history of the African negotiations has been, however, more troubled, and so far the EU has not been able to achieve all the goals of its strategy.[9]

Facing the impossibility of concluding trade deals as comprehensive as the Caribbean one, the EU Commission at first modified the strategy and concluded simpler agreements with the available countries.[10] These agreements, called interim economic partnership agreements, concentrate only on some of the trade issues the EU wanted to include at the beginning of the negotiations. Notwithstanding their name, interim trade agreements are permanent free trade treaties of the kind allowed by Article XXIV GATT. Notably, all the interim agreements concluded so far regulate the import and export of food and are substitutes for WTO law in the relationship between the EU and the countries involved. For this reason even though the EU trade strategy in sub-Saharan Africa is not completed the agreements concluded so far provide a clear picture of the direction of the negotiations and their consequences for the right to food.

[6] This group includes: Burundi, Kenya, Rwanda, Tanzania, Uganda.

[7] This group includes: Angola, Botswana, Lesotho, Mozambique, Namibia and Swaziland.

[8] S Bartelt, 'ACP-EU cooperation at a crossroads? One year after the second revision of the Cotonou Agreement' (2012) 17 *European Foreign Affairs Review* 1; P Draper, 'EU-Africa Trade Relations: The Political Economy of Economic Partnership Agreements', Jan Tumlir Policy Essays 02/2007, European Centre for International Political Economy, Brussels <http://www.ecipe.org/app/uploads/2014/12/eu-africa-trade-relations-the-political-economy-of-economic-partnership-agreements.pdf>; AM Mansoor, V Bassant and S Samen, 'Strengthening Economic Partnership Agreements and the Future of the EU-Africa Trade Relationships in the Next Decade' in *The next decade of EU trade policy: Confronting global challenges?* (Overseas Development Institute, 2012).

[9] International Food and Agricultural Trade Policy Council, 'Economic Partnership Agreements and African Regional Integration: Have negotiations helped or hindered regional integration?', Issue Brief August 2011; Andrew Bounds, 'African states refuse to join EU trade deal' (*Financial Times*, 4 December 2007) available at: <http://www.ft.com/cms/s/0/c757bcf2-a1f2-11dc-a13b-0000779fd2ac.html#axzz2Y4HpPV1W> accessed 14 June 2013. In sub-Saharan Africa several NGOs and civil society groups are opposing the conclusion of the trade agreements. See for instance the websites http://stopepa.twnafrica.org/ and http://www.twnafrica.org/.

[10] For instance the agreements do not include regulation of trade in services, intellectual property and competition policies.

This study includes six free trade agreements with sub-Saharan countries: three with single countries and three with four or more countries. The treaties with single countries are the agreement between the EU and Côte d'Ivoire,[11] the agreement between the EU and Ghana[12] and the agreement between the EU and Cameroon.[13] The agreement between the EU and Eastern and Southern Africa includes Mauritius, Seychelles, Zimbabwe and Madagascar[14] and the agreement with the Eastern African Community involves Burundi, Rwanda, Tanzania, Kenya and Uganda.[15] Botswana, Lesotho, Swaziland and Mozambique also concluded a free trade agreement with the EU.[16] All these agreements are similar to each other. Since they are all relevant for the realisation of the right to food, they will be analysed in the sections below.

III. SUB-SAHARAN AFRICA'S ECONOMIC AND LEGAL SETTING

This section takes into account the economic and legal settings of the African states. The paradox of most of these countries is that they are at the same time extremely exposed to poverty and hunger and very rich in natural resources. In fact, despite the very low per-capita income of these countries, they are among the main exporters of raw materials to the EU. In addition, sub-Saharan Africa has a particular legal status in WTO law since it contains numerous least-developed countries, which are exempt from several key WTO obligations.

A. Economic Setting

The economic and social situation of the countries involved in the free trade negotiations is extremely difficult. Of the 45 sub-Saharan countries taking

[11] Stepping Stone Economic Partnership Agreement between Côte d'Ivoire, of the one part, and the European Community and its Member States, of the other part [2009] OJ L59/3.

[12] Stepping Stone Economic Partnership Agreement between Ghana, of the one part, and the European Community and its Member States, of the other part.

[13] Interim Agreement with a view to an Economic Partnership Agreement between the European Community and its Member States, of the one part, and the Central Africa Party, of the other part [2009] OJ L57/2.

[14] Interim Agreement establishing a framework for an Economic Partnership Agreement between the Eastern and Southern Africa States, on the one part, and the European Community and its Member States, on the other part [2012] OJ L111/2.

[15] Agreement establishing a framework for an Economic Partnership Agreement between the European Community and its Member States, on the one part, and the East African Community partner states on the other part.

[16] Interim Agreement with a view to an Economic Partnership Agreement between the European Community and its Member States, of the one part, and the SADC EPA States, of the other part.

part in the negotiations with the EU, 27 are on the Food and Agriculture Organization's list of low-income food-deficit countries.[17] Moreover, the large majority of the African countries that concluded the free trade agreements are net food importers dependent on third countries to satisfy their food security needs.[18] In addition, the countries involved are often at the very bottom of international rankings on social and industrial development and capacity to compete on the international market. For instance, most of the countries involved in the free trade agreements are below the 150th position on the UN Human Development Index.[19] All these elements make sub-Saharan Africa an area of the world exposed to the vagaries of the international food market whereby the right to food remains largely unrealised.[20]

At the same time, sub-Saharan countries are among the richest of the world in several raw materials and natural resources crucial for the development of the EU economy. In fact, African countries are among the main exporters of gold, oil, diamonds and aluminium and are the providers of a substantial proportion of the raw coffee and cocoa imported into the EU.[21] In addition, several countries own the reserves of critical rare materials that are scarce or absent in the territory of the European Union. Rwanda, for instance, is one of the main exporters of tantalum, a rare metal used in electronic components, which the EU Commission identified as one of the key objectives of the Raw Materials Initiative.[22] From the official documents of the EU Commission it emerges that the EU approached the negotiations with Africa giving particular attention to the clauses influencing the supply of raw materials to EU processing industries.[23] Since sub-Saharan countries are also among those most exposed to hunger and malnutrition, the free

[17] The list contains the 62 most food insecure countries, namely countries that are unable to satisfy their food security needs through domestic supply and have a very low per-capita income. See Chapter 3 of this book.

[18] WTO, WTO list of net food-importing developing countries for the purposes of the Marrakesh ministerial decision on measures concerning the possible negative effects of the reform programme on least-developed and net food-importing developing countries, G/AG/5/Rev.10 (2012).

[19] The exact ranking of the countries involved is as follows: Côte d'Ivoire 168th, Ghana 135th, Cameroon 150th, Mauritius 80th, Seychelles 46th, Zimbabwe 172nd, Madagascar 151st, Burundi 178th, Rwanda 167th, Tanzania 152nd, Kenya 145th, Uganda 161st, Botswana 119th, Lesotho 158th, Swaziland 141st, Mozambique 185th. Most of these countries are below the 170th position of the UN index with regard to poverty and health.

[20] FAO, Regional Office for Africa, *Programme Review 2011*; FAO, *FAO Statistical Yearbook 2012, Africa Food and agriculture* (FAO, 2012).

[21] See Chapter 3 of this book.

[22] See Chapter 4 of this book for an introduction to the Raw Materials Initiative and its role in the EU external trade policy. European Commission, Report of the Ad-hoc Working Group on defining critical raw materials, available at <http://ec.europa.eu/enterprise/policies/raw-materials/files/docs/report-b_en.pdf> accessed 24 June 2017.

[23] See for instance the Annual Reports of the EU Raw Materials Initiative.

trade agreements between the EU and Africa are an ideal setting to evaluate the effectiveness of the EU Policy. Coherence for Development initiative, which should conciliate the economic objectives of the EU Commercial Policy with non-trade goals.

Finally, in certain sub-Saharan countries an emerging middle-class is increasing the value of sub-Saharan Africa as an export market. The spending capacity of African people is, however, unequal between countries and between social sectors. Moreover, there is a very high level of social inequality even in the richest and most developed African countries. This means that even in emerging African states a large part of the population is prone to hunger and malnutrition.[24] Accordingly, any strategy of the EU to improve the presence of EU companies in sub-Saharan Africa should avoid affecting the most disadvantaged groups of African society. In particular, if the EU promotes the reduction or abolition of import tariffs on food it should avoid increasing the exposure of vulnerable groups to import surges of EU products in African markets. As shown in previous chapters, this market failure is particularly dangerous when it disrupts the livelihoods of local vulnerable producers. The economic setting of sub-Saharan Africa is particularly predisposed to import surges, since malnourished people in this area often depend on fragile agricultural markets.[25] In addition, in Africa, local farmers receive limited public subsidisation to support their competitiveness, and comprehensive public programmes in support of technological development are rare and often inefficient.[26] This puts local producers in an exceptionally weak position when they face competition from developed countries such as the EU in their own domestic market.[27] Accordingly, a sudden increase of the imports of these food products from the EU, displacing local producers, is likely to affect the realisation of the right to food in the area.

[24] United Nations Development Programme, 'Income Inequality Trends in Sub-Saharan Africa', available at <file:///Users/grunig/Downloads/undp-rba_Income%20Inequality%20in%20SSA_Infographic%20Booklet_EN%20(1).pdf> accessed 27 December 2017.

[25] A report funded by the European Development Fund identified the weakness of African agricultural markets as one of the main reasons of African fragility: see European Report on Development 2009, 'Overcoming Fragility in Africa Forging a New European Approach'.

[26] FAO, *Food security and agricultural development in sub-Saharan Africa* (FAO, 2006), available at <http://www.fao.org/docrep/009/a0627e/a0627e00.htm> accessed 27 December 2017.

[27] See Manitra A Rakotoarisoa, Ramesh P Sharma and D Hallam, *Agricultural import surges in developing countries Analytical framework and insights from case studies* (FAO, 2011). For an example of an import surge in one of the countries involved in the negotiations with the EU, see FAO, *United Republic of Tanzania: Rice Maize and Dairy Products, FAO Briefs on Import Surges* (FAO, 2006). The Brief reports an escalation of import surges in the period of implementation of the Uruguay Round.

B. Sub-Saharan Africa in WTO Law

Thirty-four sub-Saharan countries are classified by the United Nations as 'least-developed countries'. The United Nations selects these countries on the basis of their low per-capita income, the instability of their agricultural production, the vulnerability of their economies and their low levels of food security, health, education and adult literacy. As noted in Chapter six, this category is relevant for WTO law because when a country is on this list it is granted additional preferential treatment. This includes the exemption of least-developed countries from several commitments and additional time to implement certain clauses contained in WTO treaties. This category is particularly relevant for the object of this research because the Agreement on Agriculture provides that least-developed countries are exempt from the WTO reduction commitments on agricultural products. This means that under WTO law least-developed countries retain considerable space to protect their markets from import surges of food when the product is regulated by the Agreement on Agriculture.[28] Therefore, when a least-developed country concludes a trade agreement with the EU, it is giving away the exemption granted by WTO law. This is so because least-developed countries are not mentioned in Article XXIV GATT and are subject to the general obligation to eliminate import tariffs when concluding a free trade agreement just like any other WTO Member. This increases the legal impact of free trade agreements because with these treaties least-developed countries are accepting binding obligations on tariffs applicable to food products imported from the EU for the first time. In the six agreements in sub-Saharan Africa considered here, there are seven least-developed countries involved: Madagascar, Burundi, Rwanda, Tanzania, Uganda, Lesotho and Mozambique. Overall, there are 26 least-developed countries involved in the African leg of the Global Europe Strategy. This is a major legal difference from the Caribbean context where, with the only exception of Haiti, the countries involved are not classified as least-developed countries and were already subject to some legal constraints on the import of food under WTO law.

IV. IMPORT RESTRICTIONS

All the six African trade agreements produce a profound modification of the maximum tariffs applicable to the products traded between the EU and African countries. This section will consider the specificities of the regulation

[28] Most food products are regulated by the Agreement on Agriculture. See Chapter 5 of this book.

applicable to food products from the perspective of its effect on the realisation of the right to food in vulnerable African countries.

A. African Products Imported into the EU

As far as African imports in the EU are concerned, the trade agreements eliminate the large majority of tariff barriers. This means that under the trade agreements African products enter the EU market duty-free. This rule applies to all products exported by African countries with no exception.[29]

The effects of this arrangement on the realisation of the right to food could be positive as long as the agreements facilitate the presence of African vulnerable producers in the EU common market. However, the benefits of the agreements for vulnerable individuals are not immediate, because the EU is granting similar preferences to other trade partners. The risk is that the free trade regime imposed by the trade agreement will only benefit the few countries and private companies that are already equipped to compete at international level.[30] De Schutter notes that the creation of a level playing-field between countries that have different levels of development polarises the gains to the most developed countries.[31] This mechanism could produce the consequence that African countries will be unable to benefit from the tariff reduction whenever more advanced countries with similar agreements with the EU (such as Mexico or South Korea) export the same products. If this happens, the free trade agreements will not interrupt the economic marginalisation of African countries. Notwithstanding this critical aspect it is positive that all the agreements, by eliminating any import tariff, forbid the use of trade instruments such as tariff escalations and tariff peaks.

B. European Food Products Imported into African Countries

For the realisation of right to food, a crucial part of the treaties is that regulating the tariffs on food products imported from the EU into sub-Saharan countries. This is so because, since European countries are extremely competitive exporters able to produce virtually every product, the quick opening of African markets risks benefiting the EU export business at the expense of vulnerable African producers. In addition, the elimination of tariff barriers

[29] The Annexes to the treaties do not include any exception to the elimination of tariffs. There is only a transitional procedure on sugar affecting African exports until 2015.

[30] J Stiglitz, *Making globalization work* (Penguin Books 2006) 54.

[31] See Olivier De Schutter, 'International trade in agriculture and the right to food', Dialogue on Globalization Occasional Paper No. 46, November 2009, available at <http://library.fes.de/pdf-files/bueros/genf/06819.pdf> (accessed 19 June 2013).

on food products has been linked to the increase of import surges of food in vulnerable countries.[32]

Each of the six trade agreements between the EU and Africa attempts to limit the exposure of African countries to import surges by exempting several food products from the process of liberalisation. For instance, in the Agreement between the EU and Côte d'Ivoire, products are classified into four categories (A, B, C, D) and category D, which includes certain live animals, cereals and vegetables, is exempt from full liberalisation. In a similar vein the agreement with Cameroon arranges products into five categories and allows the imposition of import tariffs only on the goods included in category 5. Every agreement has a similar mechanism to leave certain sensitive products out of the process of liberalisation.[33]

Looking at this regulatory choice from the perspective of the right to food, four shortcomings can be identified. First, the food products comprised in the categories exempted from liberalisation are very limited. In fact, the treaties forbid the imposition of tariffs on most meat and dairy products imported from the EU. In the same vein, agreements never exclude more than three kinds of cereals. For instance, in the agreement with Cameroon the only exempted cereals are wheat and rice. The import of the rest of agricultural products is completely liberalised with very few exceptions for certain kinds of fruit and vegetables. Notably, no exception is made with regard to least-developed countries.

Second, when a food product is exempted from liberalisation the treaties still define as a maximum ceiling the tariff that African countries were applying at the moment of the conclusion of the treaty. This means that the treaties froze tariffs at the level that African countries were imposing on sensitive products in 2008. However, the tariffs levied on these products were extremely low at the time because the treaties were negotiated right in the middle of the global food crisis, when food prices on the international market were very high. The tariffs were low because African countries were trying to diminish the price of food on their territory by eliminating any tax imposed on these products. For instance, Ivory Coast was imposing a tariff of only five per cent on rice to favour the import of the cereal into its territory.[34] This was a temporary policy, prompted by the global food crisis

[32] See above Chapter 5 of this book.

[33] Article 5 of the trade agreement between the EU and Cameroon; Article 13 and Annex 2 of the trade agreement between the EU and Ghana; Annex 2 to the trade agreement between the EU and Côte d'Ivoire; Article 25 and Annex 2 of the trade agreement between the EU and Southern Africa Development Community; Article 11 and Annex 2 of the trade agreement between the EU and the Eastern African Community.

[34] FAO, 'Policy measures taken by governments to reduce the impact of soaring prices (as of 15 December 2008)', available at <http://www.fao.org/giews/english/policy/1.asp> (accessed 13 June 2013).

but the free trade agreements make these very low tariffs permanent. If in the future the international price of food goes down and African countries need to raise the tariffs to avoid import surges of food, they will be forbidden to do so. The alternative would have been to define as the maximum applicable tariff not the tariff levied at the moment of the conclusion of the treaty, but the one required by WTO law. In failing to do so, the treaties impose lower tariffs than what WTO requires. This outcome increases the exposure of vulnerable producers to import surges of food products from the EU whenever their protection would require an import tariff higher than what allowed in the treaty.

Since African countries use import tariffs to produce public revenues their elimination weakens the capacity of those countries to intervene at the occurrence of food shortages on their territories. This negative effect is present also in the Caribbean treaty but the consequences for African countries could be particularly grave because of their weak systems of taxation and dependency on trade revenues. In fact, there is evidence that African countries are among the most dependent on trade taxes and that they find it extremely difficult to replace them with alternative instruments of taxation.[35] This is particularly so when the country involved in the free trade agreement has a weak state apparatus or a history of persistent domestic instability.[36] In this situation it is possible that only a small part of lost revenues is recouped through internal taxation and that the trade agreements will have a clear impact on the resources available to African countries to intervene at the occurrence of food shortages.

Finally, since most of the countries involved in the agreements with the EU have limited industrial capacity, the majority of vulnerable individuals living outside the capital cities have access to food that is produced through traditional instruments and without advanced mechanical support.[37] This means that the realisation of the right to food in these countries requires also the development of the independent technological know-how required to boost domestic production and diminish the dependency on the international food market.[38] This is particularly so since the countries that signed the free trade agreements with the EU are mainly net food importers still unable to achieve domestic food security without food imports from third countries. Development economics, however, has demonstrated that technological

[35] See S Bilal, M Dalleau and D Lui, 'Trade Liberalisation and Fiscal Adjustments: The Case of EPAs in Africa', European Centre for Development Policy Management Discussion Paper No. 137. See also above Chapter 6 section III.B.

[36] This is the case for instance of Zimbabwe, Uganda and Burundi which still have unstable or undemocratic governments.

[37] World Bank, *Cultivating Knowledge and Skills to Grow African Agriculture* (World Bank, 2007).

[38] J Fanzo, 'The Nutrition Challenge in Sub-Saharan Africa', WP 2012-012 (January 2012), United Nations Development Programme.

development is less likely when a developing country with almost no industrial capacity is involved in a free trade regime with an advanced economy. This is so because in the absence of progressive import tariffs on technological goods produced in the developed countries, there is little economic incentive to produce such goods in the developing countries.[39] Since buying chemicals and machinery from the EU is cheaper than developing domestic technologies and the free trade agreement forbids tariffs on these products, the trade agreement discourages technological development in the African states. The free trade agreements between the EU and Africa do just the opposite, enforcing a complete liberalisation of the trade of technological goods between the countries involved. Within this regime EU companies are likely to improve their presence in African domestic markets, discouraging the development of an advanced food industry in the area. In other words, the free trade agreements increase the dependency of African countries not only on EU food exports but also on the technologies involved in the production of food.

The regulation of tariffs by the agreements between the EU and Africa shows the limits of an international legal system that does not allow differential treatment even when advanced economies conclude a trade deal with some of the poorest countries of the world. This is a serious human rights handicap, since the treaties are likely to benefit the EU export business even when the expansion of EU trade directly affects vulnerable producers in African countries. The absence of differential treatment in these agreements is particularly regrettable since the countries involved are among the most exposed to food insecurity and the least equipped to cope with international competition and the vagaries of the international food market. In the absence of public policies to cope with this new scenario, the risk is that the new trade agreements will directly affect the realisation of the right to food in sub-Saharan Africa.

V. SAFEGUARDS

Since the clauses on tariffs considerably restrict the space for intervention of African countries at the occurrence of import surges, an advanced system of safeguards would be essential in order to ensure that price fluctuations on the international food market do not hurt vulnerable individuals in African countries. However, the regulation of safeguards by the six trade agreements

[39] In a monograph published in 2003 Chang argues that tariffs on technological goods imported from third countries played a major role during the industrial development of all Western countries. See H-J Chang, *Kicking away the ladder* (Anthem Press, 2003). In the same vein Joseph Stiglitz maintains that a free trade regime between a developed country and a developing one can discourage in the latter the creation of a technologically advanced food industry. See J Stiglitz and A Charlton, *Free trade for all* (Oxford University Press, 2005).

the EU has concluded so far with African states does not take into account this necessity and provides a system of safeguards similar to that of the Caribbean agreement. Accordingly, the African agreements always create a supranational body that supervises the adoption of safeguards, do not include an automatic mechanism like the WTO Special Safeguard and do not provide substantial differential treatment in favour of African countries. The only main difference between the African treaties and the Caribbean one is that the African agreements do not include safeguards dedicated to the protection of food security in African states.

This regulatory choice leaves African countries without an efficient mechanism to react to the consequences for domestic food security of the permanent elimination of import tariffs. In particular, the use of the same safeguards as the Caribbean agreement extends the shortcomings of that agreement also to the African context. This means that the safeguards are too slow to implement, are less effective than the ones provided in WTO law and do not take into account the difference in development between the EU and African states. Moreover, the absence of any reference to food security makes the trade agreements prone to legal interpretations that exclude the use of safeguards on the occurrence of import surges of food from the European Union. In fact, since the African countries involved in the agreements are among the least literate in issues of international trade, the decision not to make explicit the link between tariff reduction and food security could have the consequence that African countries remain unaware that they are entitled to activate the safeguards at the occurrence of food crisis due to import surges of food. There is extensive evidence in WTO practice that overcomplicated regulations or omissions in the enumeration of the risks of a trade agreement for food security have the consequence that the most disadvantaged countries do not seize the opportunity to use protective instruments even when the agreements they have concluded would allow them to do so.[40]

Finally, the fact that the regulation of safeguards by all six of the agreements is similar to what we found in the Caribbean case hints at the fact that the agreements were concluded with scant attention to the specific vulnerabilities of each African country. In particular, their similarities suggest that the EU Commission was the actor that drafted the core of all agreements and promoted their conclusion across the developing world.[41] The absence

[40] See S Joseph, *Blame it on the WTO?* (Oxford University Press, 2011) 53.

[41] The idea that free trade agreements with developing countries are mainly an EU initiative finds support in several Communications from the Commission which present free trade agreements with Africa as an EU policy to make its relation with the developing world WTO compliant. The Communications present the trade agreements as a development policy even though, as seen in Chapter 4 they are designed by the Directorate-General of Trade. See Communication from the Commission, 'Regional integration for development in ACP countries' COM(2008) 604 final; Communication from the Commission, 'Economic Partnership Agreements' COM(2007) 635 final.

of substantial differences between the treaties show manifestly that the contribution of African countries to their drafting was minimal and that their content is mainly the result of the EU's external policies. This conclusion also appears the most likely, since most of the African countries involved in the agreements already find it difficult to participate in the production of international trade law within the WTO and have no record in the international trade Dispute Settlement System because they lack the necessary legal and economic know-how.[42] From a human rights perspective, it is regrettable that during the trade negotiations with an area of the world extremely vulnerable to hunger and malnutrition, the EU resorted to a standardised blueprint and did not design a system of food safeguards tailored to the specific necessities of each African country.

In conclusion, the safeguard regulation by the trade agreements between the EU and African countries presents evident shortcomings even though the economic setting of the African countries involved is more disadvantaged than the Caribbean one and the exposure to food insecurity more evident. The similarities between the regulation of safeguards by the African agreements and the Caribbean one make clear the EU strategy to reach uniform agreements with developing countries on the basis of a text prepared by the EU Commission.[43] Arguably, a more comprehensive involvement of African states in the negotiations would have allowed a clearer definition of the risks of the agreements for the realisation of the right to food, and would have made evident the necessity to endow the trade agreements with an automatic safeguard mechanism similar to the WTO Special Safeguard.

VI. EXPORT RESTRICTIONS

All six agreements the EU concluded with African countries contain clauses applicable to exports of food that are more restrictive than WTO law. In fact, in the three separate Interim Economic Partnership Agreements that the EU concluded with Ivory Coast,[44] Ghana,[45] and Cameroon[46] quantitative

[42] S Joseph, *Blame it on the WTO?* (Oxford University Press, 2011).

[43] For instance Article 25 of the Caribbean free trade agreement, the article creating the supranational committee and including the administrative process to be followed, was copied and pasted into the African agreements.

[44] Articles 16 and 18 of the Stepping Stone Economic Partnership Agreement between Côte d'Ivoire, of the one part, and the European Community and its Member States, of the other part [2009] OJ L59/3.

[45] Articles 16 and 18 of the Stepping Stone Economic Partnership Agreement between Ghana, of the one part, and the European Community and its Member States, of the other part.

[46] Articles 15 and 22 of the Interim Agreement with a view to an Economic Partnership Agreement between the European Community and its Member States, of the one part, and the Central Africa Party, of the other part [2009] OJ L57/2.

export restrictions are prohibited and there is no reference to the exception of Article XI.2(a) GATT on export restrictions to prevent or relieve food shortages. In these three treaties new taxes are forbidden and existing export taxes can be increased only in case of serious public finance problems, greater environmental protection or protection of infant industries and then only after consultation with the EU. Also the trade agreement between the EU and Comoros, Madagascar, Mauritius, Seychelles, Zambia and Zimbabwe prohibits the use of quantitative restrictions, without reproducing the exception of Article XI.2(a) GATT on food shortages.[47] Only two free trade agreements with African countries maintain the food exception of article XI.2(a) GATT even though they impose severe limitations on the use of customs duties on exports. These are the Interim Economic Partnership Agreement between the EU and Burundi, Kenya, Tanzania, Uganda and Rwanda[48] and the Interim Economic Partnership Agreement between the EU and Botswana, Lesotho, Mozambique, Namibia and Swaziland.[49] Also in this last agreement new export taxes can be introduced only after consultation with the EU.

This section divides the clauses on export restrictions of the African agreements into two groups. In the first group there are the agreements with Cameroon, Ghana, Ivory Coast and Eastern and with Southern African countries that do not reproduce the food security exception of Article XI.2(a) GATT. The second group includes the other two agreements that contain the food security exception allowing export restrictions to relieve food shortages on the territory of the country. The analysis of the two groups of agreements will be tackled separately, since they present several specific elements with regard to the consequences for the realisation of the right to food of the countries involved. The section concludes with a comment on the influence of the EU Raw Materials Initiative on the regulation of export restrictions by the trade agreements.

[47] Article 17, Interim Agreement establishing a framework for an Economic Partnership Agreement between the Eastern and Southern Africa States, on the one part, and the European Community and its Member States, on the other part [2012] OJ L111/2.

[48] Articles 15 and 17 of the Agreement establishing a framework for an Economic Partnership Agreement between the European Community and its Member States, on the one part, and the East African Community partner states on the other part.

[49] Articles 24 and 35 of the Interim Agreement with a view to an Economic Partnership Agreement between the European Community and its Member States, of the one part, and the SADC EPA States, of the other part.

A. Agreements Not Including the Food Security Exception of Article XI.2 GATT

The four agreements with Cameroon, Ghana, Ivory Coast and Eastern and Southern African countries that do not allow the application of Article XI.2(a) GATT to the exports of food and other goods, have consequences similar to a complete ban on export restrictions. In particular, in case of food shortages on their territory these countries are not allowed to limit their exports of food to the European Union. Even though the discipline is slightly less stringent than that of the Caribbean agreement, the consequences for food security are the same. In fact, quantitative limitations on the export of food are forbidden across the board and even though existing export taxes are allowed in certain cases, the protection of food security is not one of them. For these reasons, Cameroon, Ghana, Ivory Coast, Mauritius, Seychelles, Zimbabwe and Madagascar have lost the prerogative to intervene on their food exports to protect and fulfil the realisation of the right to food of their citizens.

B. Agreements Including the Food Security Exception of Article XI.2 GATT

The two remaining agreements, which include the food security exceptions of Article XI.2 GATT, provide African countries with an instrument of quick intervention in the case of food shortages on their territory. In fact, reducing food exports these countries can increase the quantity of food available on their territory and drive local prices down. However, the discipline of export restrictions is considerably different from WTO law, since it restricts the legal space to levy export taxes on goods that African countries export to the EU. For this reason, even if Article XI.2(a) GATT is maintained, the agreements produce a change in the attitude of international trade law towards African countries that, as seen in Chapter five, had remained free under WTO law to tax the exports of their natural resources to produce public revenues. Since the public revenues of several African countries involved in the agreements with the EU are heavily dependent on the export of natural resources, the agreements weaken their capacity to collect public funds to finance social policies such as food security policies. Accordingly, at the occurrence of a food shortage on their territory the African countries involved in this group of agreements can limit the quantity of food exported but do not have any trade instrument to raise public funds to deal with the emergency. Since the trade agreements will have already produced a considerable loss of revenues through the elimination of the large majority of import taxes, the prohibition of taxing the export of natural resources introduces an additional weakness to the capacity of African countries to raise public revenues at the occurrence of food crises. With less public revenues available and with no instruments to raise revenues quickly in case of emergency, African countries could find it more difficult to design social policies targeted to vulnerable groups.

C. The Raw Materials Initiative and the Right to Food

In different ways all the six agreements diminish the policy space of African countries to intervene in case of food shortages on their territory. Four of the agreements do so by forbidding the use of all kind quantitative restrictions on food exports, and two of them by eliminating export taxes far beyond what is provided by WTO law. To what we have observed above one observation can be added. The policy paper of the EU Commission and the public debate surrounding the negotiations concentrated mainly on the effect of the treaty on the exploitation of African natural resources. This is justified by the fact that the impact of the agreements on this issue is relevant.[50] The focus on raw materials, however, produced the consequence that in all the agreements the negotiators overlooked the consequences that a more stringent regulation on export restrictions could produce on the availability of *food* on the territory of African countries. This resulted in the conclusion of a batch of agreements that eliminates or weakens the exceptions that in WTO law allow vulnerable countries to intervene in their external trade of food to protect the food security of their citizens. This result highlights the absence of coordination between the EU external trade policy and the EU external food security policy, and a marked dominance of the first over the second. This issue is particularly flagrant in the African agreements, since sub-Saharan Africa is at the same time one of the main exporters of oil and raw materials and one of the areas of the world characterised by extreme poverty and widespread food insecurity.

VII. CONCLUSIONS

This chapter produced six trade agreements regulating the trade in goods between the EU and Africa, which involved 16 African states. These agreements contain innovative regulation on the import and export of food and, despite their name, are permanent treaties, fully enforceable under international law from the date of their ratification. The six free trade agreements

[50] M Curtis, *The New Resource Grab: How EU Trade Policy on Raw Materials is Undermining Development* (Oxfam Germany, Traidcraft Exchange, WEED, AITEC and Comhlámh, 2010).

provoked a substantial modification of the law on the trade of food between the EU and the African countries involved. Notably, the trade agreements concern countries extremely vulnerable to hunger and malnutrition which are severely affected by the instability of the international food market.

The chapter has shown that even though the African economic context should have required particular attention to the effect of a free trade deal on the realisation of the right to food, the human rights deficiencies of the EU–Caribbean free trade agreement are present also in the African treaties. In fact, the regulation of all the trade instruments considered here (tariffs, safeguards and export restrictions) includes additional elements of concern. First, the regulation of import tariffs applicable to EU food imported into African countries leaves little space to intervene on the trade flows. This is particularly so because the treaty imposes a maximum tariff even on the food products that negotiators considered sensitive for African countries. This choice exposes African countries to import surges of food produced in the EU which benefit EU export business but could significantly impoverish local producers. In addition, the treaties enforce a level playing-field on advanced goods which might deepen the dependency of African food production on foreign technologies. More generally, the new treaties do not support food self-sufficiency of African countries, favouring the import of food from the EU.

Second, even though the deep liberalisation of food imports from the EU should have required an efficient system of protection, the regulation on safeguards does not take into account food security. In particular, the treaties do not include any automatic safeguard mechanism to ensure that the process of liberalisation does not result in additional import surges in African countries. As in the Caribbean treaty, safeguards are slow to implement and, based on the WTO experience, it is doubtful that they would make any difference at the occurrence of import surges of food produced in the EU. Furthermore, the similarities in the wording of the clauses to those of the Caribbean agreement point to the fact that all the treaties are based on the same blueprint drafted by the European Commission. This manner of operating discourages the involvement of African countries in the negotiation process and makes the resulting agreement dependent on policy decisions made in Brussels. The chapter has suggested that more attention to the specific vulnerabilities of each African state might have conducted to a different outcome more attentive to the realisation of the right to food.

Finally, the clauses on export restrictions increase the constraints on the use of these instruments at the occurrence of food shortages on the territory of African states. Four agreements do so by forbidding any form of export restriction and omitting to reproduce Article XI.2(a) GATT. The two agreements maintaining the exception of Article XI.2(a) GATT still impose severe limits on export taxes. In the first group of treaties the effects on the realisation of the right to food are analogous to those identified in the Caribbean case study. Even at the occurrence of major food shortages African countries are not allowed to intervene in food exports and are obliged to keep exporting food to the EU. In the second group of agreements African countries can limit the quantity exported even though they are not allowed to use taxes on exports to raise public revenues to invest in food security policies. Overall, the six agreements constitute a change of attitude by international trade law towards the African continent. Under the WTO system in fact Africa has a wide policy space to impose both quantitative restrictions and taxes on the export of food and other products, especially in situations of emergency.

This chapter confirms the picture of an external trade policy of the European Union that is not attentive to the effect of free trade agreements on the realisation of the right to food in vulnerable countries. Even in a context of extreme poverty and severe exposure to hunger and malnutrition, the trade treaties are dismissive of human rights objectives and pursue the main goal of eliminating any form of trade barrier. This is done to an extent that is unprecedented in the law of the external relations of the EU. Notably, the process of trade liberalisation of the agreements between the EU and Africa go well beyond WTO requirements in all the instruments analysed. This is done also with regard to least-developed countries that in WTO law are exempt from most of the obligations on import and export of food. In terms of EU policymaking the African treaties show manifestly the failure of the Policy Coherence for Development initiative of the EU Commission and of the other attempts to conciliate the EU external trade policy with non-trade objectives. More generally, with the African agreements the EU betrayed the mandate of Article 21 of the Treaty on the European Union to pursue the realisation of human rights, including economic and social rights in all segments of its external action.

8

Conclusions

I. INTRODUCTION

THIS BOOK HAS considered the outcome of the trade negotiations of the EU with some of the most vulnerable countries of the world in the Caribbean and Sub-Saharan Africa. It has shown that the trade agreements that the EU concluded with these countries reduce their capacity to realise the right to food of their citizens. This is so because several clauses on import and export of food create legal constraints on the trade policies that can be implemented to react to food shortages. This chapter recapitulates the main results of the book and reflects on the consequence of the findings for the external action of the EU towards developing countries. Section two of this conclusion summarises the results of each chapter and section three recaps the findings of the case studies. Finally, section four argues in favour of defragmenting EU external policies and world trade law to overcome their shortcomings in terms of the realisation of the human right to food.

II. SUMMARY OF THE MAIN FINDINGS OF THE FIRST FOUR CHAPTERS

The book started with an introductory chapter on the normative content of the right to food in international law. The chapter identified the principal international treaties and conventions that include the right and followed the evolution of the right to food from its early codifications until recent years. The chapter identified the International Covenant on Economic Social and Cultural Rights as the most relevant legal source and looked into the interpretations of the right provided by the International Committee on Economic Social and Cultural Rights. In doing so the chapter recognised the main human rights duties stemming from the human right to food (duty to respect, duty to protect and duty to provide) and clarified their meaning. Moreover, Chapter two investigated whether the Committee provided interpretations of the right generating legal duties that are applicable to the negotiations of international trade treaties. The chapter concluded that the normative content of the right to food also applies to the external economic policies of states. Notably, the Committee explicitly referred to WTO law as one of the stumbling blocks preventing the realisation of the right to food in vulnerable countries. Members of the Covenant in fact are not exempt from supporting the realisation of the right when drafting international trade treaties regulating the import and export of food. In particular, all Members to the Covenant have the duty to ensure that the instability on the international food market does not affect the realisation of the right at domestic level. This duty is particularly relevant in the context of the recent globalisation and liberalisation of international trade, since the relevance of the international food market has increased its significance for the realisation of the right. This was evident for instance between 2007 and 2008 when the upward fluctuation of the price of food on the international food market triggered a global food crisis noticeably affecting the realisation of the right to food.

Chapter three analysed the functioning of the international food market and identified its main failures. In addition, the chapter provided the categories of countries and individuals that are particularly vulnerable to the instability of the international food market. The market failures taken into account are volatility of food prices, negative incentives on domestic food production and concentration of market power. From this chapter emerged the picture of a highly unreliable international food market which can influence vulnerable countries towards the production of food products that do not contribute to their domestic food security. Moreover, the chapter argued that the participation of countries in the global food market is highly unequal and a very few countries export the large majority of the food available. This group of countries dominates the system and can influence the international price of food. Accordingly, the large majority of the international community provides very little contribution to the international food market and most countries participate in it only as importers of food to ensure domestic food security in the absence of adequate local supply. From the analysis of the failures of the global food market Chapter three identified three categories of countries that are particularly vulnerable. These are developing countries, net-food importers and agricultural economies. The chapter concluded, clarifying the duty of the international community to ensure that market failures do not affect the realisation of the right to food at domestic level from the perspective of the external action of the EU. In the chapter we maintained that the EU, when negotiating trade agreements with third countries, should pay attention to the role of the international market in the realisation of the right to food. In fact, these treaties provide the legal infrastructure for the international exchange of food products between countries. Influencing the trade policies of the signatory states of international trade agreements can affect the capacity of vulnerable countries to protect their citizens from the vagaries of the international food market. Accordingly, when the EU concludes trade agreements with vulnerable states it should promote their inclusion in the global food market and ensure that the clauses on import and export of food do not hamper their capacity to intervene in food shortages at domestic level.

Chapter four examined the details of the external action of the EU, identifying the legal competences of the EU in the areas of international trade law and the right to food and describing its main policies. The chapter showed that the EU is highly influential in the evolution of international trade law since it has exclusive competence to negotiate and conclude trade agreements on behalf of its 28 Member States. At the same time, the EU has an explicit mandate in its founding treaties to contribute to the realisation of economic and social rights through its external action. This legal mandate has been strengthened through the inclusion of human rights clauses in development cooperation agreements and trade treaties with vulnerable countries. Furthermore, the EU has developed specific policies to prioritise development objectives when concluding trade agreements with vulnerable countries. Through these policies the EU aims to address the main deficiencies of the present system, supporting the development of vulnerable states and the realisation of non-trade objectives such as food security and public health. Notwithstanding this effort, the analysis also showed that EU policymaking on international trade law has maintained a strong connection with the EU business community, which takes part in the design of the policies and the identification of the priorities to be pursued when negotiating trade agreements with third countries.[1] Accordingly, the chapter recognised two distinct visions of the participation of the EU in the creation and modification of international trade law. The first one is rooted in the necessities of EU exporters, and sees international trade law mainly as a support to the economic development of the EU. The second vision sees international trade law as a support to development policies and the promotion of non-trade objectives in vulnerable countries. This second perspective promotes the drafting of trade treaties that support the inclusion of vulnerable states in the global economy and do not expose them to the instability of the international market. The chapter concluded that these two interpretations of the EU role in the evolution of international trade law co-exist in EU policymaking and is not clear which one would prevail over the other in case of conflict. For this reason the relation between recent EU trade treaties and the realisation of the right to food can be assessed only through the analysis of the specific included in these agreements.

Chapter five provided the analysis of the regulation on the import and export of food in the law of the WTO. The chapter clarifies the international obligations that the EU has to respect when concluding trade agreements

[1] See Chapter 4 for an analysis of the institutionalisation of the participation of private companies in EU external action.

with countries vulnerable to food shortages. The chapter also looked at WTO law on the import and export of food from the perspective of the realisation of the right to food. The chapter identified several shortcomings that limit the contribution of WTO law to the realisation of the right. The chapter then gave attention to the part of WTO law (Article XXIV GATT) allowing WTO Members to conclude free trade agreements outside the WTO framework. The chapter noticed that through this article the EU is enabled to conclude free trade agreements with countries that are vulnerable to food shortages and when concluding a trade deal of this sort, WTO law requires the elimination of the large majority of import barriers. This has to be done even when the agreement is concluded between developed countries and countries vulnerable to food shortages and even when the elimination of trade barriers increases the exposure of those vulnerable countries to market instability. In contrast, with regard to other trade instruments relevant for the realisation of the right to food such as safeguards and export restrictions, WTO law leaves wide space of action and the EU is free to negotiate clauses that do not affect the realisation of the right. The chapter concludes that if the EU aims to conciliate international trade law with the realisation of the right to food it has to move in two directions. On the one hand it has to work within the WTO towards the modification of WTO law whenever the existing regulation is an obstacle to the realisation of the right. On the other, it has to avoid increasing the exposure of vulnerable countries to the failures of the global food market when concluding free trade agreements with them under Article XXIV GATT.

III. MAIN FINDINGS OF THE CASE STUDIES

The book includes the case study of seven free trade agreements between the EU and countries vulnerable to food shortages. Chapter six analysed, from the perspective of the human right to food, the trade agreement between the EU and 15 Caribbean countries, one of the most comprehensive trade agreements the EU has concluded so far with vulnerable states. Chapter seven took into account a group of six trade agreements between the EU and countries in Sub-Saharan Africa. From the case studies, it emerged that all the clauses on import and export of food (tariffs, safeguards and export restrictions) reduce the capacity of the developing countries involved to react to food shortages. First, all the agreements, in order to respect the prescriptions of Article XXIV GATT, eliminate at least 80 per cent of tariff protection, exposing vulnerable countries to increasing competition from the EU and limiting their capacity to intervene at the occurrence of import surges of food from the EU. The Food and Agriculture Organization considers import surges to be dangerous for the realisation of the right to food because they disrupt the livelihood of vulnerable farmers already exposed to hunger. To avoid this issue, all the treaties exclude certain sensitive products from the obligation to eliminate import tariffs. Notwithstanding these exceptions, the large majority of EU products will be imported into the Caribbean and African countries duty free. The African agreements include additional limitations on the maximum tariff applicable to sensitive food products imported from the EU. This new regulation promotes EU food exports in vulnerable countries even when this exposes vulnerable groups to food insecurity. The treaties are also likely to affect public revenues of developing countries, hampering their capacity to organise policies to realise the right to food. Overall, the analysis of the clauses on tariffs demonstrated the necessity of revising Article XXIV GATT to allow differential treatment when vulnerable countries are involved in trade agreements with the EU. Certain aspects of the regulation of tariffs, however, show that the negotiators also pursued the objective of imposing limits on developing countries beyond what is required by WTO law. For instance, this is the case in respect of the inclusion of a maximum tariff for sensitive products imported into African countries, which is lower than what is required by WTO law.

Second, the assessment of the clauses on import safeguards showed that during negotiations very little effort was made to provide Caribbean and African countries with an efficient mechanism of protection against the occurrence of import surges of food from the EU. In particular, the treaties do not include a special safeguard system like that of the WTO Agreement on Agriculture, which would have allowed automatic protection of domestic markets in adverse market conditions. The safeguards provided are slow to implement, are supervised by a supranational authority and contain almost no differential treatment between the EU and vulnerable countries. In addition, in the African agreements there is no reference to the possibility of using safeguards to protect food security. The safeguards contained in the Caribbean agreement contain a reference to food security which, even if relevant in terms of interpretation of the treaty, looks rhetorical, since it does not make the safeguards easier to implement. The similarities between the regulation of safeguards of all the seven treaties taken into account in Chapters six and seven show that little efforts were made to tailor the food safeguards to the specific needs of each vulnerable country.

Finally, the regulation of export restrictions in all the agreements limits considerably the capacity of developing countries to use them to intervene in the quantity of food exported abroad at the occurrence of food shortages. This is particularly evident in the Caribbean case and in four of the African treaties, which ban export quotas and most of export taxes. It is particularly regrettable that in these five treaties the negotiators decided not to reproduce the exception in Article XI.2(a) GATT, which in the WTO system allows the use of export quotas to relieve food shortages. Two of the African agreements maintained the exception even though they include a regulation of export taxes considerably more restrictive than WTO. Moreover, the prohibition of export taxes is likely to affect public revenues especially in the African countries which are scarcely industrialised but rich in natural resources. This decision deprives vulnerable countries of an additional source of revenues even if the clauses on tariffs already have an impact on public funding. The deficiencies of the regulation of exports are particularly relevant for the examination of the EU's external action because in this case WTO law explicitly provides that there is no obligation to eliminate export restrictions when concluding a free trade agreement under Article XXIV GATT. This means that at least in this area the EU had a very wide space to develop clauses that were fully supportive of the realisation of the right to food in vulnerable states. The case studies hint at the fact that since exports of industrial products, natural resources and food are regulated by the same Article, the EU might have prioritised the objective of ensuring the supply of raw materials to its EU processing industries. This conclusion seems to be justified by the fact that the EU has a well-developed external policy on raw materials, whereas there is limited policymaking on the relation between export restrictions and food security.

In conclusion, all seven of the treaties taken into account in this book diminish the capacity of developing countries to realise the right to food of their citizens. In doing so the treaties increase the gap between international trade law and the realisation of the right to food, creating new challenges for the realisation of the right that are not present in the WTO system. This outcome was influenced by Article XXIV GATT only with regard to tariffs, since WTO law would have allowed the EU and its partners to design a regulation of safeguards and export restrictions more protective of the right to food.

IV. AN EU TRADE POLICY FOR GLOBAL FOOD SECURITY

The book has highlighted the shortcomings of the external trade policy of the EU which is shaping international trade law in a way that does not take into account the realisation of the right to food in vulnerable countries. Recent trade agreements between the EU and developing countries also demonstrate the incapacity of EU organs to implement the mandate received in Article 21 of the Lisbon Treaty to include the realisation of economic and social rights in any area of EU external policymaking. This chapter identifies two directions of reform which could allow the EU to develop a deeper understanding of the interactions between trade law and the right to food and approach international trade negotiations accordingly: defragmenting EU external policies and defragmenting international trade law.

These proposals do not involve any dramatic modifications of EU external policies and can all be implemented within existing EU competences as provided by the Lisbon Treaty. The reforms would simply allow the EU, within its existing prerogatives, to pursue its external commercial policy avoiding the outcome that the finalised version of the treaty includes clauses with the potential to stop vulnerable countries from implementing policies which are needed to realise the right to food on their territory.

A. Defragmenting EU External Policies

As highlighted in Chapter four, the EU rarely uses human rights language in its external policy when dealing with economic and social rights and prefers to use terms with a less clear normative content such as 'food security' and 'sustainable development'. An expression of this attitude is the preparation of Sustainability Impact Assessments (SIA) of free trade agreements which are reports about the consequences of the trade agreement for several social parameters including food security. The SIAs are today the principal attempt to provide an analysis of the trade agreement on the basis of non-commercial interests. The SIAs of some of the treaties analysed in this book had in fact identified some reasons for concern in the drafts, which had been duly highlighted. For instance the SIA of the trade treaty between the EU and the Caribbean noticed that: 'Besides economic and social potential negative impacts, reciprocity might strengthen vulnerability in terms of increased dependency for food security'.[2] The Caribbean SIA also highlights that '[t]he impact of external sources on local and regional agricultural products is to undermine the security of the domestic food supply and nutritional standards in the region.'[3] In a similar vein the SIA of the trade agreement between the EU and West Africa noticed that:

> Among other issues … there are issues of food security associated with maintaining a viable domestic industry in key commodities, such as wheat or rice. An over-reliance on cheap imports from the EU could threaten food security in the long term and ultimately displace the cultivation of domestic crops.[4]

The SIAs, however, did not provide any comprehensive analysis of the interplay between the trade agreements and food security. In fact, the SIAs only mention examples of certain key food products that are particularly crucial for certain countries and do not include a comprehensive analysis of the potential impact of the agreements on import surges of food from the EU.

[2] PricewaterhouseCoopers, 'Sustainability Impact Assessment (SIA) of the EU-ACP Economic Partnership Agreements Regional SIA: Caribbean ACP Countries', 30 January 2004 available at <http://trade.ec.europa.eu/doclib/docs/2005/january/tradoc_121202.pdf>, p 11.

[3] Ibid, 34.

[4] PricewaterhouseCoopers, 'Sustainability Impact Assessment (SIA) of the EU-ACP Economic Partnership Agreements Regional SIA: West African ACP Countries', 30 January 2004 available at <http://trade.ec.europa.eu/doclib/docs/2005/january/tradoc_121200.pdf>, p 77.

Moreover, the SIAs do not consider that some food products have a role in the domestic food security of vulnerable countries and should not be regarded only as potential exports to the EU. In fact, only the EU–Caribbean SIA notices that it is a priority to recognise '[r]ice as a major food staple and for the issue of food security, rather than as a potential opportunity for exports to the EU.'[5] Notably, the SIAs approach food security issues without providing any analysis of how concerns for food security could translate into specific legal clauses in free trade agreements. This makes the report, which is already non-binding, even less influential on the negotiation process.[6]

A way to improve the present system, allowing negotiators to be more aware of the consequences of their activity on the realisation of the right to food, would be to substitute the SIAs with a legal review of free trade agreements on the basis of food security issues. The legal review would make specific legal proposals on how clauses on specific trade instruments (eg safeguards and export restrictions) should be drafted to take food security into account during trade negotiations. The review could be based on the normative content of the human right to food or on different qualitative frameworks and would flag specific trade clauses having the potential to affect food security in vulnerable states. In particular, the detailed legal review would have the objective of identifying any area of legislation making it more difficult for the state concerned to adapt its regulatory framework to the requirements of human rights, or to set up the institutional mechanisms that ensure domestic food security. The United Nation Human Rights Council has provided some suggestions on how such impact assessment could be performed.[7] In addition, the EU could rely on the expertise of

[5] EU–Caribbean SIA, p 77.

[6] Even though the European Parliament ratified the agreements it then published a resolution urging the Commission to be careful with its implementation because of the development disparity between the EU and the countries involved and the possible impact on ACP states. See European Parliament resolution of 5 February 2009 on the development impact of Economic Partnership Agreements (EPAs) (2008/2170(INI)). See also the Annual Reports of the EU Raw Materials Initiative. Even though the Reports concentrate on the necessity of ensuring supply of raw materials to the EU, the 2009 Report contains an extensive part on the need to conciliate the raw materials initiative with other priorities such as the sustainable development of African countries. Although this section of the Report maintains that 'situations may arise where export restrictions are important to support, for example, development objectives, protection of the environment or the sustainable exploitation of natural resources', it does not review the clauses on export restrictions of the trade agreements between the EU and Africa. In other words, the main policy assessment of the Raw Materials Initiative performed at EU level accepted the idea that a complete elimination of export restrictions might be detrimental to other interests but did not attempt any critical analysis of the clauses on export restrictions of the agreements with developing countries.

[7] United Nations Human Rights Council, 'Guiding principles on human rights assessment of trade and investment agreements', A/HRC/19/59/Add.5.

specialised agencies such as the Food and Agriculture Organization, which developed indicators to identify when countries are progressing towards domestic food security.[8]

Chapter four also showed that the EU Commission has the institutional capacity to develop a comprehensive understanding of the interactions between international trade law and non-trade objectives such as food security. The chapter also presented the Policy Coherence for Development, an internal policy of the EU Commission which has the explicit objective of making the external trade action of the EU in line with its development policy. The Communications describing the policy go as far as making a list of the reforms that the international trade system would need to support the development and improvement of living conditions in vulnerable countries. The case studies demonstrated that this policy in the end does not have any impact on the clauses regulating the trade of food products which do not take into account the needs of vulnerable states even in extreme cases, like those on export restrictions, where the new treaties directly affect the capacity of these countries to react to domestic food crisis.

The results of the case studies point at the fact that within the EU Commission there are not adequate administrative mechanisms allowing food security to be taken into account in the design of trade policy. In fact, the separation of competences between the EU Directorate General for Trade and the EU Directorate General for Development Cooperation has the consequence that the EU external commercial policy remains largely a separate policy, pursuing purely economic objectives. In fact, even if the free trade agreements mention human rights and development as main objectives, the substance of the treaties take them into account to a very limited extent. This is so even when, as in the case of safeguards and export restrictions, WTO law would have allowed the inclusion of trade clauses more attentive to food security and development concerns.

The legal review of trade agreements proposed in the previous section would provide a solution also to this administrative issue. In fact, through such food security assessment, the Policy Coherence for Development initiative could become part of the procedure for negotiating and concluding international trade agreements. The food security assessment would also provide an institutional framework within which trade specialists, food security specialists and development specialists could meet within the EU Commission in order to provide an external trade policy which is coherent with all the objectives included in the EU founding treaties.

8 A complete and regularly updated list of the FAO food security indicators is available on the FAO official website <http://www.fao.org/economic/ess/ess-fs/ess-fadata/en/#.Uyl2Ra1dWEI>.

More generally, the EU Commission could create additional internal programmes and administrative bodies where specialists of EU law and policy can develop expertise on both trade and food security. The fact that the core of trade treaties was not influenced by food security concerns might also be the consequence of the fact that there are very few specialists of both subjects, and the trade negotiators might be unaware of the interactions between trade policy and food security. To solve this issue the Commission could favour interdisciplinary research between trade and human rights through the budget lines it has available so as to train staff who are able to identify areas of trade policy that are problematic in terms of food security and human rights. The internal selection processes could also require the staff applying for a position of trade specialist to have at least a general understanding of international human rights law and food security and of the existing literature on the interactions between the two areas of policymaking.

B. Defragmenting International Trade Law

The book has showed that the WTO imposes numerous obligations when the EU is negotiating a trade agreement. Some of them limit the capacity of the EU to include food security concerns when concluding a free trade agreement with a vulnerable country. This is the case for instance regarding the rules that article XXIV GATT imposes with regard to the elimination of tariff barriers even when the trade agreement is concluded between a major trade power and a vulnerable state. This book has also showed that the EU has a 'double hat', in the sense of being subject to WTO law when concluding a free trade agreement but being also one of the driving forces of the evolution of WTO law. This means that whenever the practice of negotiating a trade agreement with a vulnerable country highlights that some human rights concerns cannot be taken into account because of WTO obligations, the EU is in a privileged position to solve the issue through its action within multilateral trade negotiations. This section provides three proposals that the EU could adopt to improve the situation and allow human rights concerns to filter into WTO legislation.

First, the EU could present a proposal for the reform of Article XXIV GATT taking into consideration that additional flexibility should be allowed when the free trade agreement involves a country vulnerable to food insecurity. A blueprint for the reform already exists in WTO law, since Article V of the General Agreement of Trade in Services provides for specific exceptions when developing countries are involved in a free trade agreement. The reform should consider that the elimination of tariffs can cause import surges of key products and the exposure of local populations to food insecurity when local farmers are displaced. The Sustainability Impact

Assessments the EU Commission requested before the conclusion of the free trade agreements with developing countries have already provided some tentative ideas on how Article XXIV GATT could be reformed to include food security concerns.

Second, the EU could use multilateral negotiations such as the Doha Round to promote the objectives identified in its Policy Coherence for Development initiative. These include the inclusion of special clauses allowing a more flexible approach to regulation when WTO obligations are applied to a country vulnerable to food shortages. The EU could also propose innovative legal instruments to prevent WTO obligations from impacting the capacity of vulnerable states to react to food shortages and to implement policies to realise the right to food. For instance the EU could work on a reform of WTO special safeguards for agricultural products, solving the problems existing in the present system.[9]

Finally, the EU could develop policies to bridge the distance between international trade institutions and human rights and food security agencies. In the present system the WTO and regional trade agreements have grown apart from the United Nations human rights framework and there are limited institutional mechanisms for dialogue between the two systems. As this book has shown, this separation between trade and food security institutions can work to the detriment of food security whenever a trade clause interferes with human rights or food security policies of vulnerable countries. This is particularly so since international trade treaties are justiciable whereas international human rights law relies on soft enforcement mechanisms. The EU being influential in the WTO, the United Nations and the Food and Agriculture Organization could propose innovative solutions to connect these institutions. This action would favour the institutional debate on the interactions between trade and the right to food and improve the awareness on these issues among international specialists. There are different strategies by which this objective could be achieved, implying different degrees of involvement of the EU. The EU could start with considering international trade negotiations in the context of the interactions that trade law has with other policy areas such as human rights, food policy or development cooperation. The EU Commission has already developed strategies to include non-trade issues in trade negotiations when certain Member States insist on doing so. This is for instance the case regarding *agricultural multifunctionality*,[10] a concept developed by EU institutions to

[9] See Chapter 5 of this book.

[10] H-U Gossl, 'EU trade policy and non-trade issues: the case of agricultural multifunctionality' (2008) 13 *European Foreign Affairs Review* 211; F Smith, 'Multifunctionality and "non-trade concerns" in the agriculture negotiations' (2000) 3 *Journal of International Economic Law* 707.

imply during trade negotiations that WTO rules on agriculture concern not only trade policy but also other aspects such as sustainable land management and environmental protection. The EU could use similar strategies to make the point that international trade rules have an impact on food availability and accessibility and that these issues should be considered during trade negotiations.

The EU could also be more proactive and start working on structural reforms of international institutions which would permanently bridge the gap between international trade law and food security. For instance, as the EU develops a procedure to perform a legal review of international trade treaties based on food security it could also propose to include similar assessments at the multilateral level. A possible approach could be to require the FAO to provide an opinion on the food security impact of trade agreements before their conclusion.

V. THE EU, THE RIGHT TO FOOD AND DEVELOPING COUNTRIES

The seven trade agreements taken into account in this book pose profound questions about the relation between the EU and countries vulnerable to hunger and malnutrition. First, the fact that the Caribbean and African free trade agreements went through the entire process of negotiation and adoption at EU level—which involves the European Commission, the Council and the European Parliament—without their deficiencies with regard to the realisation of the right to food being identified, emphasises that the EU might lack the institutional 'antibodies' to prevent its external action from creating food security issues in vulnerable countries. Accordingly, it is necessary to improve the EU mechanisms of review of free trade agreements to ensure that those agreements are examined on the basis of their effects on food security before their conclusion. In particular, the treaties demonstrate the failure of the Policy Coherence for Development initiative of the EU Commission which should have ensured the reconciliation between the EU external trade objectives and development goals. In fact, the treaties demonstrate that in EU external policymaking, commercial objectives and the support of EU export business are dominant and that the realisation of the right to food and food security is in a marginal position.

To avoid such an outcome in the future the EU should utilise the entire policy space left by the WTO to design trade clauses that do not diminish the capacity of vulnerable countries to react to food shortages. This space is particularly wide in the case of safeguards and export restrictions, which WTO law allows parties to maintain when concluding a free trade agreement under Article XXIV GATT. In particular, the EU should develop an advanced system of automatic safeguards based on that of the WTO Agreement on Agriculture but without the issues that made it ineffective. A draft of the new special safeguard could be based on some of the proposals already circulated in the Doha Round.[11] With regard to export restrictions, the fact that the EU external action on raw materials is overachieving with a group of small developing countries suggests that EU policymaking should concentrate more on the limits that trade clauses should have when treaties are concluded with vulnerable states. In particular, the EU would need a policy on export restrictions on food that is detached from the EU raw materials initiative and which is fully dedicated to the solution of the problems that export restrictions cause during global food crises. In the same vein, the EU should negotiate clauses on restrictions on exports of food separately from the clauses on raw materials. In particular, the regulation of export restrictions included in the free trade agreements should not hamper the capacity of vulnerable countries to use them as emergency mechanisms or as a source of revenue.

In addition, whenever the WTO is not sufficiently flexible and obliges the EU to include clauses in trade agreements that are potentially harmful for the realisation of the right to food, the EU should favour their modification in the WTO. This is particularly so with regard to Article XXIV GATT, which obliges states to eliminate the large majority of trade barriers even when a developed country concludes a trade agreement with vulnerable states. This clause could be easily modified, since the clause that regulates free trade agreements on services already provides for the possibility of concluding non-reciprocal agreements when this is necessary to protect developing countries. A copy and paste of a few words would allow the EU and other developing countries to conclude free trade agreements while respecting the principle of differential treatment under Article XXXIV: 8 GATT. It is regrettable that notwithstanding the centrality of this principle in the Doha Declaration there is no advanced proposal for the modification of the article. A starting point for the revision of Article XXIV could be the introduction of an exception to the requirement of liberalising 80 per cent of trade for least-developed countries or for the countries included in the FAO list of low-income-food-deficit countries. This would create the legal space to solve some of the most relevant issues of the agreements between the EU and Africa.

In conclusion, the EU and developing countries in their free trade agreements have not duly considered the consequences of such agreements on the right to adequate food of vulnerable states and categories of people.

[11] See Chapter 5 of this book.

Yet, the EU is perfectly placed to revise such agreements to include technical solutions in world trade law fully taking into account food security when concluding free trade agreements. Some such solutions, like the special safeguard mechanism or flexibilities with regard to export restrictions, are already present in WTO law or have been discussed in the Doha Round. The EU has the competences and leverage to take a role of international leadership in the design of such a sustainable world trade law.[12] Will the EU be ambitious enough?

[12] G Gruni, 'Towards a Sustainable World Trade Law? The Common Commercial Policy of the European Union after Opinion 2/15' (2018) 13 *Global Trade and Customs Journal* 4.

Bibliography

Abbott FM, Kaufmann C and Cottier T (eds), *Trade and Human Rights: foundations and conceptual issues* (Michigan University Press, 2006).

Abbott R, 'Are developing countries deterred from using the WTO dispute settlement system?' ECIPE Working Paper 01/2007.

Abass A, 'The Cotonou Trade Regime and the WTO' (2004) 10 *European Law Journal* 439.

Adlung R and Molinuevo M, 'Bilateralism in services trade: is there fire behind the (BIT-) smoke?' (2008) 11 *Journal of International Economic Law* 365.

Ahmed B, 'The impact of Globalization on the Caribbean Sugar and Banana Industries' The Society for Caribbean Studies Annual Conference Papers, vol 2 (2001) <http://community-languages.org.uk/SCS-Papers/olv2p1.pdf> accessed 29 March 2011.

Ahmed T and de Jesús Butler I, 'The European Union and Human Rights: An International Law Perspective' (2006) 17 *European Journal of International Law* 771.

Aksoy MA, 'Global Agricultural Trade Policies' in M Ataman Aksoy and John C Beghin (eds), *Global Agricultural Trade and Developing Countries* (World Bank, 2005).

Alston P and Robinson M (eds), *Human Rights and Development* (Oxford University Press, 2005).

Alston P and Tomasevski K (eds), *The Right to Food* (Martinus Nijhoff, 1984).

Arezki R, *Commodity price volatility and inclusive growth in low-income countries* (International Monetary Fund, 2012).

Azmanova A, 'The crisis of Europe: democratic deficit and eroding sovereignty—not guilty' (2013) 24 *Law and Critique* 23.

Babarinde O and Faber G (eds), *The European Union and the Developing Countries: The Cotonou Agreement* (Martinus Nijhoff, 2008).

Bagwell K and Staiger RW, 'An Economic Theory of GATT' (1999) 89 *American Economic Review* 215.

—— *The Economics of the World Trading System* (MIT, 2002).

Baldwin R, 'Resolving the conflict leading to the collapse of the Doha Round', VOX CEPR's Policy Portal, available at <http://voxeu.org/article/how-resolve-doha-stalemate-better-agricultural-safeguard-trigger> accessed 2 January 2016.

Barnard C, 'The External Dimension of Community Social Policy: The Ugly Duckling of External Relation' in N Emiliou and D O'Keefe (eds), *The European Union and World Trade Law* (John Wiley, 1996) 149.

Barral V, 'Sustainable development in international law: nature and operation of an evolutive legal norm' (2012) 23 *European Journal of International Law* 377.

Barrett CB and Maxwell DG, *Food Aid After Fifty Years* (Routledge, 2005).

Barteit S, 'ACP-EU development cooperation at a crossroads? One year after the second revision of the Cotonou Agreement' (2012) 17 *European Foreign Affairs Review* 1.

Bartels L, 'The EU's approach to social standards and the TTIP' in S Khorana (ed), *The Transatlantic Trade and Investment Partnership (TTIP) Negotiations between the EU and the USA* (Barcelona Centre for International Affairs (CIDOB), 2015).

—— 'The Trade and Development Policy of the European Union' in M Cremona (ed), *New Developments in the EU's External Relations Law, Collected Courses of the Academy of European Law* (Oxford University Press, 2008).

—— 'The WTO Enabling Clause' in B Remiche and H Ruiz-Fabri (eds), *Le commerce international entre bi et multilatéralisme* (Larcier, 2010) 249.

—— 'The Trade and Development Policy of the European Union' in M Cremona (ed), *New Developments in the EU's External Relations Law, Collected Courses of the Academy of European Law* (Oxford University Press, 2008) 128.

—— 'A Legal Analysis of Human Rights Clauses in the EU's Euro-Mediterranean Association Agreement' (2004) 9 *Mediterranean Politics* 368.

—— 'Human Rights and Sustainable Development Obligations in EU Free Trade Agreements' University of Cambridge Legal Studies Research Paper Series, Paper No. 24/2012.

—— 'The trade and development policy of the European Union' (2007) 18 *Journal of International Economic Law* 715.

—— 'The WTO enabling clause and positive conditionality in the European Community's GSP programme' (2003) 6 *Journal of International Economic Law* 507.

—— 'The WTO legality of the EU's GSP+ arrangement' (2007) 10 *Journal of International Economic Law* 869.

—— 'Trade and Human Rights' in *Max Planck Encyclopedia of Public International Law* (August 2011 edn) <http://www.mpepil.com/subscriber_article?script=yes&id=/epil/entries/law-9780199231690-e1550&recno=1&searchType=Quick&query=trade+and+human+rights> accessed 17 January 2012.

Bartels L and Haberli C, 'Binding Tariff Preferences for Developing Countries under Article II GATT' (2010) 13 *Journal of International Economic Law* 969.

Bartels L and Ortino F (eds), *Regional trade agreements and the WTO legal system* (Oxford University Press, 2006).

Bartelt S, 'ACP-EU cooperation at a crossroads? One year after the second revision of the Cotonou Agreement' (2012) 17 *European Foreign Affairs Review* 1.

Baunsgaard T and Keen M, *Trade Revenue and (or?) Trade Liberalization*, International Monetary Fund Working Paper WP/05/112 (International Monetary Fund, 2005).

BBC News, 'US, EU and Japan challenge China on rare earths at WTO' available at <http://www.bbc.com.uk/news/business-17348648>.

Berry C, *Globalisation and ideology in Britain Neoliberalism Free Trade and the Global Economy* (Manchester University Press, 2011).

Bhagwati J, 'Free Trade: Old and New Challenges' (1994) 104 *The Economic Journal* 231.

—— *In defense of globalization* (Oxford University Press, 2007).

—— *International trade: selected readings* (MIT Press, 1996).

—— *Termites in the Trading System: How Preferential Agreements Undermine Free Trade* (Oxford University Press, 2008).

Bhagwati J, Greenway D and Panagariya A, 'Trading Preferentially: Theory and Policy' (1998) 108 *Economic Journal* 1128.

Bilal S, Dalleau M and Lui D, *Trade Liberalisation and Fiscal Adjustments: The Case of EPAs in Africa*, European Centre for Development Policy Management Discussion Paper No. 137.

Blake C, 'Moral damages in investment arbitration: a role for human rights?' (2012) 3 *Journal of International Dispute Settlement* 371.

Blyberg A, 'The case of mislaid allocation: economic and social rights and budget work' (2009) 11 *International Journal on Human Rights* 123.

Bounds A, 'African states refuse to join EU trade deal' (*Financial Times*, 4 December 2007) available at: <http://www.ft.com/cms/s/0/c757bcf2-a1f2-11dc-a13b-0000779fd2ac.html#axzz2Y4HpPV1W> accessed 14 June 2013.

Bonarriva J, Koscielski M and Wilson E, *Export controls: an overview of their use, economic effects and treatment in the global trading system*, US International Trade Commission, Office of Industries Working Paper No. ID-23, available at <http://www.usitc.gov/publications/332/working_papers/ID-23.pdf> accessed 9 January 2012.

Borchert I, 'Trade diversion under Selective Preferential Market Access' (2009) 42 *Canadian Journal of Economics* 1390.

Bouet A and Laborde D, 'Assessing the potential cost of a failed Doha Round' (2010) 9 *World Trade Review* 319.

Brandtner B and Rosas A, 'Human Rights and External Relations of the European Community: An Analysis of Doctrine and Practice' (1998) 9 *European Journal of International Law* 468.

Bretherton C and Vogler J, *The European Union as a Global Actor* (Routledge, 1999).

Brown ME, *Food security, food prices and climate variability* (Routledge, 2014).

Capps P, *Human Dignity and the Foundations of International Law* (Hart Publishing, 2009).

Cardwell PJ, 'EuroMed, European neighbourhood policy and the Union for the Mediterranean: overlapping frames in the EU's governance of the Mediterranean' (2011) 49 *Journal of Common Market Studies* 219.

Ceballos F, Hernandez MA, Minot M and Robles M, 'Transmission of food price volatility from international to domestic markets: evidence from Africa, Latin America, and South Asia' in M Kalkuhl, J von Braun and M Torero (eds), *Food price volatility and its implications for food security and policy* (Springer, 2016).

Chang H-J, *23 Things they don't tell you about capitalism* (Penguin Books, 2010).

—— *Bad Samaritans* (Bloomsbury Press, 2008).

—— *Kicking away the ladder* (Anthem Press, 2003).

Chavas JP, Hummels D and Wright B, *The economics of food price volatility* (The University of Chicago Press, 2014).

Cheng F, 'Tariff Escalation in world Agricultural Trade' in P Pinstrup-Andersen and F Cheng (eds), *Case studies in food policy for developing countries—Volume III Institutions and International Trade Policies* (Cornell University Press, 2009).

Ching LL, Edwards S and Scialabba N, *Climate Change and Food Systems Resilience in Sub-Saharan Africa* (Food & Agriculture Organization, 2011).

Clapham A, *Human Rights Obligations of Non-State Actors* (Oxford University Press, 2010) 162.

Collier P, *The Bottom Billion* (Oxford University Press, 2008).

Coomans F, 'The extraterritorial scope of the International Covenant on Economic, Social and Cultural Rights in the work of the United Nations Committee on Economic, Social and Cultural Rights' (2011) 11 *Human Rights Law Review* 1.

Corden WM, *Trade Policy and Economic Welfare* (Oxford University Press, 1997).

Cottier T, Pauwelyn J and Burgi Bonanomi E (eds), *Human rights and international trade* (Oxford University Press, 2005).

Cremona M, 'A Policy of Bits and Pieces? The Common Commercial Policy After Nice' (2001) 4 *Cambridge Yearbook of European Legal Studies* 61.

—— 'Balancing Union and Member State interests: Opinion 1/2008, choice of legal base and the common commercial policy under the Treaty of Lisbon,' (2010) 35 *European Law Review* 678.

—— 'The Completion of the Internal Market and the Incomplete Commercial Policy of the European Community' (1990) 15 *European Law Review* 283.

—— 'EC External Commercial Policy after Amsterdam: Authority and Interpretation within Interconnected Legal Orders' in JHH Weiler (ed), *Towards a Common Law of International Trade?: The EU, the WTO and the NAFTA* (Oxford University Press, 2000).

—— 'Economic and Social Rights in EU External Policy' in Francesco Bestagno (ed), *I diritti economici sociali e culturali* (Vita e Pensiero, 2009).

—— 'External Relations of the EU and the Member States: Competence, Mixed Agreements, International Responsibility, and Effects of International Law' EUI Working Paper LAW No. 2006/22.

—— 'Human Rights and democracy clauses in the EC's trade agreements' (1995) *Law & Justice* 105.

Curtis M, *The New Resource Grab: How EU Trade Policy on Raw Materials is Undermining Development* (Oxfam Germany, Traidcraft Exchange, WEED, AITEC and Comhlámh, 2010).

Daly M and Kuwahara H, 'The impact of the Uruguay Round on Tariff and non-Tariff Barriers to Trade in the Quad' (1998) 21 *The World Economy* 207.

Davidson C and Matusz SJ, 'Trade liberalization and compensation' (2006) 47 *International Economic Review* 723.

Davidson C, Matusz S and Douglas RN, 'Can Compensation Save Free Trade?' (2006) 71 *Journal of International Economics* 167.

Davies A, 'One step forward, two steps back? The *Viking* and *Laval* cases in the ECJ' (2008) 37 *Industrial Law Journal* 126.

Davitti D, 'On the meanings of international investment law and international human rights law: the alternative narrative of due diligence' (2012) 12 *Human Rights Law Review* 421.

de Beco G, 'The interplay between human rights and development the other way round: the emerging use of quantitative tools for measuring the progressive realisation of economic, social and cultural rights' (2010) 4 *Human Rights and International Legal Discourse* 265.

de Schutter O, 'International Trade in Agriculture and the Right to Food', Dialogue on Globalisation, Occasional Papers Geneva No. 46/November 2009 (Frederich Ebert Stiftung, 2009).

—— *Trade in the service of sustainable development linking trade to labour rights and environmental standards* (Hart, 2017).

—— (ed), *Transnational Corporations and Human Rights* (Hart, 2006).
—— 'Mission to the WTO', Human Rights Council, A/HRC/10/5/Add.2.
—— 'The World Trade Organization and the Post-Global Food Crisis Agenda', Activity Report, November 2011, p. 11, available at <http://www.wto.org/english/news_e/news11_e/deschutter_2011_e.pdf> accessed 2 January 2012.
—— *Food Commodities Speculation Food Price Crises*, United Nations Special Rapporteur on the Right to Food Briefing Note 02, available at <http://www.srfood.org/images/stories/pdf/otherdocuments/20102309_briefing_note_02_en_ok.pdf> accessed 19 February 2012.
—— *International Trade in Agriculture and the Right to Food* (Friedrich Ebert Stiftung, 2009).
—— *The role of development cooperation and food aid in realizing the right to adequate food: moving from charity to obligation*, Report of the Special Rapporteur on the Right to Food to the Human Rights Council (11 February 2009) A/HRC/10/5.
Deep Ford JR, dell'Aquila C and Conforti P, *Agricultural trade policy and food security in the Caribbean* (FAO, 2007).
Dixit A and Norman V, 'Gains from trade without lump-sum compensation' (1986) 21 *Journal of International Economics* 111.
Doyle C, 'Millennium development goals and human rights: in common cause or uneasy partners?' (2009) 13 *International Journal of Human Rights* 5.
Drahos P, 'Four lessons for developing countries from the trade negotiations over access to medicines' (2007) 28 *Liverpool Law Review* 1.
Draper P, 'EU-Africa Trade Relations: The Political Economy of Economic Partnership Agreements', Jan Tumplir Policy Essay 02/2007, European Centre for International Political Economy.
Droege S et al, 'The trade system and climate action: ways forward under the Paris Agreement' Climate Strategies Working Paper, October 2016.
Easterly W, *The white Man's Burden: Why the West's Efforts to Aid the Rest Have Done So Much Ill and So Little Good* (Penguin, 2007).
Easterly W and Pfutze T, 'Where does the money go? Best and worst practices in foreign aid' (2008) 22 *Journal of Economic Perspectives* 29.
Eeckout P, *EU External Relations Law* (Oxford University Press, 2011).
Eide A, 'Human rights requirements to social and economic development: The case of the right to food and nutrition rights' in Uwe Kracht and Manfred Schulz (eds), *Food security and nutrition* (St. Martin Press, 1999).
—— 'The Importance of Economic and Social Rights in the Age of Globalization' in Wenche Barth Elde and Uwe Kracht (eds), *Food and Human Rights in Development* (Intersentia, 2005).
—— 'The right to adequate food and to be free from hunger', United Nations Economic and Social Council.
—— 'The Right to Adequate Standard of Living Including the Right to Food' in *Economic, Social and Cultural Rights—A textbook* (Martinus Nijhoff, 2001).
Elsig M, 'The EU's Choice of Regulatory Venues for Trade Negotiations: A Tale of Agency Power?' (2007) 45 *Journal of Common Market Studies* 927.
European Parliament, Directorate-General for External Policies, *Human rights mainstreaming in EU external relations*. Available at <http://www.eiuc.org/tl_files/EIUC%20MEDIA/Docs/EST28775.pdf> accessed 11 July 2013.

European Report on Development 2009, *Overcoming fragility in Africa—Forging a New European Approach*. Robert Schuman Centre for Advanced Studies, European University Institute, 2009.

Fanzo J, 'The Nutrition Challenge in Sub-Saharan Africa', Working Paper 2012-012, January 2012, United Nations Development Programme.

FAO, 'Global hunger declining but still unacceptably high', available at <http://www.fao.org/docrep/012/al390e/al390e00.pdf> accessed 13 December 2011.

—— 'Towards improving the operational effectiveness of the Marrakesh Decision on Measures Concerning the Possible Negative Effects of the Reform Programme on Least-Developed and Net Food-Importing Developing Countries', available at <http://www.fao.org/DOCREP/005/Y3733E/y3733e09.htm> accessed 24 January 2012.

—— *Agricultural import surges in developing countries* (FAO, 2011). For the relationship between import surges and trade instruments see chapter 5.

—— *Agricultural Import Surges in Developing Countries*, available at <http://www.fao.org/docrep/014/i1952e/i1952e.pdf> accessed 19 February 2012.

—— *Food Export Restriction: Reviews of the 2007–2010 Experience and Consideration for Disciplining Restrictive Measures*, FAO Commodity and Trade Policy Research Working Paper No. 32, available at <http://ictsd.org/downloads/2011/05/sharma-export-restrictions.pdf> accessed 19 February 2012.

—— *Food security and agricultural development in sub-Saharan Africa* (FAO 2006).

—— *Voluntary guidelines to support the realisation of the right to adequate food in the context of national food security* (FAO, 2005).

—— *Institutional requirements for the implementation of Special Safeguard Mechanism*, FAO Brief on Import Surges No. 5, available at <ftp://ftp.fao.org/docrep/fao/009/ah490e/ah490e00.pdf> accessed 8 January 2011.

—— Regional Office for Africa, *Programme Review 2011* (FAO, 2011).

—— *FAO Statistical Yearbook 2012, Africa Food and agriculture* (FAO, 2012).

—— *Resilient livelihoods. Disaster risk reduction for food and nutrition security* (2011) available at <http://www.fao.org/docrep/015/i2540e/i2540e00.pdf> accessed 19 February 2012.

—— *Responding to the food crisis: synthesis of medium-term measures proposed in inter-agency assessment* (FAO, 2009).

—— *The Breakdown of the Doha Round Negotiations. What Does it Mean for Dealing with Soaring Food Prices?*, FAO Economic and Social Perspective, Policy Brief No. 3, August 2008, available at <ftp://ftp.fao.org/docrep/fao/011/aj221e/aj221e.pdf> accessed 9 January 2012.

—— *The state of food insecurity in the world 2003* (FAO, 2003).

—— *The state of food insecurity in the World 2011* (FAO, 2011).

—— *The State of food insecurity in the world 2013* (FAO, 2013).

—— *The State of Agricultural Commodity Markets* (FAO, 2009), p 9, available at <ftp://ftp.fao.org/docrep/fao/012/i0854e/i0854e01.pdf> accessed 19 February 2012.

—— Trade Policy Technical Notes on issues related to the WTO negotiations on Agriculture, *A special safeguard mechanism for developing* countries, Technical Note No. 9, available at <ftp://ftp.fao.org/docrep/fao/008/j5425e/j5425e00.pdf> accessed 8 January 2012.

—— *Trade reforms and food security: conceptualizing the linkages* (FAO, 2003).
—— *United Republic of Tanzania: Rice Maize and Dairy Products, FAO Briefs on Import Surges* (FAO, 2006).
—— *Voluntary guidelines to support the realisation of the right to adequate food in the context of national food security* (FAO, 2005).
Finger JM, 'A special safeguard mechanism for agricultural imports: what experience with other GATT/WTO safeguards tells us about what might work' (2010) 9 *World Trade Review* 289.
Flint A, *Trade, Poverty and the Environment: The EU, Cotonou and African-Caribbean-Pacific Bloc* (Palgrave Macmillan, 2008).
Follesdal A and Hix S, 'Why there is a democratic deficit in the EU: a response to Majone and Moravcsik' (2006) 44 *Journal of Common Market Studies* 533.
Foltea M, *International Organizations in WTO Dispute Settlement How Much Institutional Sensitivity?* (Cambridge University Press, 2014).
Forman L, 'An elementary consideration of humanity? Linking trade-related intellectual property rights to the human right to health in international law' (2011) 14 *Journal of World Intellectual Property* 155.
Fredman S, "New horizons: incorporating socio-economic rights in a British Bill of Rights" (2010) Public Law 297.
—— *Human Rights Transformed* (Oxford University Press, 2008).
Gehring MW and Cordonnier-Segger M-C, *Sustainable development in world trade law* (Kluwer Law International, 2005).
George C and Kirkpatrick C, 'Trade and development: assessing the impact of trade liberalisation on sustainable development' (2004) 38 *Journal of World Trade* 441.
Geraets D, 'The case of shale gas extraction regulation in light of CETA and TTIP: another example of the frackmentation of international law' (2016) 24 *Environmental Liability* 16.
Gerlach C, 'Famine responses in the world food crisis 1972–1975 and the World Food Conference 1974' (2015) 22 *European Review of History* 929.
Goldin I and van der Mensbrugghe D, 'Assessing agricultural tariffication under the Uruguay Round' in Will Martin and L Alan Winters (eds), *The Uruguay Round and the developing countries* (The World Bank, 1996).
Gossl HU, 'EU trade policy and non-trade issues: the case of agricultural multifunctionality' (2008) 13 *European Foreign Affairs Review* 211.
Grimes WS, '2021: International Trade Ten Years From Now: International trade law: wealth distribution, free trade, and competition law' (2011) 18 *Southwestern Journal of International Law* 65.
Grossman G and Sykes A, 'A Preference for Development: The Law and Economics of GSP' (2005) 4 *World Trade Review* 41.
Gruni G, 'Towards a Sustainable World Trade Law? The Commercial Policy of the European Union after Opinion 2/15' (2018) 13 *Global Trade and Customs Journal* 4.
—— 'Labor Standards in the EU-South Korea Free Trade Agreement' (2017) 5 *Korean Journal of International and Comparative Law* 100.
—— 'Law or Aspiration? The EU Proposal for a Labour Rights Clause in the Transatlantic Trade and Investment Partnership' (2016) 43 *Legal Issues of Economic Integration* 399.

—— 'Going from one extreme to the other: food security and export resrtrictions in the EU-CARIFORUM Economic Partnership Agreement' (2013) 19 *European Law Journal* 864.

Gurkan AA, Balcombe K and Prakash A, 'Food import bills: experiences, factors underpinning changes and policy implications for food security of least developed and net food-importing developing countries', FAO, available at <http://www.fao.org/docrep/006/y5117e/y5117e04.htm> accessed 13 December 2011.

Hadfield A, 'Janus advances? An analysis of EC development policy and the 2005 Cotonou Partnership Agreement' (2007) 12 *European Foreign Affairs Review* 39.

Hall RB and Biersteker TJ (eds), *The Emergence of Private Authority in Global Governance* (Cambridge University Press, 2002).

Hallaert JJ, *Special Agriculture Safeguards: Virtual Benefits and Real Costs-Lessons for the Doha Round* (International Monetary Fund, 2005).

Harrison J, 'Incentives for development: the EC's generalized system of preferences, India's WTO challenge and reform' (2005) 42 *Common Market Law Review* 1663.

Harvey C and Rooney E, 'Integrating human rights? Socio-economic rights and budget analysis' (2010) 3 *European Human Rights Law Review* 266.

Harvey D, *A Brief History of Neoliberalism* (Oxford University Press, 2007).

Hathaway DE and Ingco MD, 'Agricultural liberalization and the Uruguay Round' in *The Uruguay Round and the developing countries* (The World Bank, 1996).

Hepburn J, 'Evaluating agriculture in the Nairobi package', ICTSD Bridges Africa, available at <https://www.ictsd.org/bridges-news/bridges-africa/news/evaluating-agriculture-in-the-nairobi-package> accessed 21 December 2017.

Hepple B, *Labour Laws and Global Trade* (Hart, 2005).

Hillion C and Koutrakos P, *Mixed Agreements Revisited: The EU and its Member States in the World* (Hart, 2010).

Hoda A, *Tariff negotiations and renegotiations under the GATT and the WTO* (Cambridge University Press, 2001).

Hoda A and Gulati A, *WTO Negotiations on Agriculture and Developing Countries* (The Johns Hopkins University Press, 2007).

Hope T, Elizabeth M, *Climate Change and Food Security: Africa and the Caribbean* (Routledge, 2016).

Hornbeck JF, 'CARICOM: Challenges and Opportunities for Caribbean Economic Integration', CRS Report for Congress, available at <http://doczine.com/bigdata/2/1367212967_0be99a5735/crscaricom_challenges_e.pdf> accessed 12 February 2014.

Horng D-C, 'The human rights clause in the European Union's external trade and development agreements' (2003) 9 *European Law Journal* 677.

Huda FA, 'Process of global shocks transmission to domestic food price level: case of Bangladesh' (2014) 2 *International Journal of Food and Agricultural Economics* 97.

ILO, *Investing in food security as a driver to better jobs*, available at <http://www.ilo.org/global/publications/books/WCMS_170026/lang--en/index.htm> accessed 14 December 2011.

Ingco MD, 'Agricultural Trade Liberalization in the Uruguay Round. One Step Forward, One Step Back?', World Bank, Policy Research Working Paper 1500, August 1995.

—— 'Tariffication in the Uruguay Round: How Much Liberalisation?' (1996) 19 *The World Economy* 425.

International Assessment of Agricultural Knowledge, Science and Technology for Development, *Agriculture at the Crossroads* (IAASTD, 2009).

International Commission of Jurists, 'Courts and the legal enforcement of economic, social and cultural rights: comparative experiences of justiciability', Human Rights and Rule of Law Series No. 2, available at <http://www.refworld.org/docid/4a7840562.html>.

International Food & Agricultural Trade Policy Council, 'Economic Partnership Agreements and African Regional Integration: *Have negotiations helped or hindered regional integration?*', Issue Brief August 2011.

Irwin DA, *Free Trade Under Fire* (Princeton University Press, 2009).

Ismail F, 'An assessment of the WTO Doha Round July–December 2008 collapse' (2009) 8 *World Trade Review* 579.

Jackson JH, 'Global economics and international economic law' (1998) 1 *Journal of International Economic Law* 1.

Janeway W, 'The Retreat from Hyper-Globalization', Institute for New Economic Thinking, 1 December 2016, available at <https://www.ineteconomics.org/perspectives/blog/the-retreat-from-hyper-globalization> accessed 27 December 2017.

Jansen M and Lee E, *Trade and Employment* (Secretariat of the World Trade Organization and International Labour Office, 2007).

Jarvis LS, 'The rise and decline of rent-seeking activity in the Brazilian coffee sector: Lessons from the imposition and removal of coffee export quotas' (2005) 33 *World Development* 1881.

Jessem A and Rodriguez E, 'The Caribbean Community: Facing the Challenges of Regional and Global Integration', ITD Occasional Paper 2, available at <http://books.google.be/books?id=W8XcZ_51wbAC&pg=PA42&lpg=PA42&dq=caricom+external+relations&source=bl&ots=ynKEjqVFd3&sig=YmQ_h10ZAW3QIxX8VelyvcyGNaY&hl=en&sa=X&ei=Pn_7UtXoOc2qhQeN3YH4Cg&ved=0CD4Q6AEwBA#v=onepage&q=caricom%20external%20relations&f=false> accessed 12 February 2012.

Jones E, *Negotiating Against the Odds: A Guide for Trade Negotiators from Developing Countries* (Palgrave Macmillan 2013).

Jones E, *Manoeuvring at the Margins: Constraints Faced by Small States in International Trade Negotiations* (Commonwealth Secretariat 2010).

Joseph S, *Blame it on the WTO? A human rights critique* (OUP 2011) 200.

Karapinar B, 'Export Restrictions and the WTO Law: "Regulatory Deficiency" or "Unintended Policy Space"' in *World Trade Report* (World Trade Organization, 2010).

Kemp MC and Wan HY, 'Gains from trade with and without lump-sum compensation' (1986) 21 *Journal of International Economics* 99.

Kim J, *Recent Trends in Export Restricitons*, OECD Trade Policy Working Papers, available at <http://www.oecd-ilibrary.org/docserver/download/fulltext/5kmbjx63sl27.pdf?expires=1326112273&id=id&accname=guest&checksum=1950BFC3DD46E666F4CD102AF1AB6848> accessed 9 January 2012.

King J, 'The Justiciability of Resource Allocation' (2007) 2 *Modern Law Review* 197.

—— *Judging Social Rights* (Cambridge University Press. 2012).

Kingah S, 'The revised Cotonou Agreement between the European Community and African, Caribbean and Pacific States: innovations on security, political dialogue, transparency and social responsibility' (2006) 50 *Journal of African Law* 59.

Kirby M, 'Intellectual property law, human rights and the HIV/AIDS pandemic—the urgent need for a Luther of jurisprudence' (2011) 42 *International Review of Intellectual Property and Competition* Law 251.

Kleimann D, 'Taking stock: EU Common Commercial Policy in the Lisbon Era', Centre for European Policy Studies Working Document No. 345, April 2011.

Koizumi T, *Biofuels and food security* (Springer, 2014).

Koutrakos P, *EU International Relations* Law (Hart, 2006).

Kretzmer D and Klein E (eds), *The concept of human dignity in the human rights discourse* (Kluwer Law International, 2002).

Krugman P and Venables AJ, 'Globalization and the Inequality of Nations' (1995) 110 *The Quarterly Journal of Economics* 857.

Kuijper PJ, 'Conflicting rules and clashing courts: the case of environmental agreements, free trade agreements and the WTO', International Centre for Trade and Sustainable Development, Issue Paper No. 10.

Kunnemann R, 'Violations of the Right to Food' in T van Boven, C Flinterman and I Westendorp (eds), *The Maastricht Guidelines on Violations of Economic, Social and cultural Rights*, Netherlands Institute for Human Rights (1998) *SIM Special* 20.

Lal R, *Climate Change and global food security* (Taylor and Francis, 2005).

Lang A, *World trade law after neoliberalism. Reimagining the Global Economic Order* (Oxford University Press, 2011).

Lang R, 'Renegotiating GATT Article XXIV—a priority for African countries engaged in North-South trade agreements', United Nations Economic Commission for Africa African Trade Policy Centre, Work in Progress No. 33.

Langford M, 'Domestic adjudication on economic social and cultural rights: a socio-legal review' (2009) 11 *International Journal on Human Rights* 91.

—— 'The justiciability of social rights: from practice to theory' in M Langford (ed), *Social rights jurisprudence: emerging trends in international and comparative law* (Cambridge University Press, 2009).

—— (ed), *Social rights jurisprudence* (Cambridge University Press, 2009).

Lapper R, 'A bitter harvest: the Caribbean faces the prospect of a life without sugar', *Financial Times* (15 August 2005) <http://www.ft.com/cms/s/0/97801242-0d28-11da-ba02-00000e2511c8.html#axzz1G1M0B0r4> accessed 29 March 2011.

Leal-Arcas R, 'The European Community and mixed agreements' (2001) 6 *European Foreign Affairs Review* 483.

Leckie S, 'Violations of Economic Social and Cultural Rights' (1998) *Sim Special* 20.

Lee HH and Park CY, 'International Transmission of Food Prices and Volatilities: a Panel Analysis' Asian Development Bank Working Paper Series No. 373.

Lindland J, 'The impact of the Uruguay Round on tariff escalation in agricultural products' (1997) 22 *Food Policy* 487.

Lobell D, *Climate change and food security: adapting agriculture to a warmer world* (Springer, 2010).

Lord JE, Suozzi D and Taylor AL, 'Lessons from the experience of UN Convention on the Rights of Persons with Disabilities: addressing the democratic deficit in global health governance' (2010) 38 *Journal of Law, Medicine and Ethics* 564.

Mahony H, 'Mandelson Defends Third-World Free Trade', *Bloomberg Businessweek*, 16 October 2006, available at <http://www.businessweek.com/stories/2006-10-16/mandelson-defends-third-world-free-trade> accessed 15 October 2012.

Mandelson P, 'Free trade is our only way forward', *The Telegraph*, 6 July 2008, available at <http://www.telegraph.co.uk/comment/personal-view/3560228/Free-trade-is-our-only-way-forward.html> accessed 15 October 2012.

Mansoor AM, Vishnu Bassant and Salomon Samen, 'Strengthening Economic Partnership Agreements and the Future of the EU-Africa Trade Relationships in the Next Decade' in *The next decade of EU trade policy: Confronting global challenges?* (Overseas Development Institute, 2012).

Marceau G, 'WTO Dispute Settlement and Human Rights' (2002) 13 *European Journal of International Law* 75.

—— (ed), *A History of Law and Lawyers in the GATT/WTO* (Cambridge University Press 2015).

Marceau G and Wyatt J, 'Dispute settlement regimes intermingled: regional trade agreements and the WTO' (2010) 1 *Journal of International Dispute Settlement* 67.

Matthews A, 'Food Security and WTO Domestic Support Disciplines post-Bali', ICTSD Issue Paper No. 53.

Matsushita M, 'Regionalism and the disciplines of the WTO: analysis of some legal aspects under Article XXIV of the GATT' (2005) 13 *Journal of International Economic Law* 191.

Matsushita M and Lee YS, 'Proliferation of Free Trade Agreements and Some Systemic Issues—In Relation to the WTO Disciplines and Development Perspectives' (2008) 1 *The Law and Development Review* 3.

Matsushita M, Schoenbaum TJ and Mavroidis PC, *The World Trade Organization. Law, Practice, and Policy* (Oxford University Press, 2006).

McCrudden C, 'Human Dignity and Judicial Interpretation of Human Rights' (2008) *European Journal of International Law* 655.

—— 'In pursuit of human dignity: an introduction to current debates', University of Michigan Public Law Research Paper No. 309.

McCrudden C and Davies A, 'A Perspective on Trade and Labor Rights' (2000) 3 *Journal of International Economic Law* 43.

Mechlem K, 'Harmonizing Trade in Agriculture and Human Rights: Options for the Integration of the Right to Food into the Agreement on Agriculture' (2006) 10 *Max Planck UNYB* 127.

—— 'Food security and the right to food in the discourse of the United Nations' (2004) 10 *European Law Journal* 631.

Mersing J, 'How to Phase Out Rich Country Agricultural Subsidies Without Increasing Hunger in the Developing World' in Olivier De Schutter and Kaitlin Y Cordes (eds), *Accounting for Hunger* (Hart, 2012).

Messenger G, *The Development of World Trade Organization Law* (Oxford University Press, 2016).

Messerlin PA, 'The influence of the EU on the World Trade System' in M Daunton, A Narlikar and RM Stern (eds), *The Oxford Handbook on the World Trade Organization* (Oxford University Press, 2012).

Meunier S, *Trading Voices: The European Union in International Commercial Negotiations* (Princeton University Press, 2005).

Meunier S and Nicolaidis K, 'The European Union as a Trade Power' in Christopher Hill and Michael Smith (eds), *The International Relations of the European Union* (Oxford University Press, 2005).

—— 'The European Union as conflicted trade power' (2006) 13 *Journal of European Public Policy* 906.

Michalopoulos C, 'The Role of Special and Differential Treatment for Developing Countries in GATT and the World Trade Organization', Policy Research Working Paper 2388 (World Bank, 2000).

Mildner SA and Lauster G, 'Settling Trade disputes over Natural Resources: Limitations of International Trade Law to Tackle Export Restrictions' (2011) 3 *Gottingen Journal of International Law* 251.

Millennium Project, *Halving Hunger: It Can be Done, Summary Version of the Report of the Task Force on Hunger* (The Earth Institute at Columbia University, 2005) 6.

Milton C and Ochieng O, 'The EU-ACP economic partnership agreements and the "development question": constraints and opportunities imposed by Article XXIV and special and differential treatment provisions of the WTO' (2007) 10 *Journal of International Economic Law* 363.

Moyo D, *Dead Aid* (Farar Straus and Giroux, 2009).

Muller A, 'Limitations to and derogations from economic, social and cultural rights' (2009) 9 *Human Rights Law Review* 557.

Narlikar A, *International Trade and Developing Countries* (Routledge, 2003).

Naylor RL, Liska A, Burke M, Falcon WP, Gaskell J, Rozelle S and Cassman K, 'The Ripple Effect: Biofuels, Food Security and the Environment' (2007) 49 *Environment* 30.

Ng F and Aksoy MA, 'Who Are Net Food Importing Countries?' World Bank Policy Research Working Paper No. 4457.

Newbery DMG and Stiglitz J, 'Pareto Inferior Trade' (1984) 51 *The Review of Economic Studies* 1.

Nogues JJ, 'Comment to "Trade, Growth, and Poverty–A Selective Survey" by Andrew Berg and Anne Krueger, and "Doha and the World Poverty Target" by L. Alan Winters'. Commentary presented at the Annual World Bank Conference on Development Economics, 10–11 May 2002, Brussels.

Nolan A and Dutschke M, 'Article 2(1) ICESCR and state parties' obligations: whither the budget?' (2010) 3 *European Human Rights Law Review* 280.

Nolan A, Porter B and Langford M, 'The justiciability of social and economic rights: an updated appraisal', Center for Human Rights and Global Justice Working Paper No. 15, 2007 available at <http://www.chrgj.org/publications/docs/wp/NolanPorterLangford.pdf>.

Novitz T, 'Legal Power and Normative Sources in the Field of Social Policy: Normative Power Europe at Work?' in Jan Orbie (ed), *Europe's Global Role: External Policies of the European Union* (Ashgate, 2008).

O'Keeffe D (ed), *The European Union and World Trade Law: After the GATT Uruguay Round* (John Wiley & Sons, 1996).

Odell JS (ed), *Negotiating Trade Developing Countries in the WTO and Nafta* (CUP 2006).

OECD, *The Uruguay Round Agreement on Agriculture. An Evaluation of its Implementation in OECD Countries* (OECD, 2001) 32.

Ofodile UE, 'Foreign investment in land and the clash of regimes: mapping the role of international investment law and international human rights law' (2013) 7 *Human Rights and International Legal Discourse* 56.

Ostry S, 'The Uruguay Round North-South Grand Bargain: Implications for Future Negotiations' in Daniel M Kennedy and James D Southwick (eds), *The Political Economy of International Trade Law: Essays in Honor of Robert E. Hudec* (Cambridge University Press, 2002).

Oxfam, *Weighing the options*, Briefing note prepared for the Pacific Trade Ministerial, Port Vila, Vanuatu, 31 July–1 August 2007, available at <http://www.acp-eu-trade.org/library/files/Oxfam_EN_310707_Oxfam_Weighing-the-options.pdf> accessed 7 January 2012.

Ozden C and Reinhardt E, *The Perversity of Preferences: The Generalized System of Preferences and Developing Country Trade Policies, 1976–2000*, Policy Research Working Paper No. 2955 (World Bank, 2003).

Papadopoulos S, *The International Dimension of EU Competition Law and Policy* (Oxford University Press, 2010).

Pauwelyn J, 'Interplay between the WTO Treaty and Other International Legal Instruments and Tribunals: Evolution after 20 years of WTO Jurisprudence' in CE Cote, V Guevremont and R Ouellet (eds), *Proceedings of the Quebec City Conference on the WTO at 20* (Presses de l'Université de Laval, 2018).

—— 'Sources of International Trade Law: Mantras and Controversies at the World Trade Organization' in S Besson and J d'Aspremont, *Oxford Handbook on the Sources of International Law* (Oxford University Press, 2016).

—— 'The Role of Public International Law in the WTO: How Far Can We Go?' (2001) 95 *American Journal of International Law* 535.

Peng J and Cunningham N, 'WTO case analysis, suggestions and impacts: China-Measures Related to the Exportation of Various Raw Materials' (2012) 7 *Global Trade and Customs Journal* 27.

Picart CJS and Fox M, 'Beyond unbridled optimism and fear: indigenous peoples, intellectual property, human rights and globalisation of traditional knowledge and expression of folklore' (2014) 16 *International Community Law Review* 3.

Pillay A, 'Economic and social rights adjudication: developing principles of judicial restraint in South Africa and the United Kingdom' [2013] *Public Law* 599.

Pinelli C, 'The discourses on post-national governance and the democratic deficit absent an EU government' (2013) 9 *European Constitutional Law Review* 177.

Pinstrup-Andersen P, *Food price policy in an era of market instability: a political economy analysis* (Oxford University Press, 2015).

Plameter D and Mavroidis PC, 'The WTO legal system: sources of law' (1998) 92 *American Journal of International Law* 398.

PricewaterhouseCoopers, 'Sustainability Impact Assessment (SIA) of the EU-ACP Economic Partnership Agreements Regional SIA: Caribbean ACP Countries',

30 January 2004 available at <http://trade.ec.europa.eu/doclib/docs/2005/january/tradoc_121202.pdf>, p 11.

—— 'Sustainability Impact Assessment (SIA) of the EU-ACP Economic Partnership Agreements Regional SIA: West African ACP Countries', 30 January 2004, available at <http://trade.ec.europa.eu/doclib/docs/2005/january/tradoc_121200.pdf>, p 77.

—— 'Sustainability Impact Assessment (SIA) of the EU-ACP Economic Partnership Agreements Regional SIA: Caribbean ACP Countries', 30 January 2004, available at http://trade.ec.europa.eu/doclib/docs/2005/january/tradoc_121202.pdf.

Prowse S, 'Responses to the International trade and aid community to food security' in Baris Karapinar and Christian Haberli (eds), *Food Crisis and the WTO* (Cambridge University Press, 2010).

Puig GV and Al-Haddab B, 'The common commercial policy after Lisbon: an analysis of the reforms' (2011) 36 *European Law Review* 289.

Raffaelli M, *The rise and demise of commodity agreements* (Woodhead Publishing, 1995).

Rai S, *Recognition and Regulation of Safeguards Measurer Under GATT/WTO* (Routledge, 2011).

Rakotoarisoa MA, Sharma RP and Hallam D, *Agricultural import surges in developing countries Analytical framework and insights from case studies* (FAO, 2011).

Rapsomanikis G, 'Price transimission and volatility spillovers in food markets' in A Prakash (ed), *Safeguarding Food Security in Volatile Global Markets* (FAO, 2011).

Rapsomanikis G and Mugera H, 'Price Transmission and Volatility Spillovers in Food Markets of Developing Countries' in I Piot-Lepetit and R M'Barek (eds), *Methods to analyse agricultural commodity price volatility* (Springer, 2011).

Redondo ED, 'The Millennium Development Goals and the human rights based approach: reflecting on structural chasm with the United Nations system' (2009) 13 *International Journal of Human Rights* 29.

Reid E, *Balancing human rights, environmental protection and international trade* (Hart, 2017).

Riddel RC, 'Does Foreign Aid Really Work?' (Oxford University Press, 2007).

Roach K, 'The challenges of crafting remedies for violations of socio-economic rights' in M Langford (ed), *Social rights jurisprudence: emerging trends in international and comparative law* (Cambridge University Press, 2009).

Rodrik D, 'Populism and the Economics of Globalization' NBER Working Paper No. 23559.

—— 'Straight talk on Trade', Project Syndicate 15 November 2016, available at < https://www.project-syndicate.org/commentary/trump-win-economists-responsible-by-dani-rodrik-2016-11?barrier=accessreg>.

—— *Straight Talk on Trade: Ideas for Sane World Economy* (Princeton University Press, 2017).

—— *Has Globalization gone too far?* (Columbia University Press, 1997).

Rodriguez PM, 'Safeguards in the World Trade Organization ten years after: a dissociated state of the law?' (2007) 41 *Journal of World Trade* 159.

Rolland SE, 'Developing countries coalitions at the WTO: in search of legal support' (2007) 48 *Harvard International Law Journal* 483.

Ruse-Khan HG, 'A real partnership for development? Sustainable development as treaty objective in European economic partnership agreements and beyond' (2010) 13 *Journal of International Economic Law* 139.

Samuels WJ, 'Economics as a Science and Its Relation to Policy: The Example of Free Trade' (1980) 14 *Journal of Economic Issues* 163.

Schill SW, 'Cross-regime harmonization through proportionality analysis: the case of international investment law, the law of state immunity and human rights' (2012) 27 *ICSID Review* 87.

Schmidt-Traub G, 'The Millennium Development Goals and human rights-based approaches: moving towards a shared approach' (2009) 13 *International Journal of Human Rights* 72.

Schumacher R, 'Deconstructing the Theory of Comparative Advantage' (2013) 2 *World Social and Economic Review* 83.

Sciarra S, 'Viking and Laval: Collective Labour Rights and Market Freedoms in the Enlarged EU' (2008) *Cambridge Yearbook of European Law*.

—— 'Notions of solidarity in times of economic uncertainty' (2010) 39 *Industrial Law Journal* 223.

Sen A, 'Entitlements and the Chinese Famine' (1990) 15 *Food Policy*.

—— 'Food and freedom' (1989) 17 *World Development* 769.

—— 'Food Entitlement and Economic Chains' in LF Newman (ed), *Hunger in History* (Blackwell, 1990).

—— 'On the Approach to Planning Against Hunger' (July–August 1977) 58 *CERES: FAO Review on Agriculture and Development*.

—— 'Public Action to Remedy Hunger' (1991) 16 *Interdisciplinary Science Reviews* 324.

—— *Hunger and Entitlement* (World Institute of Development Economics Research, 1987).

—— *Poverty and Famines: an Essay on Entitlement and Deprivation* (Oxford University Press, 1983).

—— *The Political Economy of Hunger* (Clarendon Press, 1990).

Sen A and Drèze J, *Hunger and Public Action* (Clarendon Press, 1989).

Sharma R, 'Agriculture in the GATT: An Historical Account' in *Multilateral Trade Negotiations in Agriculture* (FAO, 2000), available at <http://www.fao.org/docrep/003/x7352e/x7352e04.htm> accessed 16 December 2011.

—— 'Effective special safeguards mechanism' in JR Deep Ford, C dell'Aquila and P Conforti, *Agricultural trade policy and food security in the Caribbean* (FAO, 2007).

—— *Food Export Restrictions: Review of the 2007–2010 Experience and Considerations for Disciplining Restrictive Measures*, FAO Commodity and Trade Policy Research Working Paper no. 32 (FAO, 2010).

Shi J, *Free trade and cultural diversity in international law* (Hart, 2013).

Singh R, 'The World Trade Organization and legitimacy: evolving a framework for bridging the democratic deficit' (2008) 42 *Journal of World Trade* 347.

Singham S, *A General Theory of Trade and Competition: Trade Liberalisation and Competitive Markets* (Cameron May, 2007) 182.

Skogly SI, 'Right to adequate food: national implementation and extraterritorial obligations" (2007) 11 *Max Planck United Nations Yearbook* 329.

Smith F, 'Multifunctionality and "non-trade concerns" in the agriculture negotiations' (2000) 3 *Journal of International Economic Law* 707.

Steger MB, *Globalization: A very short introduction* (Oxford University Press, 2017).

Steinberger E, 'The WTO Treaty as a mixed agreement: problems with the EC's and EC Member States' membership of the WTO' (2006) 17 *European Journal of International Law* 837.

Steiner S, 'The External Dimension of the European Fundamental Rights Agency' (2006) 11 *Austrian Review of International and European Law* 105.

Stewart TP, *The GATT Uruguay Round. A Negotiating History, Volume IV: The End Game* (Kluwer, 1999).

Stiglitz J, *Making globalization work* (Penguin Books 2006).

Stiglitz J and Charlton A, *Fair trade for all* (Oxford University Press, 2007).

Strydom H, 'Will the Cotonou agreement succeed where Lomé I-IV have failed?' (2007) 32 *South African Yearbook of International Law* 125.

Sykes AO, 'Comparative advantage and the normative economics of international trade policy' (1998) 1 *Journal of International Economic Law* 49.

—— *The WTO Agreement on Safeguards: a Commentary* (Oxford University Press, 2006).

Syrpis P and Novitz T, 'Economic and social rights in conflict: Political and judicial approaches to their reconciliation' (2008) 33 *European Law Review* 411.

Trakman LE, 'The Proliferation of Free Trade Agreements: Bane or Beauty?' (2008) 42 *Journal of World Trade* 367.

United Nations Human Rights Council, Report of the Special Rapporteur on the right to food, Olivier de Schutter 'Mission to the World Trade Organization', available at <http://carnegieendowment.org/files/Summary_of%20report%20of%20the%20Special%20Rapporteur%20on%20the%20right%20to%20food.pdf> accessed 29 December 2017.

United Nations, *The Global Social Crisis* (United Nations, 2011).

United Nations Development Programme, *Human Development Report 1997: Human Development to Eradicate Poverty* (Oxford University Press, 1997).

United Nations Ministerial Conference of the Least Developed Countries, *Globalization, Agriculture and the Least Developed Countries*, available at <http://www.unohrlls.org/UserFiles/File/LDC%20Documents/Turkey/20June07-Agriculture-Final.pdf> accessed 13 December 2015.

Vakericks TV, *Antidumping, Countervailing Duties and Other Trade Actions* (Practising Law Institute, 1987).

Valdes A and Foster W, 'Special safeguards for developing country agriculture: a proposal for WTO negotiations' (2003) 2 *World Trade Review* 5.

VanGrasstek C, *The History and Future of the World Trade Organization* (WTO, 2013).

Van den Bossche P and Zdouc W, *The Law and Policy of the World Trade Organization* (Cambridge University Press, 2013).

van der Marel E, 'Polly wants a Doha deal: what does the trade community think?' (2011) 10 *World Trade Review* 551.

van der Meulen B, 'The global arena of food law: emerging contours of a meta-framework' (2010) 4 *Erasmus Law Review* 217.

Voiculescu A, 'Unorthodox human rights instruments: the ACP-EU development co-operation from the Lome Conventions to the Cotonou Agreement' (2006) 4 *Journal of Commonwealth Law and Legal Education* 85.

Vranes E, *Trade and the Environment Fundamental Issues in International Law, WTO Law, and Legal Theory* (Oxford University Press, 2009).

Ward A, 'Community Development Aid and the Evolution of the Inter-institutional Law of the European Union' in A Dashwood and C Hillion (eds), *The General Law of EC External Relations* (Sweet & Maxwell, 2000).

Westhoff PC, *The economics of food: how feeding and fueling the planet affects food prices* (FT Press, 2010).

Wolfe R, 'The special safeguard fiasco in the WTO: the perils of inadequate analysis and negotiation' (2009) 8 *World Trade Review* 117.

World Bank, 'Transmission of Global Food Prices to Domestic Prices in Developing Countries' Contribution to the G20 Commodity Markets Working Groups.

—— *Cultivating Knowledge and Skills to Grow African Agriculture* (World Bank, 2007).

—— *Global Economic Prospects June 2011*, p 8, available at <http://siteresources.worldbank.org/INTGEP/Resources/335315-1307471336123/7983902-1307479336019/Full-Report.pdf> accessed 19 February 2012.

WTO, 'The WTO and the International Trade Centre (ITC)', available at <https://www.wto.org/english/thewto_e/coher_e/wto_itc_e.htm> accessed 21 December 2017.

—— *From GATT to the WTO: the multilateral trading system at the Millennium* (Kluwer Law International, 2000).

—— *The WTO and preferential trade agreements: From co-existence to coherence*, World Trade Report 2011, available at <www.wto.org/english/res_e/booksp.../world_trade_report11_e.pdf> accessed 15 October 2012.

—— *Handbook on Notification Requirements Under the Agreement on Agriculture* (WTO, 2015).

Ziegler J, 'Peasant Farmers and the Right to Food a History of Discrimination and Exploitation', Requests Addressed to the advisory committee stemming from human rights council resolutions: right to food, A/HRC/AC/3/CRP.5.

Ziegler J, Golay C, Mahon C and Way S-A, *The Fight for the Right to Food Lessons Learned* (Palgrave MacMillan, 2011).

Zimmermann H, 'Realist Power Europe? The EU in the Negotiations about China's and Russias's WTO Accession' (2007) 45 *Journal of Common Market Studies* 813.

Index

www.ingramcontent.com/pod-product-compliance
Ingram Content Group UK Ltd.
Pitfield, Milton Keynes, MK11 3LW, UK
UKHW021816051026
15470UKWH00025B/1151

9 781509 916207